CLERGY
WORLDVIEWS

Now the Men's Voices

Martha Long Ice

Westport, Connecticut
London

Library of Congress Cataloging-in-Publication Data

Ice, Martha Long.
    Clergy worldviews : now the men's voices / by Martha Long Ice.
      p.   cm.
    Includes bibliographical references and index.
    ISBN 0–275–94968–0 (alk. paper)
    1. Clergy—Attitudes—Sex differences. 2. Pastoral theology—
Public opinion. 3. Theology—Public opinion. 4. Church and social
problems—Public opinion. 5. Postmodernism—Religious aspects—
Christianity. I. Title.
BV660.2.I5   1995
253′.081—dc20   94–42838

British Library Cataloguing in Publication Data is available.

Library of Congress Catalog Card Number: 94–42838
ISBN: 0–275–94968–0

First published in 1995

Praeger Publishers, 88 Post Road West, Westport, CT 06881
An imprint of Greenwood Publishing Group, Inc.

Printed in the United States of America

The paper used in this book complies with the
Permanent Paper Standard issued by the National
Information Standards Organization (Z39.48–1984).

10 9 8 7 6 5 4 3 2 1

To the clergymen who gave their stories for this study;
and to my lifeline of family and friends.

Contents

Acknowledgments

A 1992 Centennial Scholars Summer Grant from Concordia College allowed me to begin the clergy interviews whose narrative content is the heart of this study. I am grateful for that help to support the data-gathering phase of the research.

The following year, after my retirement from full-time teaching, I began the editing and writing tasks. Colleagues in the Sociology/Social Work Department at the college continued to encourage me in countless ways. My gratitude to the department's office manager, Jo Engelhardt, is profound. The speed, flexibility, and good humor with which she turns my handwritten manuscript into word-processed pages makes her a true joy as a clerical worker.

Faculty friend Alfhild Ingberg agreed to read certain portions of the manuscript and offered criticism that I found very helpful.

Above all, I deeply appreciate the informants' contributions to this work. I thoroughly enjoyed the hours with the nineteen men interviewed. Their willingness to share life stories and ministerial experiences serves to enrich the literature of clergy studies, my life, and (I hope) theirs.

Chapter 1

Project Overview

This is a study of nineteen clergymen. It is an attempt to present careful documentation of their self-reported life experiences, with special attention to their insider views on theological, moral, and administrative aspects of professional ministry.

About ten years ago I began an investigation of clergywomen's perspectives. Initially I had no plan to follow up with a study of clergymen. At that time my interest was to find out how the role of clergywoman was emerging among female professional ministers in traditionally male-formed institutions and how women's presence as official leaders might be expected to influence religion in the United States.

It was a complex study with four parts: (1) a review of the literature of cultural futurism, which looks at how worldview paradigms are shifting and what further changes may be expected; (2) a review of gender differentiation literature; (3) interviews with seventeen clergywomen; and (4) integration of the findings from all three information sources.

I compared my informants' thinking with some broad conclusions from both literatures; that is, with what worldview orientations are said to be emergent and/or needed for species vitality, and with what gender differences are said to be evident in human life orientation, at least in the United States. I was curious about how professional ministerial women were developing their tasks and roles in a social sector shaped traditionally through male activities and rationales. As the women shared self-perceptions in the interviews, they revealed primary worldviews substantially in harmony with both the one said to be more associated with women than men and the one said by the futurists to be increasingly needed for coping with our changed and changing global society.

An absorbing interest for me is the sociology of knowledge, especially of scientific and religious knowledge. Thus my focus is on the cultural worlds of meaning that people construct—largely unconsciously—in the ongoing quest to make sense of their life circumstances.

In recent years, as I made conference presentations of data about clergy-women, audiences raised questions about how ministerial men's views would now differ from women's, if at all. I found myself addressing the question of whether or when I would be doing interviews with clergymen. I emphasized the fact that my findings are not drawn from the kind of sample suitable for making valid and reliable generalizations over the larger population of clergywomen or for making statistical comparisons with clergy-men. Narrative data have an alternative set of strengths. Nonetheless, colleagues indicated a strong desire to hear the clergymen's voices in a parallel study. They suggested that clergymen are deeply divided over the epistemological issues that are affecting the terms and consequences of general social dialogue. They often threw in observations such as, "Men have been changing a lot in recent years; they sound different from the way they did in the past"; or "Men in religious ministries would probably not be as male-typical as other men in the society."

Over time, I began to share the interest in hearing the male voices explicitly through the same kind of phenomenological approach to research that I had used with the women. I came to see such work as a potentially important complement to existing survey data and denominational publications that regularly exhibit clergy views. At any rate, I now have gathered the interview data from clergymen.

Almost a decade has elapsed since inception of the earlier investigation. Scholarship in gender and reality orientation has exploded during that time, making epistemology—how we know what we know—a hot academic and journalistic topic. In and about such terms as *postmodern deconstruction of texts, new paradigm thinking*, and *social inclusivity* we glimpse the struggle between traditionally modern ideas of objectively established truths and postmodern assumptions that all knowledge (no matter how scientific, religious, or "folk") is a dynamic product of interactive social processes.

Scholars across the various academic disciplines have been giving increasing attention to bedrock ideals and assumptions that constitute our mostly taken-for-granted orientation to life as humans. The literature of cultural futurism I reviewed points to the rift becoming increasingly evident throughout Western World institutions, between an established (conventionally modern) worldview accenting competitive mastery goals, hierar-

chical relationships, abstract principles of morality, and highly compartmentalized professional knowledge specialties; and an alternative worldview emphasizing democratic cooperation, equalitarian discourse, morality
based on mutual respect and responsible caring, and holistic, integrative,
contextualized views of how knowledge is constructed.

Throughout the affairs of Western society we see much evidence of this
split in reality paradigms—in the social sectors of corporate business,
government, education, medicine, religion, and family. Within religion, for
example, as well as within specific denominations and individual congregations, strong polarities have emerged, with some people drawn to traditional, right-or-wrong certainties and others drawn to dialectical knowledge
perspectives that recognize ongoing processes of social meaning construction.

As denominational constituencies agonize in debilitating controversies
over such matters as statements about sexuality, ordination, criteria for
permissible language for imaging God, and economic justice, it is often
clear that these disagreements are instances of a more fundamental division
over the nature of truth.

Orthodoxies of all stripes now appear to be under attack, as are also
critical thinking approaches, which are often branded as mere floating
relativism. One side fears the obstruction of free inquiry, illuminating
discourse, and healthy human development; the other fears loss of familiar
truth-grounding premises.

The present era is frequently identified as a time of fundamental life
orientation shifts, with radical revisions in cultural assumptions about the
nature of reality. So-called new-paradigm ideals generally have been associated more with women's ways—the yin aspects of life—though they are
often valued and articulated by men. Currently, in many sectors of U.S.
society, proponents of new-paradigm ideals are putting them forward as a
balancing corrective—an important humanizing dynamic in Western institutions that are heavily tilted toward hierarchical and abstract efficiencies
of bureaucratic organization.

Some of the informants in this study show considerable influence from,
and interest in, what can be recognized as new-paradigm views. Others
appear relatively untouched by, or resistant to, such perspectives. In the
quotations from the clergymen these contrasts will be evident.

The phenomenological approach I have employed seeks accurate documentation of informants' self-interpreted, subjective realms of meaning.
Such a study looks at the ways people choose to describe their own life
experiences. It is designed to honor the uniqueness of the informants' views
and metaphors as they spontaneously reveal them during relatively free-

format interviews. It can thus pay attention to such matters as levels of tentativity, retractions and clarifications delivered, connections noted, caveats, and telling witticisms. It can yield a wealth of fine-grained information about how these clergy see their work, as well as what biographical particulars form the context for their ministerial functioning and growth.

The narrative data are valuable for glimpsing the processes at work in the perceived reality worlds of professional religious leaders. This is the investigation's primary contribution to scholarly knowledge. The quotations also can serve as an exploratory resource for discovering appropriate survey research categories, and they can yield nuanced understandings for enriching the interpretation of quantitative findings; but neither of these latter fruits is their central significance here.

The nineteen informants are what Michael Quinn Patton calls a "purposeful sample" of "information-rich" cases—in this instance, a "maximum heterogeneity" sample.

> The logic of purposeful sampling in qualitative methods is quite different from the logic of probabilistic sampling in statistics. The power of statistical sampling depends on selecting a truly random and representative sample which will permit confident generalization from the sample to a larger population. The power of purposeful sampling lies in selecting *information-rich cases* for study in depth. Information-rich cases are those from which one can learn a great deal about issues of central importance to the purpose of the evaluation. (1990, 51–52)

The participants were selected with an eye to variety—a characteristic selection strategy in this type of research, since the interviews are lengthy and the number of cases relatively small. Thus the clergymen differ substantially as to age, race, marital and parental status, type of congregation, education, economic status, denominational affiliation, and family background, though they are alike in having professional reputations for doing solidly good work in their congregational ministries. One value of using a wide range of informant subtypes is that if identifiable patterns of expression do emerge in the data across these variations, they warrant framing as hypotheses for systematic testing, using scientific sampling techniques, quantifiable survey responses, and mathematical models for analysis. Meanwhile, apart from any patterns of similarity, the approach delivers an empirically informed, textured sense of real-life experiences as interpreted by the experiencers.

The decision for homogeneity with regard to reputational success was made to intensify the informants' representative value. After all, who ends up identified as successful, who gets offered the choicest opportunities, whose voice carries most weight—such things say as much about the community's operating ideals as about the leader.

Most of the men were curious about how I had selected them, and the reader may be, too. I approached people who had broad knowledge of clergy in a region (typically staff in judicatory offices and interdenominational agencies). After describing my connections and my project, I asked for names of nonmarginal clergy—clergy who are considered "good ministers," "strong preachers," "successful," according to congregants and colleagues. I said I was not looking for a "stars" list and I wanted a variety of persons who range from conservative to liberal, dignified to bombastic, intellectual to practical, and so on. I also mentioned variety in age, race, and marital status, along with the size and location (urban, suburban, or rural) of the parish.

Usually I received a list of twelve to fifteen names with brief and basic descriptive comments. I intended to interview only one or two from any such list and indicated to the suppliers that I would not share with them information about who was selected.

As agreements were made I adjusted subsequent choices toward maximum variety until I had my full complement of twenty interviewees. (A man who would have been the oldest in the study needed to drop out because of severe illness in his family, so I ended up with nineteen.)

The clergy I approached were interested in what would be done with the information. Most seemed to find the idea of an academic study appealing, but a few said they'd feel their time was better spent if the study were used to accomplish something specific, beyond the mere delivery of information.

Each of the participants was interviewed for a total of four hours, in two, two-hour sessions. I asked them to share their perspectives on the central tasks of their ministries, namely, theological, moral, and administrative leadership. Prior to the first meeting I provided each informant with a list of subtopics I was interested in hearing them discuss. I stood ready to make suggestions at interview time but encouraged them to chart their own direction and talk about the things that interested them most.

I made all arrangements, conducted all interviews, and handled all editing myself. I assured the participants of strict confidentiality, though a few indicated that they were telling others about their participation. Some wondered about the need for or desirability of confidentiality but, after the interviews, commented that they had been more comfortable and free with sensitive information knowing that the terms of privacy had been established.

My attempt to preserve anonymity for the informants involves sharing with others neither their names nor my appointment destinations and delivering the edited data according to topical areas rather than whole stories.

The body of this text is devoted to displaying for the reader what the interviewees did, in fact, say on an array of topics. Since the informants were encouraged to speak freely and not confine themselves to strict rubrics of focus, the quotations often show the connective bridges in their thought.

A few words about editing strategies may be helpful here.

As media reporters have become more aggressively clever in making fun of public figures, many have gleefully documented spontaneous utterances, verbatim, making the speaker sound like an idiot. I seek to avoid such malice masquerading as accuracy. Informal oral delivery presents special problems for displaying the sense of interviews responsibly, especially when the central interest is ideas, impressions, attitudes—subjective experiences that are complex, hard to describe, and reported to someone not well known to the interviewee. Informant statements contain numerous parenthetical insertions, self-interruptions, references to other interview topics, and partial sentences, even when the speaker is highly articulate. I tried hard to make judicious editing cuts that preserve the full "color" of comments yet rake out excessive debris of false starts, "yaknows," "ers," "ums," in the interest of clarity and efficient use of book space. If intent was not plain to me during the interview, I asked the informant to clarify. Related comments from different parts of the interviews are sometimes pulled together into a single presentation for maximum coherence. My overall goal is to provide a true sense of the interviews, lifting out the most revealing comments and intentionally suppressing no discrepant material. In the end, credibility in both quantitative and qualitative research findings depends on trust that the researcher is being scrupulously honest with information, whether in table, quotation, or description form.

Most commonly the use, in quotations, of brackets indicating editorial insertion, signifies one of two patterns: (1) The words were contained in a question I had just asked or a subject the informant had introduced already; thus a minister's words, "As long as they wouldn't have to give up anything they'd be all *for* it," needs to be contextualized by replacing "it" with "[economic justice]." (2) Words of the informant may need to be *de*contextualized for confidentiality; "[it's an] all white congregation," is my rendering of a sentence in which the man had named and located his church explicitly. Likewise, "[My denomination]" is my substitution for a national executive's name used to designate a church body affiliation.

Vagueness about numbers in reporting data ("most," "almost all," "very few," "close to two-thirds") represents my respect for the nature of free-format data. All of the men do not speak on all of the same themes. Therefore, when I say "Over half of the men . . . " I am confident that my statement is empirically based in the nineteen interviews; but the remaining ("less than half") cases contain both alternative views and interviews that have no material on the theme.

Sometimes a statement I wanted to use could not be quoted directly. Certain voices did not record distinctly on all parts of the tapes. In those cases I worked between my notes and the tapes to paraphrase what I could be absolutely certain was there; and I did not present it in quotation format.

Existing studies of clergy do not fit together neatly like pieces of a jigsaw puzzle. According to researcher interests and opportunities they emerge to deliver information that may or may not mesh well with other studies—filling gaps, extending and challenging them in coherent ways. A few examples will show the spread in focus and methodology.

Jackson Carroll, Barbara Hargrove, and Adair Lummis (1983) compare women and men as to circumstances of family background, career choices, seminary education, career entry and development, congregational life, and interpersonal relationships; they also compare their respondents on a long list of attitudes and preferences in ministry. This quantitative study surveys more than a thousand ministers in nine "mainstream" Protestant denominations.

Edward Lehman's 1985 study looks at congregants' thinking about women pastors and adds some observations from the women pastors themselves. The study is limited to the Presbyterian denomination. Lehman's 1993 work focuses on statistical comparisons of male and female clergy attitudes and preferences. It involves approximately 300 clergy respondents from four Protestant denominations.

Ruth Wallace's work (1992) is a qualitative investigation of the pastoral experiences of twenty Catholic women "entrusted by their bishops with the pastoral care of parishes where there are no resident priests." Through extensive interviews and participant observations Wallace gathers data about the women's work as nonordained but officially designated ministers.

In conference papers since 1992 the many clergy research projects reviewed have included the following: a Paula Nesbitt analysis of about 200 clergy career and biography files (male and female) in two Protestant denominations, seeking comparative information on quality of career entrants and career opportunities; a Lynn Gesch case study of an especially charismatic woman minister; and Frederick Schmidt's qualitative data from fifty interviews with ministerial women in five denominations (Catholic and four Protestant), attempting to identify and assess "the significance of bureaucratic and cultural linkages that mitigate against or facilitate the inclusion of women." There are numerous other projects, including my own phenomenological studies of clergymen and clergywomen.

In spite of the disparity of projects, the increasing body of clergy research establishes a sturdy and rapidly expanding resource for understanding vocational circumstances; role occupants; issues, problems, and perspectives; and numerous other aspects of professional ministerial work.

Sociological knowledge expands from two broadly complementary methods of study: the qualitative, descriptive inquiries that produce a sense of how people see their own situations and the quantitative studies that assess how representative a given experience, interpretation, or trait may be for a larger population of similarly selected respondents. My work lies in the descriptive tradition.

In Chapter 2 I address some knotty and persistent epistemological issues attached to contemporary discourse, scholarly and ordinary. My hope is to provide reference points that will be serviceable for illuminating interview material. Chapter 3 introduces the men who were interviewed. The concrete particulars of the autobiographical stories can provide grounding for the voices to be heard later. In Chapter 4 the clergymen's self-described theological resources and views are revealed. Chapter 5 shows moral perspectives the men shared with the interviewer—both general ideas about morality and specific comments about more narrowly focused areas of moral choice. Chapter 6 presents a wide range of clergy observations about administrative aspects of professional ministerial work. Chapter 7 deals with gender comparisons and with important issues that have arisen connected with such work. It also includes what the informants say about differences between men and women clergy and describes my impressions of differences in my two sets of data. Finally, Chapter 8 contains concluding comments about the project as a whole.

Chapter 2

How Do We Know?
(Epistemological Issues)

In recent decades several mainstream U.S. Protestant denominations and Roman Catholicism have been shaken and deeply divided over doctrinal issues centered in social justice and morality concerns. Some of the most acrimonious debates focus on women's status in the church and human sexuality teachings. Sociology of religion scholars Robert Wuthnow, Wade Clark Roof, and others suggest that the current chasms within major Christian denominations in the United States are deeper and more disabling in church life than the chasms between denominations.

These chasms are no simple differences in strength of adherence to denominational beliefs; they often represent radical differences in religious knowledge orientation, and in underlying worldviews. It is the distinction between knowledge seen as verified fact items—acquired, accumulated, and sorted into categories—and knowledge seen as ongoing construction of meaning worlds—where percepts, concepts, and language are forming dialectically through social intersubjectivity. While these two perspectives seldom if ever exist in mutually exclusive, pure forms, and while balanced living seems to draw freely from versions of both, the tendencies are conceptually distinguishable. They constitute correctives to each other's excesses of overapplication and have different modes of fruitfulness for seeing and saying and doing.

The contrasting social perspective systems of which I speak are operating all over society—at the heart of arguments being made in committee meetings, in letters to the editor, in courts of law and legislatures, in scholarly journals, in families. This means that many discussions reach frustrating impasses, with parties to the debate despairing of the other side's ability or desire to see clearly, when the essential split is really about *how* truth in a matter is established. I suspect it would be immensely helpful in our society if we could be attuned to the broader life orientations represented in all this discussion, recognizing them more easily in their everyday manifestations.

I see this chapter as crucial for understanding what follows, in two ways: (1) It prepares an interpretive frame for comments I will be making in the final chapters, as well as from time to time in the upcoming data display chapters. (2) It alerts the reader to these differences in lifestance as they emerge in the clergy voices.

ALTERNATIVE WORLDVIEWS

The distinction between contrasting knowledge models is part of a more comprehensive distinction many scholars now make between general life orientation models. Such models operate mostly below the surface of consciousness to organize people's basic frames of meaning in life—for interpreting their observations, their memories, their feelings and actions, their intentions and judgments—everything.

In making personal and collective decisions at the conscious level, it matters what we assume to be the nature of reality. Our taken-for-granted real worlds are the cultural milieus in which we try to make sense of symbolically delivered impressions and expressions throughout life. So I will start off with a brief description of these larger frames of meaning and then proceed to focus on subthemes with special relevance for this study.

When I did the study of clergywomen I was interested in alternative worldview paradigms much discussed, then and now, in the literature of cultural futurism. Paradigms constitute fundamental perceptual and conceptual frameworks of assumptions within which specific phenomena are noticed, described, analyzed, discussed, located, used. Paradigms function as largely "unarguable" knowledge providing the terms for discourse in a given knowledge community. Physicist Fritjof Capra gives an illustration from science.

> In order to do science, you need a certain framework, and you want to work within this framework. If you questioned everything all the time, you wouldn't be able to do science. But if you never question anything, you won't make progress. Ideally you should pursue a scientific activity within a certain framework, but you should be ready to question any part of that framework at any time. (Capra, Steindl-Rast, and Matus 1991, 150)

Whether in architecture, government, psychotherapy, astronomy, relig-ion, or the everyday existence of ordinary folk, socially shared visions of the nature of reality "hold the world in place"ing with mundane events on a continuing basis.

Thomas Kuhn in *The Structure of Scientific Revolutions* (1962) stimu-lated awareness of knowledge paradigms and their significance for scien-tific knowledge development. Others have expanded and adapted these insights for focusing on parallels in other realms of meaning and in culture per se. Kuhn talks about the attendant concept and communication disorder experienced by many when the reigning truth paradigm itself is challenged as deficient, distorted, or false. If a credible alternative is proposed as a successor, it may encounter vigorous (even devious or violent) resistance from those who find the new reading of reality literally disorienting and fantastic, relative to their perceived experiences.

Public arenas of knowledge and discourse inevitably come, over time, to be permeated by the expressive metaphors of the dominant reality para-digms that have captured the collective imagination and/or been the oper-ating terms of socialization. Thus, ordinary conversations nowadays contain knowing references to "circling the globe," "bureaucratic redtape," "subconscious motives," "assembly lines," "world government," "laser surgery," and "microchips" that would have been truly unthinkable in other eras, let alone part of common parlance.

There is widespread agreement with the Berger, Berger, and Keller assertion (1973) that Western World modernization themes of technological progress and bureaucratic organization gradually influenced the mental operations through which we see and say what's so for us, in general. The themes did not just stay contained in, or tied to, the concrete activities of industrial and bureaucratic structures in modern societies. Berger et al. conclude that much of the present-day sense of personal "lostness" stems from uncritical adoption of technological and bureaucratic ideals and values as mental grids for understanding life in general, including the personal realm.

This conventionally modern worldview, with its hallmark emphases on linear logic, rational control of goal-focused processes, hierarchical con-ceptual and social arrangements, and compartmentalized expert specialties, is now being countered with a postmodern worldview. This alternative orientation emphasizes integrative, dialectical ways of clarifying thought, developmental attention to processes as more than mere means to ends, equalitarian conceptual and social arrangements, and a balanced concern for the interdependent parts of a system as well as the whole of it.

For a much more thorough review of scholarly thinking about the significance and consequences of these worldview alternatives, see my *Clergy Women and Their Worldviews* (1987) on the perspectives of clergy-women, especially Chapter 9. Here I shall merely list some of the representative polarities and later discuss their implications for contemporary concerns about how best to *know*.

In order to construct such a list and make such distinctions, one necessarily creates an abstraction that exists nowhere in real life in this clear-cut kind of division. It sets up what sociologist Max Weber called an *ideal type*—a definitional model that provides conceptual clarity for discursive references but describes no concrete phenomena, as such. Weber, for example, gave us a definitive description (an ideal type) of bureaucracy— the bureaucratic features that make a bureaucracy a bureaucracy. A number of social thinkers have described the features of modernity that make a modern worldview modern and the features of the "rising," or "postmodern," worldview that makes it identifiably postmodern. No actual corporate entity exists as a pure form of bureaucracy. So, also, no actual person or group has an orientation to reality that is purely "old paradigm" or "new paradigm."

Among scholars pointing to social pathologies rooted in modernity I know of none who suggests that obliteration of modern perspectives is required for human health. They claim, rather, that it is the inappropriate hegemony of modern perspectives that requires radical revision. Balance is a key element of new-paradigm thinking—balanced, equalitarian consideration and respect for ideas, persons, social sectors, and peoples; and overall part/whole balance in systems between the parts and the whole.

All of us can look at the following listings and see ourselves on both sides. Yet our fundamental assumptions about reality—conscious or unconscious—predispose us toward patterns of response that tend to lean one way more than the other for supporting what we judge to be realistic views and responses. One way more than the other will tend to hold for each of us more fearsome social dangers.

Because most of a worldview is "soaked up" and expressed unconsciously in daily living, we are seldom good at identifying or analyzing our own worldviews and how they operate in our actions. As the world becomes "smaller," and we are exposed more often to different perspectives, we may become somewhat more aware of our own. But it is still very easy for all of us to avoid genuine involvement with other perspectives and their personal bearers—to discount and dismiss as crazy, immoral, or unrealistic views that challenge our own.

In these listings I've assembled a wide range of terms from numerous sources.

Common Labels for Alternative Worldview Orientations

yang	yin
old paradigm	new paradigm
modern	postmodern
established	emergent
ego-centric (including community or nation as "ego")	eco-centric
structuralist	poststructuralist

Common Types of Ideals, Assumptions, and Relations Associated with Alternative Orientations Toward Reality

hierarchical	equalitarian
elitist, authoritarian	democratic, communitarian
pyramidal influence structures	network influence strucures
competitive mastery	cooperative synergy
dualistic-exclusive	pluralistic-inclusive
power over	power with
extrinsic authority	intrinsic authority
imposed order	emergent order
given ("natural") order	negotiated order
fundamental order	constructed order
objectivist	intersubjectivist
instrumental	developmental
essentialist	existentialist
absolutist	dialectical
rationalist	humanist
principled justice	responsible caring
correctness and purity	authenticity and openness
segmented specialties with attention to hierarchical coordination of compartmentalized operations	integrative systems with holistic attention to the interdependence of component parts
the personal as private	the personal as societal
individualistic	communal

Now if you are at all like most people in classes I've taught during the past quarter century (mainly college undergraduates but also other adults at other ages), your responses are likely to include the following (regardless of whether you are female or male):

1. There is conscious preference for, and greater comfort with, the right-hand columns. They seem less threatening, more admirable, more ideal, better, nicer, friendlier (according to spontaneous feedback). Most people claim they'd love to live in a world where human relations could be described in such terms; but they say they couldn't invest themselves fully in trying to bring it about because it's totally unrealistic and impossible among actual people. "Maybe in heaven," a few remark. Also it looks disturbingly fuzzy and up in the air and—well, yes—boring; nothing could ever get settled or won, once and for all.

2. There is general acceptance of the left-hand columns as characteristic of the real world, real life, the way things actually happen and can be handled. It's the way things are, the way things work, the way things have to be and always will be. Sure, people admit, it looks a little (sometimes a lot!) nasty and unfair and oppressive; but they are also attracted to its promise of what seems to them like more excitement, personal challenge, and overall satisfaction. They like what appears to them as its greater familiarity and predictability; they sense it as a social order they can deal with more confidently and succeed in more definitively.

3. There is a tendency to regard the columns as narrowly exclusive and to offer examples of crossover persons and situations as assumed evidence that the distinctions themselves are invalid.

4. Identification of the columns with either male/female tendencies or public/private realms sometimes leads in the direction of justifying and accusing debates rather than illuminating exchanges.

The listings are provisional, incomplete, and redundant; the pairing notably imperfect. "Humanist," for example (given certain interpretations), might be claimed—or disclaimed—for either column. This whole attempt to clarify alternative worldviews for the reader could be seriously misleading insofar as any conceptual distinctions were taken to be mutually exclusive and/or fully or ideally separable in real experience. The listings are merely a crude tool for understanding why so many discussions of fact, value, and policy nowadays break down around discrepant (usually unstated) assumptions and grounding rationales about what's true, good, and possible for humans. It is a framework for identifying features of alternative life orientations that are much talked about currently.

KNOWLEDGE PARADIGMS

Perhaps the two new-paradigm elements that have attracted greatest popular attention and had greatest impact on public discourse are the social-justice concern for equalitarian inclusion of all people in social benefit/opportunity structures and the epistemological concern for how knowledge, as such, is established among humans. Social-justice and social-meaning concerns are closely related. De-privileging categories of social entitlement in social institutions and de-privileging categories of conventional knowledge in classical texts are interpenetrated endeavors. It has been said that not only do people have ideas, but ideas have people. Equalitarian respect for people requires equalitarian consideration of ideas that are important to them. Likewise the critical thinking disciplines now broadly encouraged across academia cannot achieve their objectives of intellectually equalitarian comparisons of views apart from equalitarian respect for persons who hold such views.

Feminist and minority scholarship has by now produced a growing literature of considerable breadth, depth, and sophistication. Among other things, it clarifies the ways certain social location factors enter into world-view formation. What we see and how we interpret things, given the interests and constraints of our lives, are crucial factors in how we construct intellectual or ethical assertions. Being young, black, intelligent, poor, and male or being old, wealthy, female, ill, and deaf are sets of facts affecting our sets of facts. So is being white, male, educated, and economically successful, though the perspectives of this set of facts are less noticeable, as such, in a society where they generally blend into the dominant culture climate. As interest mounts, in some quarters at least, for "deconstructing" assertions and ascertaining how the world looks to different categories of people, we see just how complicated and rich our crosscutting social memberships make our points of view.

The traditionally modern worldview assumes a firm givenness of physical and social realities, about which we can gain irrefutable knowledge through expert disciplines of observation and analysis. It frames conceptual and moral truths as trustworthy ideas capturing the essential nature of phenomena that are objectively and continuingly so.

By contrast, the emergent worldview emphasizes the social development of truth and goodness as ongoing social meaning constructions that vary according to time, place, and demographic category and need endless interpretive discourse (from highest erudition to simplest transaction) for establishment, clarification, and development. The number of people, even in academic circles, who have stomach for chewing their way through the tough texts about interpretation of texts (e.g., by such authors as Michel Foucault, Jacques Derrida, Kenneth Burke, and M. M. Bakhtin) is doubtless quite small. Yet the implications of such watershed scholarship are apparent in recent decades, throughout works that are more palatable fare for broader audiences.

Critical thinking as a developmental ideal for college students has arrived at the precarious edge of general acceptability where its textbook "how-to" formulas and its virtual buzzword status may cause people to discard it as stale before it is comprehended fully or assimilated into ordinary discourse. Nonetheless, critical thinking perspectives and disciplines pervade under-graduate study at this point in history and they are clearly postmodern in their overall processual thrust.

Critical thinking is not put forth in current U.S. pedagogy as a point-on-point exercise in assertion and refutation. It recognizes a set of clarifying procedures that do not reduce knowledge to linear logic, right/wrong perspectives, or probabilistic calculations. It involves a wide range of disciplines focused on clarifying the view *point* along with the view *object*. Among the inquiry approaches it accents for establishing the status of an assertion the following commonly appear:

clarifying component aspects of propositions, such as how certain terminology, concepts, and references are being employed

identifying contexts for the assertion—personal, social, intellectual, institutional

identifying embedded assumptions, values, implications, and commitments

evaluating logical and empirical bases for the rational consistency and validity or reliability of evidence

evaluating cause-and-effect assertions for both independent and proposition-supporting validity

comparing, challenging, and integrating a proposition with alternative relevant assertions

The central themes of critical thinking appear nowadays in many adaptations. Maxine Greene in *The Dialectic of Freedom* (1988) talks about the dialectical conditions for experiencing human freedom, using arguably postmodern terms. Dialectical conditions are conditions in the process of mutual formation, dynamically embedded in each other's development and significance. Among the conditions Greene identifies for negotiating one's own autonomy are such knowledge-clarifying exercises as the following:

recognizing and realistically assessing obstacles to be transcended

developing critical, dialectical, and integrative thinking skills imagining alternatives preferable to existing circumstances

recognizing the situatedness, connectedness, imbeddedness, and constructedness of life events

developing interest in growing, becoming, overcoming, and transcending

But Greene is clear that freedom is not found merely by way of sophisticated critical thinking processes. According to her, crucial dynamics in the "dialectic of freedom" also include the following:

accepting accountability for authoring one's life according to one's own stated commitments

communicating authentically with thoroughgoing honesty and integrity

developing and steadily participating in a mutually supportive community of discourse and commitment

If this list sounds somewhat religious, there are good reasons why that might be. On the one hand it suggests organizational premises clearly appropriate for the kind of religious community that aspires to embody human freedom, integrity, accountability, authenticity, development, mutual support, and openness to experience. On the other hand, it runs counter to interpretations of postmodern orientation that caricature postmodernism as mere relativistic intellectual and moral chaos—personal "drift" from moorings of origin or destination. Life lived relative to one's momentary whims might, indeed, come to deliver substantial existential chaos; but that is just the point: relativity requires an object—a "to something." Life lived relative to evolving care commitments—to self, others, community, cosmos—could deliver substantial coherence at all levels. Einstein's theory of relativity, for example, is not about how nothing can be known with confidence but about how certain familiar dimensions of experience (in this case time and space) must henceforth be thought of in terms of each other. The growing consciousness that everything truly is related to everything else in the universe, likewise, is not about how truth and goodness are now impossible to comprehend but about how familiar cognitive and moral ideals must henceforth be thought of relative to the complex terms of their social construction—that is, as dynamic human projects in concrete social contexts.

As a responsible awareness, learning, and relating agenda, this consciousness can seem overwhelming. It should be obvious that no one always could keep it all available to attention without experiencing what one person calls "enormity paralysis." If, however, we do not back off from this postmodern orientation as hopelessly confusing—if, instead, we ponder it seriously as the best "take" our best contemporary minds now offer on the nature of reality—grounding then we may continue to reap its fruits for grounding a revised personal confidence and cultural coherence. The orientation opens the possibility of incorporating adapted strengths of the modern framework into the postmodern framework as limited balancing influences.

SAMPLING POSTMODERN PERSPECTIVES

Perhaps it would be helpful at this point to give some sense of the many voices contributing to the postmodern way of viewing the world. Philosophic grounding for the postmodern knowledge perspective is often attributed to specific scholars, such as Michel Foucault and Jacques Derrida, though many others are conspicuous contributors. Against such modern ideas as primary principles, rational-empirical establishment of objective truth, and authentic centers of meaning, they speak credibly about knowledge as always and only *under construction* in the elements of discourse. Linguistic transactions, as such, thus become a crucial focus for all searches into the nature of the world. No matter how refined, sophisticated, and illuminating they are, linguistic/conceptual attempts to frame objects in experience are never to be equated with the objects themselves. Thus no object of human attention is available to that human attention except through the "dark glass" of language/culture/person filters. Direct apprehension/comprehension of any object by any subject is, in this view, acknowledged as impossible.

Derrida's *Of Grammatology* (1976) emphasizes in myriad ways that the *signifier* (language term) and the *signified* (object of reference) are never in a truly stable union. Every signifier is "under erasure," according to Derrida, in that it is both necessary in communication and inevitably inadequate in communication. This consideration has special importance in theology. It implies that certainly (but not only) when expressing experiences of transcendent presence all terms for God (though necessary signifiers of something we may find important to communicate) are forever under erasure as conveyers of that God and that importance. It constitutes a new call (echoing and reframing some older calls) to appropriate humility, tentativity, and openness in religious discourse.

Traditionalists are immensely fearful of what they see as postmodern erosion of a solid culture base for life-ordering projects. They talk much about descent into chaotic relativism, often envisioned as pure privatized and self-serving subjective preference.

People with a developmental view of reality are, instead, fearful of an institutionalized social formalism that tends to reify and enforce its perspectives as the true, objective, and natural order and is neither capable of realistic self-criticism nor open to considering the full developmental requirements of diverse social systems.

Philosopher Richard Rorty observes,

As soon as one says that objectivity is intersubjectivity one is likely to be accused of being a relativist. . . . But this epithet is ambiguous. It can name any of three different views. The first is the silly and self-refuting view that every belief is as good as every other. The second is the wrong-headed view that "true" is an equivocal term, having as many meanings as there are contexts of justification. The third is the ethnocentric view that there is nothing to be said about either truth or rationality apart from descriptions of the familiar procedures of justification which a given society—*ours*—uses in one or another area of inquiry.

[. . .]

To say that we must be ethnocentric may sound suspicious, but this will only happen if we identify ethnocentrism with pig-headed refusal to talk to representatives of other communities. In my sense of ethnocentrism, to be ethnocentric is simply to work by our own lights. The defense of ethnocentrism is simply that there are no other lights to work by. (In Nelson, Megill, and McCloskey 1987, 42–43)

From here on, I shall offer, with minimal interspersed commentary a sampling of quotations from an array of scholars—scientific, philosophical, theological, literary. My hope is to provide representative postmodern observations that give a feel for the fundamental perspectives.

In our culture the notions of "science," "rationality," "objectivity," and "truth" are bound up with one another. Science is thought of as offering "hard," "objective" truth: truth as correspondence to reality, the only sort of truth worthy of the name. Humanists like philosophers, theologians, historians, and literary critics have to worry about whether they are being "scientific"—whether they are entitled to think of their conclusions, no matter how carefully argued, as worthy of the term "true." We tend to identify seeking "objective truth" with "using reason," and so we think of the natural sciences as paradigms of rationality. We also think of rationality as a matter of following procedures laid down in advance, of being "methodical." So we tend to use "methodical," "rational," "scientific," and "objective" as synonyms.

[. . .]

The rhetoric of the Enlightenment praised the emerging natural sciences in a vocabulary which was left over from a less liberal and tolerant era. This rhetoric enshrined all the old philosophic oppositions between mind and world, appearance and reality, subject and object, truth and pleasure. [John] Dewey thought that it was the continued prevalence of such opposition which prevented us from seeing that modern science was a new and promising invention . . . something which required new rhetoric rather than justification by an old one.

Suppose that Dewey was right about this, and that eventually we learn to find the fuzziness which results from breaking down such oppositions spiritually comforting rather than morally offensive. (Rorty, in Nelson, Megill, and McCloskey 1987, 38, 51)

The point is not to find the new, true perspective; the point is to strive for impartiality by admitting our partiality. The perspective of those who are labeled "different" may offer an important challenge to those who imposed the label, but it is a corrective lens, another partial view, not the absolute truth. (Minow 1990, 376)

Scholarship uses argument, and argument uses rhetoric. The "rhetoric" is not mere ornament or manipulation or trickery. It is rhetoric in the ancient sense of persuasive discourse. In matters from mathematical proof to literary criticism, scholars write rhetorically. Only occasionally do they reflect on that fact.

[. . .]

To admit these rhetorical dimensions of inquiry has seemed dangerous to modernists, who crave certainty.

[. . .]

Two barriers sometimes frustrate efforts at rhetoric of inquiry. One is the philosophical tendency to contrast rhetoric and rationality, taking rhetoric to endorse radical relativism (or mere nihilism). The other is the failure to examine rhetoric within actual practices, academic or otherwise.

[. . .]

Rhetoric of inquiry reflects a renewed concern for the quality of speaking and writing in scholarship. It emphasizes the interaction of style and substance. But mostly it tries to improve the conduct of inquiry, inside and outside the academy, by learning from its diversity. As immanent epistemology, within particular fields, rhetoric of inquiry shows what we are really doing and how to criticize it. As comparative epistemology, across different fields, rhetoric of inquiry shows what others are doing and how to learn from it. Rhetoric of inquiry explores how reason is rhetorical. (Nelson, Megill, and McCloskey 1987, 3, 8, 14, 17)

Increasingly, scholars in a wide variety of disciplines are recasting what they are about in rhetorical terms.

[. . .]

[There is] a widespread recognition among scholars in diverse disciplines that rhetoric's disputes are their disputes; that the objectivist presuppositions on which their fields depended no longer can be defended; . . . that what they are engaged in is more akin to persuasion than to proof.

[. . .]

The trope of tropes . . . in the rhetoric of inquiry . . . is that of irony; its message of messages that things are not what they seem; its lesson of lessons (if there be one), that there is a covert, ideological text in everything that is communicated— hence, that we had best attend self-reflexively to our own tropologies, our own ways of constructing the world. (Simons 1989, 1, 5, 7)

For [anthropologist Clifford] Geertz, the devil to be avoided has two faces; an insufficient appreciation of the "localness" of one's own culture; and the use of a universe of discourse insufficient to account for the social semiotic of cultures other than one's own.

[. . .]

Both translation and interlocution require the ethnographer to put his/her own world "at risk." In fact, they mandate the development of vocabulary and concepts sufficiently powerful to describe social realities fundamentally differ- ent from one's own without denying those differences. The result is a rhetorical form which . . . is explicitly self-reflexive, . . . determinedly flexible in its logics . . . explicitly open-minded . . . [and] transparently rhetorical. (W. Barnett Pearce and Victoria Chen, in Simons 1989, 128, 130)

We suggest that the media, rather than ruining communication (via the manipu- lation of images) in fact reveal something profound about communication that was easier to leave implicit in earlier times: the constructedness of reality and the reality of construction.

[. . .]

Human society is best characterized by its being made. In it facts and fictions coexist as siblings, separated only by the relative density of interconnections to other human productions, and not by any essential (ontological) difference. The terms *fact* and *fiction* etymologically are related: both are things that are made.

[. . .]

Experience is not something raw and dumb that gives our words their meaning; rather, our words give meaning to our experiences.

[. . .]

The discovery that all the world is symbolic doesn't call for a rejection of the world, but a more appropriate understanding of how it works. (John Durham Peters and Eric W. Rothenbuhler, in Simons 1989, 11, 17)

Fritjof Capra, David Steindl-Rast, and Thomas Matus entered into a conversation about new-paradigm thinking that was published in 1991 as *Belonging to the Universe*. With extremely broad academic and religious backgrounds, including all having experiences with both Eastern and West- ern religions, they were, at the time of the conversation, a physicist (Capra) and two Roman Catholic monks.

I have selected some quotations from the dialogue and will use first names, as they do in the book.

> FRITJOF: Science asks for the *how* and theology, the *why*. . . . But then the how and the why can not always be separated. Science asks . . . for how a particular phenomenon is connected to all other phenomena. If you include more and more connections, ultimately you will reveal the entire context, which is, in fact, the why. (19–20)
>
> [. . .]
>
> DAVID: How can we speak about God in the new paradigm? The moments of religious encounter are always moments in which something becomes meaningful. In other words, you see something in its ultimate context. We have an idiomatic expression in which we say, "It tells me something" or "It speaks to me." That idea of a dialogue is very strong in the context of finding meaning.
>
> Does it ring true to you . . . to say that through making sense of the world, through understanding this world more deeply, we have the experience of being in contact with that source of it all in the sense that it "tells us something"? It tells us something about itself; it tells us something about ourselves. The model of a dialogue is not completely inapplicable. (138)
>
> [. . .]
>
> THOMAS: Truth should never be confused with any of the ways we express truth, whether metaphorical or conceptual. That is why a number of theologians have adopted a "models" method typical of the natural sciences. . . . I think that the use of models in theology simply reflects the traditional awareness of the analogical character of all theological language. All we say about God is *analogy*—that is, whatever we affirm about God also implies God's infinite difference from everything else we know. (40)

At the beginning of the book David and Thomas expand their outline of the shift from old-paradigm to new-paradigm thinking (in theology) according to the following themes:

1. Shift from God as Revealer of Truth to Reality as God's Self-Revelation
2. Shift from Revelation as Timeless Truth to Revelation as Historical Manifestation
3. Shift from Theology as an Objective Science to Theology as a Process of Knowing
4. Shift from Building to Network as a Metaphor of Knowledge
5. Shift in Focus from Theological Statements to Divine Mysteries (xi–xv)

> [. . .]
>
> DAVID: This concept of mystery does not refer to what mystifies us because we do *not yet* grasp it; it refers to what we can *never* grasp because it is inexhaustible, as inexhaustible as life itself. (102)

Sallie McFague in *Metaphorical Theology* (1982) clarifies how such things as perceivers' interests and goals, conceptual frames, or sets of contextual particulars influence points of view and assertations about reality.

> The deconstruction and reconstruction of models by which we understand the relationship between God and the world is, in my opinion, one of the most serious tasks facing contemporary theology. . . . In many ways the traditional imagery is anachronistic and not in keeping with the contemporary cultural sensibility. . . . [Postmodern] assumptions include a greater appreciation for nature; a recognition of the importance of language to human existence; a chastened admiration for technology; an acceptance of the challenge that other religious options present to the Judeo-Christian tradition; an apocalyptic sensibility; a sense of the displacement of the White, Western male and the rise of those dispossessed due to gender, race, or class; and, perhaps most significantly, a growing awareness of the radical interdependence of life at all levels and in every imaginable way. Theological work, as is true of all constructive work, must, I believe, take place within the post-modern context if it is to address the pressing issues of our time.
>
> [. . .]
>
> Poets use metaphor all the time because they are constantly speaking about the great unknowns—mortality, love, fear, joy, guilt, hope, and so on. Religious language is deeply metaphorical for the same reason and it is therefore no surprise that Jesus' most characteristic form of teaching, the parables, should be extended metaphors. Less obvious, but of paramount importance, is the fact that metaphorical thinking constitutes the basis of human thought and language. From the time we are infants we construct our world through metaphor; that is, just as young children learn the meaning of the color red by finding the thread of similarity through many dissimilar objects (red ball, red apple, red cheeks), so we constantly ask when we do not know how to think about something, "What is it like?" Far from being an esoteric or ornamental rhetorical device super-imposed *on* ordinary language, metaphor *is* ordinary language. It is the *way* we think.
>
> [. . .]
>
> A metaphorical theology will insist that *many* metaphors and models are necessary, that a piling up of images is essential, both to avoid idolatry and to attempt to express the richness and variety of the divine-human relationship. (x–xi and 15, 20)

Kenneth Burke in *Permanence and Change* (1984) notes:

> I must keep harping on the fact that the function of analogy is not confined to its formal use, as analyzed in Aristotle. The principle is built into the very nature of language. For we can learn language only because we can apply the same terms to many different situations, yet all situations are in their details *unique*. To that extent situations cannot be identical: they can but be

analogous, and can be classed together by having in common some particular trait which is inferred to be the distinguishing characteristic in a given case, as even *verbs* classify. A cry of "Help" in effect "defines" this as a "help-situation," but the help-situation involves quite different responses if one is in a fire or drowning. (335)

At a summer 1993 conference titled "Science, Technology and the Christian Faith" at Concordia College, Moorhead, Minnesota, physicist-clergyman John Polkinghorne made the following three comments at different points in his lecture.

What we *can* know *models* the case; the temptation is to mistake it *as* the case.

This is a world of true becoming; we are about making the future toward which we are headed.

In prayer, we're offering *our* room to maneuver to *God's* room to maneuver.

Richard Busse, reporting on a 1991 Chicago symposium "Human Viability and World Religion," summarizes a presentation by University of Chicago psychologist Mihaly Csikszentmihalyi.

Instead of looking to the past for guidance concerning human viability, Csikszentmihalyi gazed toward the future. His research on human consciousness and assessment of the loss of faith in the current historical era led him to propose that religion needs to adapt to the "totality of evolving knowledge." Yet more is needed than adapting (surviving). Humans want and need to live well.

[. . .]

A faith perspective gives meaning and purpose to life, but the faith must be credible, must not conflict with empirical knowledge (which is not to say that faith is limited to empirical knowledge). The problem with many forms of religion is [that] the power to transform lives has dissipated with the refusal of religion to consider new knowledge. And further, much religious thought is too restricted, parochial, and divisive in claiming to be the sole expositor of universal truth. What is needed is a universal faith that will not divide, but enhance human consciousness as it merges toward greater and greater complexity in the future.

[. . .]

For Csikszentmihalyi a new concept of divinity will emerge out of new forms of human consciousness, a consciousness that sees itself in individual yet global identities. It has been the function of religion in the past to offer unified world views. The problem has been the limitation to one particular view. A new global consciousness, a new global religion will look to the future, and sing a new song of the emerging, interrelated, dynamic, complex, and interesting, human consciousness. (Busse 1992, 1, 7)

Early in Busse's report he makes the following statement: "This decade may well be remembered as one where humans began to consider 'viability' from an interdisciplinary and global perspective, by reimaging cultural diversity, epistemological discrepancies and disciplinary narrowness."

At a 1993 professional conference, psychologist John Ingram observed that socially constructed reality affects any given reality in ways we can't even begin to imagine, so we are rethinking the nature of reality. He cautions, however, that there can be inappropriate overemphasis, overextension, overinvestment in postmodern perspectives, as there has been with modernism, though he thinks postmodernism is a wonderful corrective to modernism, just as modernism, in a different age, was to many aspects of *its* worldview precursors. He thinks we need to recognize the limits of *all* perspectives and learn to work in multiple modes.

Postmodern acknowledgment of the infinite complexity and intersubjective dynamism of human language/culture/meaning construction returns us, in some ways, to a premodern, pre-Enlightenment humility about our capacity to comprehend the universe—a state in which awe at the incomprehensible might be carried reverently and poetically in stories, songs, and sayings. Truth myths, truth parables, truth tales, and life stories are gaining new respect and usefulness, in many quarters, as we enter new awareness that they can be powerfully evocative carriers of simple but sophisticated wisdom. Faith in goals of final mastery and absolute certainty is severely eroded in contemporary U.S. society; artistries of insight are recovering some of their ancient appeal and serviceability, as well as new realism.

Native American educator John Mohawk, speaking at a Concordia College symposium in 1992, showed keen awareness of being on the edge of a revolution in thought about the value of diversity and the potential for humans to participate consciously in species development. Ancient American Indian ways of celebrating and imaging how diversity is all part of unity—how everything is connected and sacred—may be poised now to enter mainstream thinking, not as quaint, but as restorative. The joining of earth and spirit are recurring themes among Native Americans, as are the joining of spirit and society. Mohawk says, "If your society doesn't mirror your soul you *lose* your spirit." Put in another metaphor, this saying reflects a gnawing fear voiced among many U.S. citizens.

Extensive as this discussion of reality paradigms may seem to any reader eager to plunge into the clergy interview data, it only lightly brushes the surface of what's emerging on the subject in recent years. My intention, as stated earlier, is to draw the reader deeply into the interpretive frame that is operating, for me, relative to the data.

Since the clergy interview material is multifaceted and needs to be experienced without minute dissection by an interpretive scalpel, I now want the reader to notice, throughout, the ways the voices move away from and toward the alternative reality orientations, take comfort or offense in them, comment upon them, stew and fret within or between them, weave them together, and employ them as working assumptions—with or without seeming to recognize the contrasting views explicitly.

I close this chapter with two clergy quotations about moral issues. They may serve as "practice exercises" in identifying assumptions, as "appetizers," and as a transition to the focus on clergy informants.[1]

- It's really hard to create a climate of lively debate, though I don't think people feel discounted as human beings when they disagree with me, in the sense that I won't care for them pastorally, I won't like them, I won't talk with them. . . . I don't think the congregation is a place of lively moral discourse and I think it needs to be. . . . To me it's a process issue. I don't think we have found a way to *engage*. [My denomination] came out with a document on human sexuality, inviting congregations to respond. We invited people to . . . be part of a year-long creating of our response. . . . Thirty some people have been involved in that, every week for eight months. But the continuum represented . . . is from center to left of whoopee. There isn't anybody that is in disagreement with the document or even thinks [it] went too far. And I'm *sure* there are people like that in the congregation.

- [Sources for moral guidance are] dynamic and ever changing. Yet it used to be black and white. It was very simplistic; this is what you do and this is what you don't do. Again, experience has tempered that. . . . Some of these moral issues are very complex and not always as clear-cut as my perceptions from the past.

NOTE

1. Throughout the study, the bulleted extracts will signal in informant speaking. In a series of extracts each bullet will mark the shift to a different informant.

Chapter 3

The Men

The central data in this study are the portions of interview narrative focused on theological, moral, and administrative perspectives. The biographical pieces in this chapter (beyond their obvious human interest value) can serve to supply helpful reference points for socially locating the voices that will be heard in the themes of subsequent chapters.

So I shall now introduce you to the men in the study—not with coherent personal stories about individual clergymen but with thematized biographical items from the nineteen interviews. Admittedly, there is a loss of informative connections this way; we simply cannot "see" the men as clearly through such topically grouped fragments as we could if each informant were sketched as a biographical whole. Nonetheless, the procedure is necessary in order to preserve confidentiality according to the terms of the interview arrangements. Regrettably, this procedure also causes loss of some potential challenges to stereotypical assumptions about traits tied to certain factors such as denomination, age, race, educational background, and sexual orientation. The theology and moral commitments of particular clergymen, for example, do not always display either the official or the commonest positions in their denominations. Through the interpretive comments, I've done what I can to warn the reader away from conventional assumptions that run counter to my data. I must also rely on the reader to resist constructing imaginary clergymen that are composites of items selected to fit preconceptions.

I interviewed men in Ohio, Michigan, Minnesota, and North Dakota. They serve congregations ranging in size roughly from 200 to 13,000 members. About half the men are in congregations in the 1,000–4,000 range. Four of the informants are African American, fifteen are European American. Ages spread from early thirties to mid-fifties. Sixteen are married, three are single; one of the nineteen identifies himself as gay; four are in second marriages—one, after the death of his first wife, and three, after earlier marriages ended in divorce. Two, each, come from the following affiliations: Jewish (one, Reform and one, Conservative), Roman Catholic, Lutheran (ELCA), Presbyterian (USA), United Methodist, United Church of Christ, and Baptist (one, Missionary, and one, jointly affiliated National/American). One, each, is African Methodist Episcopal, Disciples of Christ, Unitarian Universalist, Episcopal, and Assemblies of God. All but one informant, who is an associate minister, are designated sole or senior clergy in their congregations.

Two of the nineteen had full-blown careers in other areas of work before entering professional ministries. These two were a major league baseball player and an executive with a data-processing corporation. Several others had important and extensive work experiences (some lasting a few years) interspersed with years of college and/or seminary. These include teaching, sales, industrial manufacturing, social work of various sorts, and U.S. military intelligence operations.

All completed undergraduate college degrees at schools ranging through Bible colleges, state institutions, small liberal arts colleges, and nationally prestigious Ivy League institutions. One black and one white clergyman have bachelor's degrees from Harvard. All but three completed seminary degrees required by their denominations for ordination. These three are ordained in groups not requiring seminary work; two of them, at the beginning of their ministries, were mentored several years by clergy elders. One of the latter was urged to attend seminary but said he declined because, in his experience, ministers with seminary training were not "as spiritually alive" as the mentored ones. Seminaries attended, like colleges, vary in type. Many of the nineteen went to denominational seminaries, but six selected nondenominational divinity schools such as Union, Princeton, and University of Chicago. Four went on to earn Doctor of Ministry degrees, one was awarded an honorary doctorate, and several did some graduate-level study in specialized areas. One completed work for a Ph.D. in theological studies.

Five are sons of clergy fathers. One is third-generation clergy and one is fifth-generation in the male line of descent. The latter remarks, "And each of us in a different denomination!" One had a clergy grandmother; one, a clergy uncle; one, a clergy godfather. All of the latter were emotionally close to the related informant.

Each man chose the setting he preferred for the interview. For one, it was his rectory; the others opted for offices or lounges in their church or synagogue buildings. During the interviews five sat at their desks, with me on the other side; the rest selected an informal arrangement in a social-function room or an office space arranged for ministerial counseling and visiting. Some of the edifices were quite modest and plain. Others were elegantly designed and furnished complexes, with numerous staff specialists evident.

I have no way of knowing whether the clergymen met me as they might meet their parishioners or what other activities were on their respective schedules before and after our conversations, but clothing and self-presentation varied widely. About two-thirds wore business suits and the rest were informally attired in slacks or jeans and shirts or sweaters. Though levels vary, all of the men are verbally adept and show well-developed interpersonal skills—not surprising, given their chosen profession and their relatively successful performance in it.

Several were rather brisk, businesslike, and reserved in their demeanor. Their responses were somewhat measured and cautious and had a for-the-record quality that lacked spontaneity, compared to the others. More often the tone set was a sort of pleasant, confident dignity—relaxed, affable, freely expressive and engaging, though quite low-key. Six informants displayed an exceptionally high level of expressive intensity. The passion of their commitments and wide range of ideas and anecdotes (punctuated with ready humor) flowed from them in a torrent of considerable force. And then there were three who were rather conspicuously casual, for example, removing shoes, stretching and yawning frequently, exhaling dramatically, propping feet on tables or desks, draping legs over chair arms. All in all, they are a friendly, personable, attractive lot who are likely to evoke many positive impressions in public and private meetings.

According to what U.S. society judges as "good looks" in regard to facial features, body size and proportions, hair, grooming, and bearing, these men, as a group, are well above general population averages. How appearance interacts with success in various realms of endeavor is an interesting research question in itself—one that I shall not here pursue. As previously mentioned, biographical information firmly places the informants between their early thirties and middle fifties. They have a mean age of about forty-four and eight are very close to that mean. Though I did not ask interviewees for their exact ages, approximations are easy to deduce from the narratives and help clarify our picture of the men. In the selection process, as I asked for names of ministers who were broadly considered successful in their denominations, I also asked the information supplier (usually a judicatory office person) for an age estimation (to help me get variety in this respect). I subsequently became interested in how these estimations of age matched the information I received from the interviewees themselves. Two clergymen I interviewed were described to me initially as "an energetic young minister" and "a very competent older fellow." It turned out they were exactly the same age. Yet, men identified as in about the same stage of life sometimes were, in fact, quite widely separated in age. I came to realize that a kind of boyishly effervescent personality was often judged "young"; and a more conventionally manly formal reserve tended to be seen as belonging to an "older" minister. Interesting.

FAMILIES OF ORIGIN AND SCHOOLING

A great deal of interview information was shared about families of origin. None of the nineteen was born into a family suffering severe economic deprivation. The clergyman indicating the greatest economic difficulty in his childhood home says the family lived, nonetheless, with firm middle-class values and aspirations. Four informants come from lower-middle or "working class" families with varying degrees of economic stability. The rest of the early households are middle-class to upper-middle-class in their relative economic position.

Not surprisingly, given U.S. vocational mobility patterns, there were shifts in parental occupations as the men were growing up. Fathers' occupations included the following: businesses, sales work, religious ministry, law, mining, utility work, engineering, ranching, farming, carpentry, management. Mothers' occupations ranged through fashion illustration, party-planning, bookkeeping, teaching, clerking, secretarial work, mill work, postal clerking, library work, and homemaking. For about two-thirds of the men the mother's major occupation during all or part of the interviewee's childhood was primarily as homemaker. In almost all of these cases, however, she carried additional responsibilities (sometimes very heavy) for part-time employment, community leadership, or assistance to a professional or entrepreneurial husband.

Two informants are oldest among their sisters and brothers—one the oldest of five and one, of four. Six are youngest in families with two to five children. Seven occupy mid-positions among siblings in families with three to five children. Four are the only children of their biological parents but have step-siblings. One of these four was born to a teenage mother who never married his father. He and his mother lived in her parental home until her later marriage to another man and the informant's move with them to a separate house nearby. He remembers well the day several years later when his mother and stepfather set off with his infant stepsister to establish work and home in a distant city, while he was returned to the grandparental household. Everyone seemed concerned that he'd be upset and paid a lot of attention to him; but since he was still in a familiar home place, with extended family and friendly neighbors, he remembers no sadness or fear about the shift in arrangements. Nor does he remember much difficulty adjusting to the later reunion with his mother's household in their city apartment, after he was dragged by a mule and seriously injured while working on his grandpa's farm. He says he got along well with his hard-working stepfather, who was less "gruff and hard" than his equally hard-working grandfather. He remembers them both as serious, task-oriented men. His grandfather had early identified the informant as a competent worker and "a smart kid," holding him up in the family as an example of how kids should be.

I describe this childhood situation in some detail, partly in order to point out that circumstances looking on the surface like "big trouble" may contain important dynamics for stabilizing and supporting a child's development in healthy ways.

Several other clergymen had little or no contact with their biological fathers. In two cases there was a parental divorce in the informant's infancy and two others lost fathers through sudden death. One father died from an aneurysm when the son was ten days old; the other was fatally burned in a car-repairing accident when the son was four. The latter clergyman experienced the tragic death of a father a second time when, as a teenager, his stepfather died, a man who had been plagued for years with severe paranoid episodes.

More common in the interviews was the description of an "absent father"—part of the household but physically or psychologically removed from comfortable interaction with the informant as a child, owing to high levels of work involvement, alcohol problems (three instances), or a volatile temperament that kept families "walking on eggs to keep Dad from blowing up," as one put it. Two mothers are also reported as alcoholic during the son's childhood and youth. In one family both parents were problem drinkers. This clergyman recalls an exceptionally dysfunctional household in which he and his siblings groped for satisfying life supports and he accumulated many "negative values" (qualities he considered important *not* to carry forward into his own adulthood). The other two with alcoholic fathers were into their teen years before they even realized that Dad had a drinking problem; they do not remember much attendant turmoil in the family.

A second clergyman speaks of his childhood household as thoroughly dysfunctional. He remembers his alcoholic and twice-divorced, but talented and attractive, mother as emotionally volatile, vocally negative about men, and irresponsible about agreements (especially time agreements). He remembers constant frustration and embarrassment connected with waiting for her in awkward circumstances. Her second marriage resulted in much verbal fighting with her spouse, though the informant recalls some really good times with his stepfather and stepsister. After the second divorce the mother became increasingly intrusive in her son's life. Until shortly before her death, he says, she remained problematic to him with her "unreasonable and interruptive" demands on his time and attention.

A man with a "workaholic" clergy father says his childhood memories of Dad include the "ever present briefcase and papers." One image that stands out for him is the family, on vacation, with Dad at a park picnic table writing letters beside his open briefcase.

Several informants report being truly terrified of older brothers who teased them mercilessly and, in various ways, exploited the younger brother's gullibility. In one case, this included some episodes of sexual abuse. Several others remember constantly teasing their younger siblings, especially sisters.

No minister talked about physical (including sexual) abuse from parents; but four noted irritable, angry fathers who dished out what the sons remember as overly harsh punishments; and one had a mother given to extremely unpleasant punishments. A few relationships with parents sound at least borderline abusive in the verbal and psychological sense.

The only interviewee born with a physical handicap (surgically correctable, over time, and not evident to me at our meeting) remembers much verbal bullying in his family and at school. He claims that the defense he learned to rely on was a quick and acid wit. He also thinks that the trauma his parents experienced at his birth may, in part, explain his especially close relationship with his grandparents, who lived in the same block as his parents.

Other situations representing major sadness or struggle in the families of origin include debilitating terminal illnesses for two fathers and a mother when the informant was fairly young (but no longer a child), much loving care focused on a Down's syndrome sibling in one family, and several households in which one or more siblings were "always in trouble" (substance abuse and vehicle accidents, for example). Two clergymen recall being rescued from drowning at early ages.

Before concluding this meandering tour through some of the more troubling aspects of reported childhood situations, we should consider early experiences of racism from the African American ministers' stories. One, who says he "pretty much escaped the horror stories" that were all around him, needed to deal with white folks very little until, as a teenager, he became eligible to attend a magnet school for high-performing students. Persons of different races mingled freely at that school and he doesn't remember serious difficulties around issues of race. Another man, however, recalls high consciousness of racial prejudice and discrimination from a very early age as he and his sister "integrated" their grade school by being the only black youngsters enrolled. A succession of distressing, racially focused incidents and problems culminated for him in adult interests and activities addressing race-based differences in U.S. social benefits and supports. A third African American minister was in eighth grade when he first recognized pain directly attributable to racism; he lost out to a white candidate in a very close class presidency election and later found out he had actually received the greater number of votes. This bitter pill was followed by happier results in his high school, where he was elected to class presidency all four years. Later, while employed during school vacation, he was the target of blatant discrimination in an incident his father helped him identify as a deliberate setup calculated to make him fail and quit. He was able to survive with "a new determination not to be broken" and sub-sequently received a work commendation from his boss.

The remaining black minister tells a story with frightening overtones for any reader familiar with the historic Emmet Till case. As a child he periodically went with persons in his family to visit kin in the segregated South. One day he walked twelve miles with a relative to do a bit of business at the post office. The informant recalls sitting down upon arriving to rest and wait. An old white man beside him stomped his cane on the floor, saying, "Nigger, you can't sit beside me!" The informant says he jumped up and said something back but can't remember what it was. At any rate, he was immediately shipped back north by his family, for fear of severe retaliation.

All four of the black ministers in this study describe especially rich, stable, and extensive support systems in childhood. Such support doubtless constitutes a crucial resource for any minority person steering a steady life course in a racist society. Just as their childhood experiences include multiple adult models of community responsibility and leadership, so they are aware that they now function as such models in the congregations they serve.

At least two of the white ministers remember formative racial events in their youth. Around a neighborhood incident where a black family was denied residence and around the firing of a household employee these men remember sensing injustice and being angry at not getting more information from parents. Both now have longstanding reputations as highly visible, outspoken activists in the cause of racial justice.

Having spent considerable time on the more difficult, problematic, or distressing aspects of early biographical material, I'll turn now to the larger data pool of nurturant, supportive aspects that were shared.

With the exception of two cases, the ministers report strong mother parenting by women who were essentially competent, caring, responsible, steady, and, in quite a few cases, a lot of fun. I sensed that I was hearing about mothers who were not run-of-the-mill parents. Nor was I getting signals of unusual emotional dependency in the relationships described. These sons say they generally felt that their mothers understood them, enjoyed them, and helped them in their development.

Also, with few exceptions, the clergymen tell of dependable father-parenting; though (especially for the men whose fathers were absent, "absent," or negative influences) the parent was not always the biological father. Attentive fostering of youthful development frequently came from grandfathers, uncles, teachers, employers and (important in these men's lives) clergy. Later on, fathers-in-law were important positive influences for some. About half of the men describe multiple layers of female and male caretakers/mentors functioning on their behalf during formative years. These networks of support appear especially deep in the African American and Jewish narratives. For example, one black informant recalls great sadness when he was twelve and a newborn sibling died. His mother was incapacitated with grief and clinical depression for a long time; he can picture her constant rocking and crying. The extended family provided mother-substitutes, already familiar with (and to) the children, until the mother was able to function fully again. The same minister describes childhood closeness with both sets of grandparents, aunts, uncles, cousins, and assorted friends—a very stimulating, supportive, and mostly pleasant early environment for him.

- A lot of folks cared about us tremendously in our early ages and did real nice things around our birthdays and holidays and those kinds of things. . . . I've always felt loved . . . not only by my biological parents but also by the community. . . . That's a tremendous asset . . . and so that always placed a great deal of concern on my part to be able to give back to the community . . . and to be . . . supportive of the community.

Several clergymen refer to much comfortable "alone time" as small children. One of them thinks this may be connected with his intuitive, introspective strengths as an adult. Another remembers that, at eleven or twelve, he sometimes skipped school and hid in a familiar place under a bridge to play and think. He says he doesn't know what the motivation may have been, or what he was wrestling with or searching for, but "it was *my* time." By contrast, a few others describe unusually large and stable neighborhood play groups: lots of kids, lots of games, lots of fun.

Two informants had early access to many youth events of community and religious groups through being allowed to accompany older sisters on a regular basis. Roughly a third of the men grew up in families that put them into a dense milieu of religious, educational, and community activities connected with parental commitments. some of them say they were aware that they belonged to families that "carried weight" in their respective communities. Where there was comfortable closeness with the parents this seems not to have been felt as burdensome. A few, however, remember wanting to be free of that identification. The life-style may have already evoked certain self-expectations, though, since these sons moved directly into their own performance and leadership involvements. In fact, by high school, at least six informants had been singled out as school leaders; by college years, at least eleven of the nineteen were substantially invested in religious leadership of some sort (local congregations, college associations, national movements, camps, and so on).

Without exception the men were identified early as intelligent youngsters with many capabilities and interests. A few say they lacked high motivation for studying until their late teens, but all of them did reasonably well in school and about two-thirds of them were recognized as exceptionally high performers throughout their school careers. They describe numerous awards, opportunities, and achievements; but perhaps more telling is their evident pleasure in remembering for me their school years. One relatively young man, who claims he cannot recall seeing adults read in his early childhood home, talks of his great and continuing excitement at going to school. His emotion was evident as he recalled how much he loved school and especially learning to read. He seemed to savor the experience anew as he described it.

- Oh, I was excited! I remember I was *so* excited to go to school. Oh-h-h, those were the happiest days of my life up to that point—going to school. . . . I *loved* school. I really enjoyed it. It was a challenge for me. . . . One of my first teachers was an Oriental lady. I remember her working with me diligently trying to get me to pronounce "truck" properly, and "train." Playtime was nice. I enjoyed lunch and drinking the chocolate milk. The big group of children . . . I never experienced that before.

A fairly large number of ministers point to especially influential teachers who created memorable learning experiences.

- There's one person . . . whom I'll never forget. The seventh grade teacher who taught me grammar taught me how to *think*. . . . I'm eternally grateful for that kind of disciplined learning.

- Probably the [teacher] who had the most effect on me in childhood was my sixth grade teacher. . . . She was raised in the Holiness Church . . . a plain lady . . . never wore any makeup . . . but had a tremendous care for her students. . . . We would sometimes become rambunctious . . . [she] would take me out in the hallway . . . lifting me by the collar and saying to my face that she expected far more out of me than I was giving her—that I was capable of a lot more than I was being satisfied with. . . . and probably that day more than any other she woke up something inside of me that never again would allow me to be satisfied with just being part of the group.

He returned after graduation from college to tell his teacher what kind of an impact she had made on his life. Her appreciative smile is remembered by him as one of his most rewarding experiences.

Most of the men speak of their interest in sports. Ten narratives include school or public recognition of athletic excellence. Several men were high school sports stars, and there was the one (mentioned earlier) who ended high school with a professional baseball offer that he accepted. A few were recognized for athletic excellence in college, as well. Acclaim came to four men through musical performance and to five by way of dramatic productions. Three men indicate that they remain active in music or drama, two as instrumentalists, one as singer and dancer in local musicals.

The college years were extraordinarily important in the formation of these men. Since, by and large, they were already aware of their high intelligence and many competencies, college became a time and place for accelerated development in self-understanding, independent decision making, performance disciplines, and interpersonal skills. Quite a few of them tell of entering directly into leadership roles on campus or in congregations. Even more talk of their intellectual worlds opening up to events, issues, and perspectives entirely new to them. One remembers writing letters from his church college denouncing "the hypocrisy of the teachers" who "were not Christian" in their teaching about biblical criticism and social justice. In a few years he was thinking of many of those same ideas as moderate, well founded, and central to his thinking about faith.

Several describe "misunderstandings" and occasional serious tensions with campus authorities; but only one talks about his "wildness" and defiance of rules as pretty much characterizing his college years. He says, "I thrived on not being 'normal' " (at a very conservative church college).

Many of the ministers were in college during the years of "campus unrest." Their stories contain numerous instances of intense, moderate, or peripheral involvement in civil rights, antiwar, antidraft, and anti-parietal-rules movements, as well as other political activism. These were also the years of flamboyant sexual experimentation and mind-altering drug use. The human-potential movement was flourishing. Middle-class students, in huge numbers, were experiencing "the inner city" through college-related trips and projects of various sorts. The national turbulence of that time, though troubling to certain informants in some respects, was mostly fruitful for them. They were pressed steadily to rethink their taken-for-granted views. Through church and campus opportunities many found themselves in shockingly unfamiliar surroundings and had life-quaking experiences, from which they say they learned much.

A campus romance is recalled, in one case, as pivotal in a man's academic and intellectual development.

- Probably one of the best things that happened to me . . . in my sophomore year . . . I got interested in a young lady . . . who really taught me how to study. She had a system in place; if I was going to date her, we'd meet at the library at four Between four and seven every day we'd study and that's where I learned a systematic approach to studying. What that really did was free me up to be the student I was capable of being . . . and still [allows me] to enjoy weekends. My grades skyrocketed.

Given the central focus of this book, biographical accounts of early religious influences are especially interesting pieces of the life stories.

EARLY RELIGIOUS INFLUENCES

Fifteen ministers remember their childhood environments as consistently religious, largely in positive ways. These men report attendance at religious services; parental involvement in congregational offices, projects, and social events; religious instruction; and some household devotional activities. The five clergy families might be expected to fit this description; but many others were nearly as involved, it seems. Six informants went to a religious grade school and/or high school.

Three interview quotations illustrate some of the men's early memories of religious activities.

- Church formed a very important part of life . . . Sunday School and Church every Sunday. . . . I enjoyed the people. . . the kids. . . that was a lot of fun. . . . I did *not* enjoy the Sunday dinner [at a succession of parish homes] that preachers' families were always subjected to every Sunday without fail . . . and having to stay dressed up. It would have been fine if I could have gone in my play clothes. I liked the church . . . plain glass windows . . . the feeling of lightness, of airiness, of openness. . . . Home was not particularly pious.

- When I look back at . . . my upbringing there's much I've been very appreciative for . . . the clear family center in faith, . . . devotional life, . . . sharing prayer at an early age, . . . children being expected to lead in devotions, taking our turn. . . . Sunday meals were always in the dining room and devotions on Sunday were most often *every*one sharing in prayer. . . . We had a real sense of humor in our family. . . . My grandmother [part of the parental household] . . . a very quiet pietist . . . had a bun in her hair that she was always adjusting. Sometimes her prayers would get too long and I would take toothpicks and fill into her bun so afterwards when she'd shake her bun, she'd hit the toothpicks first. It was my way of saying, "Grandma, this was *too* long.". . . or I'd tie her apron strings to the chair . . . and it was all OK . . . we laughed a lot. But, my goodness! . . .we'd sing the books of the Bible as a song at the table, . . . we'd sing the Lord's Prayer to learn the words. . . . When I think of the contrast now trying to get any kind of devotional life in our family!

- Church was *big*! . . . We had to go every Sunday. Saturday and Sunday afternoons were show time. . . . If we didn't go to church we didn't go to the show . . . and that was dress up time, . . . you got to go in your Sunday shoes and you got to put on your good clothes. . . . Sunday was a real special day, so you kinda looked forward to Sunday. Sunday was family time . . . big family dinners.

The four ministers who did not have such generally consistent and positive childhood religious experiences warrant individual attention. One rabbi says that though his parents kept a kosher home for the comfort of extended family, they themselves were not observant or active in the synagogue. However, he says his childhood milieu was very Jewish and he became both observant of religious practices and active in synagogue youth functions at an early age, willingly tagging along with an older sister to synagogue events. He remembers sensing that he made his grandparents and some of his aunts and uncles very proud as he showed such strong interest in religious activities.

The two ministers who speak of their childhood families as severely dysfunctional nonetheless mention considerable religious influence in their youth and already, during their high school years, considered the possibility of clergy vocations. They remember the early family religious experiences as inconsistent and conflicted, but not overwhelmingly negative. Their religious development and attraction to ministerial work came mainly through the influence of dynamic youth ministers whom they liked and found supportive. Each had an important spiritual experience toward the end of high school. One "went forward" at a Billy Graham crusade, and the other discovered an important model for life in a leader at a youth gathering. Even more important in the life of the first mentioned was an occasion later that year when, as a freshman in college, he recalls a personal breakthrough that freed him "to let go of much family baggage" at God's invitation. From early childhood he had taken on a heavy load of responsibility as family peacemaker.

Finally, one man grew up in a family that attended church and instilled a sturdy sense of right and wrong, but he says they (including himself) "were not Christians who had a personal relationship with Jesus Christ." In fact, he says, he was quite cynical and "put off" by what he considered the hypocrisy of people "dressed up" and "showing off"—"going through religious motions" when he could not see that it made any difference in their lives.

He dates his own conversion from a time of intense searching for life direction after a girlfriend (now his wife) issued an ultimatum: "Either you become a Christian or I will not keep on dating."

- I thought, "I'm gonna give it a shot." I began to read the Bible she had given me and tried to understand how God could be personal in some sense, instead of just in the church on Sunday.

Some months later, he says, he "accepted Christ as Savior" and "began the process of making Christ Lord of [his] life." He recalls a vivid experience of abandoning profanity and pornography, as well as growing in faith and zeal and family closeness; though these changes also caused some family members to bristle at what they saw as his attempts to lay his newfound religion on them. I asked if he at that time had thoughts of going into the ministry and he responded, "Not at all; *none* at *all*!"

He was much affected, over time, by the ministry of his father-in-law and other clergy he respected. Then after years of a successful career in a data-processing corporation he claims he had (while praying) a vision of himself on a platform—Bible in hand—preaching to a large crowd.

It blew me away, to say the least. No way was I seeking that! . . . I couldn't tell my wife (I was so overcome) but she knew something had happened. When I did tell her, she said, "Finally!" She had had a prior vision of this plan for my life. She had said nothing. . . . She felt God would confirm it directly with me and she wouldn't have to do it for Him.

He considers himself cautious by nature and sought greater clarity in the matter before requesting his congregation's approval of his ministerial candidacy.

This last narrative bridges into the stories of how the men came to their vocational decisions for professional ministerial careers.

DECISIONS FOR MINISTRY

Almost all of the men talk the language of spiritual experience, one way or another. None of the nineteen speaks of the ministry purely as a professional job; for each there has been a personal need to experience for himself the dynamic truth of the traditions he is entrusted with as clergy.

The earliest remembered decision was at age ten.

- Even at an early age . . . I felt the presence of God in my life, and on my life. . . . I knew at ten I was to preach. There was no doubt! . . . [There was] an emerging consciousness. I never shifted when I talked about the ministry. I would hear older men talk about, you know, they heard God speak to them in the field . . . plowing, and God spoke to them . . . doing something and they had this vision, . . . but so I'm waiting . . . and I wasn't getting that. [Someone] explained to me that God did not deal with every man the same and that if this urge and this desire was real that God would eventually let me know . . . what I was to do . . . and at age fourteen I told them [family] I was called. . . . At that time my godfather told it to the church.

Though this man had such an early and strong call to preach and to enter ministry, he did not see himself as a parish pastor. He intended to be a teacher because he did not think clergy income could support a family. It was college time before he saw the possibility of full-time parish ministry, rather than just preaching, as realistic and desirable for himself.

Both priests had declared themselves interested in priestly vocations by the end of their grade school years and had entered "minor seminaries" (residential high school and junior college institutions expressly for students with a declared intention of entering the priesthood). One went straight through to ordination. At a time when it became clear that he was being groomed for high offices and special assignments he asked for and was granted his preferred role of parish priest. The other dropped out for five years of teaching and social-service work and only returned to formal preparation for the priesthood after a lengthy exchange with a woman in his parish. She "bugged" him constantly about becoming a priest. Finally she extracted from him a promise that he would pray about it specifically. He promised, he said, mainly to get her off his back; but after only two weeks he was convinced he should return to the seminary. He has not been sorry.

Like the man who already felt his call to preach at ten, one of these priests thinks he was likely moving toward a ministerial vocation from early childhood. He does not date any special event or decisional awareness until he entered the minor seminary. However, a great uncle whom he loved, admired, enjoyed, and was very close to was a priest and his primary male model in childhood.

- Church was a big thing. . . . [I was] very into church stuff, you know . . . devotions . . . being altar boy . . . but also being tempered by the fact that I had this human insight into what clergy were all about by going and visiting my uncle. . . . The structure . . . can do some good but it can also be a fearsome thing if you don't put the human element in it and keep it in its place; so lucky for me I had a family that helped me do that.

He describes the uncle as a caring relative—humorous, playful, down-to-earth, a hospitable host to guests. A great deal of time was spent with this uncle during the informant's early years and, already while in grade school he was forming a decision to follow his uncle's vocation. His steady commitment to the priest vocation was colored by two early spiritual experiences from his minor-seminary years.

I was in the evening study hall . . . a big room with maybe 150 desks and a priest moderator sitting on a platform. . . . It would always begin and end with prayer. . . . At the closing prayer of that night . . . [I had] one of those wonderful mystical experiences of all of a sudden having a sense of God and God's pervasive love and presence and beauty. . . . It couldn't have lasted more than a few seconds, but it forever is a touchstone for what real prayer and mystical experience is about. The other [experience was] when I was a camper . . . working toward a certain award in riflery. I had only a few targets left. . . . I remember making a good old bargain with God: If you help me get that award I'll come and say the rosary in the chapel after supper every night till the end of the period. . . . Of course, hating it after I got the award the next day . . . but being enough of a compulsive . . . sneaking into the chapel so no one could see me and then finding it nice there . . . a beginning of that hunger for a kind of contemplative, quiet prayer. It was almost like *stumbling* upon it.

Quite a few of the other participants in the study at an early age had at least glimmers of possible ministry vocations. This was especially true for clergy sons who showed leadership potential and were aware of family or community expectations.

- You know, I often talk about my call to ministry . . . [as] genetically prede-
termined! It began . . . with my father probably speaking into my mother's
womb saying, "You will be a pastor . . . you will be a pastor." I think in some
sense I fought against, rather than being drawn to, the ministry because I had
such a strong sense that being the male of the family there was such an
expectation that I would . . . be a pastor. It was a family . . . with strong
expectations of public leadership . . . I was a young person who always got
involved in leadership.

Through a series of remarkable events this man was presented during his
college years with spectacular opportunities to participate officially as a
peer among international leaders at some important councils and conferences. In addition, there were rich learnings from off-campus structured
experiences available to students. He steadily moved toward seminary
preparation that eventually culminated in ordination.

The other clergy sons' decisions for ministry follow:

- I realized pretty early [teen years] that I had the gifts [for ministry]. . . . I've
probably never been overwhelmed with a zeal to do this but it's kind of like if
you wake up in the morning with a hammer and saw in your hand you'll probably
go out and be a carpenter. Whether you want to or not, those are your tools. . . .
I realized I had the tools of being able to talk to people . . . of making sense out
of people's concerns . . . of leading worship . . . of preaching (that I loved from
the first that I stepped into the pulpit). Watching what the Lord can do through
my preaching will never cease to amaze me.

When I asked where along the line, in reviewing his strengths, this man had
developed a specific intention to enter the clergy vocation, he told about an
older brother who everyone in the family assumed was headed for ministry.
Moving into the ordination process the brother quit and "threw the whole
family into shock."

I stepped back at that point and wondered, "Am *I* following my father's
footsteps? What am I doing?"

After college this man got a job in corrections, married, and a couple of
years later applied to his denomination for entering the process leading to
ordination.

During that time I developed a sense of "Yes, this is what I want to do". . . . I
don't know if it was more. . . . part enthusiasm, part acceptance . . . and maybe
part fear that I couldn't do anything else well.

- At the age of sixteen I was asked to participate in a youth service in my dad's church . . . and the minute I stood at that podium and I looked out at those 400 or 500 people sitting out there I knew what I wanted to do. I had given my first public speech to a class at the age of twelve and had loved it and every speech I'd given since then I'd loved, but I never thought about that in the sense of a profession or a calling . . . but when I stood there at that moment I knew that I wanted to do this . . . and I wondered what to do. I remember going to my father and telling him, "I really loved that; but that's probably not a worthy reason to go into the ministry." What he told me was this: "It's not the *only* reason you should, but it's a worthy reason, because if you don't enjoy that you won't be able to take it."

He then talked seriously with a friend of his father's and became more convinced that he would move toward seminary. When he actually entered seminary, he remembers it as a disappointment—a dramatic drop in intellectual stimulation, compared to college. He describes himself as frustrated, bored, and offended at the mocking contempt directed toward theologians he had learned to appreciate. He left to enlist in the U.S. Army. Some years later he resumed theological studies at a different institution and eventually sought ordination.

- I rejected the saying that I would probably take my father's place in the ministry. Down deep I probably knew it was true . . . but didn't want it to be true. . . . [Summers during college were spent working either in an auto plant or a steel mill.] The steel mill was a great experience because I was a common laborer. I worked with everyday kind of folks and learned a lot in that process . . . worked with a lot of men who had been in the mill for thirty years but hated every day of it and made me promise them that whatever I would do would be something I loved. That has stuck with me to this day. [In the junior year of college] the Lord really began to trouble my spirit. . . . I came home at Thanksgiving, . . . rode all the way home and didn't say anything to anyone. . . . I went to church for the first time in God knows how long and that Sunday my father was preachin' about Jonah runnin' from the Lord and the more he talked the more I realized he was talkin' *to* me and *about* me. . . . That one had my name on it! Suddenly all the stuff that was inside me began to swell up and I never will forget it. I broke down and cried. . . . That's the *worst* thing a young man can do, sittin' in the church tryin' to be cool and all that. I really was overcome with emotion. . . . [I] got up to go downstairs and the next thing I remember I was up in front of the church. My dad was givin' the invitation and I just shared with the church family: "I need to talk." . . . I acknowledged my call into the ministry. . . . There was such a release of passion and energy in that. . . . It was a very emotional day for my family.

After "college drift" away from religious observances, accompanied by involvement in much political activism, work as a professional musician, and a health department job, one clergy son tells of being aggressively recruited for a position on a church judicatory office staff. At a national conference of black religious leaders he encountered "a new world of church." By way of a charismatic female minister speaking in tongues, the laying on of hands, megachurch ministries, and other experiences, he began to see what he had previously judged "fringe" activities brought into real experience for him. Recognizing his own gifts and God's equipping him for religious service, he felt the call into ministry as a hunger to develop and hone the gifts of the Spirit.

- Nothing about faith seemed out of reach. I saw that my leadership potential could be fulfilled *in* the Church.

He talks of "digging in" and "tooling up" at the seminary, finding it stimulating and satisfying.

The other clergy, who are not clergy sons, talk about decision experiences that include the following stories:

An informant whose high school peer group was involved heavily in youth activities at a local church (and greatly influenced by pastors with much appeal for them) enrolled in a church college but claims he had misgivings about choosing religious ministry as his life work. He was interested but thought it too confining. He just wasn't sure.

- At college chapel a young man got up to give testimony. . . . Most of the time they were yawners. . . . They never impressed me. He sincerely spoke of how the Holy Spirit had touched his life. Then somebody else got up and said something similar . . . then there was some singing . . . very spirited and enthusiastic. It soon became apparent that something unusual was happening. The dean got up and said, "We'll suspend classes for two hours; we certainly don't want to quench the Spirit." I took advantage of that to go to the grill to get a Coke. . . . This went on all day. I avoided it. I had a lot of work to do and I wasn't sure that it was sincere. Then at ten or twelve that night I could hear the singing and so I went over—mostly out of curiosity—and I truly had a very moving experience. I did feel the presence of God and felt my call to ministry confirmed and substantiated. Then I started to check out seminaries. . . . Also I had to contact my draft board.

A clergyman who says he went to the Bible college where his sisters had gone, fully intending after a year to join the U.S. Air Force and become an electronics specialist, found his plans changing.

- I never got around to the Air Force. My reason for going to the Bible college was I just wanted to get a good, sound basis in the Bible and my Christian faith before I went into the Air Force, and . . . after a year I really felt that I should go one more . . . then I would go on to my planned career.. . . . In the second year we were having some kind of special meeting . . . praying and I felt the Lord wanted me to prepare for the ministry. The ministry was never something I planned to do . . . nor did I look on it as a career that would be necessarily admirable. I don't mean despicable, but I mean it just did not seem like the kind of thing for me. . . . I've never had doubts or ambivalence . . . ever since that.

Discovering that his baseball career was a mixed bag of great friendships, exciting events, and tyrannical management (a "level of meanness" he had "never before witnessed"), a man who had already had some memorable religious experiences was reevaluating his life situation.

- I also had a critical religious experience during that year [second year as a professional baseball player]. . . . attending my home church that I grew up in . . . [I] suddenly felt the inspiration on a particular Sunday morning to seek a deeper, fuller religious experience. It was a really profound experience for me. I spoke with my pastor and shared with him what I was feeling . . . he counseled with me and helped me to identify what it was I was going through at the time.

This man recalls the pastor's helping him to see the experience as a call to ministry. He continues:

Out of that . . . I understood that I could not live as I had to that point, meaning I had to involve the Lord Jesus Christ in my life in conscious ways and serve Him. That was a new, eye-opening awakening for me. It caused me to give a lot of thought to what I was doing in life and how I was spending my life. I . . . felt an urgency about life that I had not experienced before.

During the following year he returned to his home church and talked with denominational elders about preparation for professional ministry.

One clergyman says that it was only after approximately twenty years in professional ministry and a brief interim of successful insurance selling that he first really "owned" his choice for ministry. He had been through a divorce and remarriage during the previous decade, and a counselor had been very helpful in guiding him into new self-knowledge. He maintains, "She wouldn't let me get by without going deep into self-understanding." He describes his original choice as probably more to please his parents and minister, as well as his fiancée and her parents—all of whom "thought it would be a fantastic thing." He refers to his ordination as an "intellectual passage into a chosen vocation, not a spiritual high," though he was genuinely religious and feels seminary was conducive to spiritual development for him.

(If the reader is counting) it is clear that all the narratives are not displayed. The telling would become far too lengthy if all data were used on each theme, so I have made editorial choices to show the range of views. Thus the omitted pieces tend to resemble, in part or whole, accounts that are included. Each story, of course, has some distinctive elements of spiritual formation, such as periods of time in Israel for the rabbis and crucial influence from two clergywomen (a campus pastor and a conference speaker) for one Protestant clergyman. Also, wives and girlfriends sometimes were part of the decisional milieu, as in the story that led into this section about vocation choice.

When parents and siblings heard about the decisions for clergy vocations they were mostly pleased, according to the informants. In a few cases the men perceived indications that a family member feared loss of closeness and spontaneity in a valued relationship. The more serious misgivings about the choice tended to come from a small number of fathers and a mother who were not negative about professional religious work, as such, but were uneasy about their sons' economic prospects; especially, their financial dependency on congregations that would need to be pleased. Contemplating the future for sons who were multitalented and personable, these parents felt some disappointment at the selection of work they judged as having inferior promise for fame, fortune, and material security, compared to alternatives. None of the men, however, faced serious attempts by family members to obstruct their progress toward ordination; nor was there ongoing alienation or criticism attributable to the career choice. The man who left well-paid corporate administration for lesser pay in the ministry was aware that his father, siblings, and former work partners saw his move as utterly incomprehensible. They were baffled by how someone could give up such a "sweet" work situation for what they saw as quite doubtful rewards from clergy work.

MARRIAGE, PARENTING, LEISURE

Nine of the sixteen married informants were married already at the time of ordination—one, to his second wife, after a divorce ended his first marriage. Five more married early in their professional ministries. The remaining two were single for several years after ordination, one of them after a divorce late in his seminary years. While the data hold no information about how the wives, families, neighbors, or congregations view these marriages, the men draw overwhelmingly positive personal vignettes when they talk about their mates. All but three had made firm plans to enter the clergy role prior to marital commitments, so mate selections may have reflected, in part, their ideals for ministers' wives and those mates' positive sentiments about having a clergy husband.

The two Catholic priests say they would have liked to marry. However, they also indicate comfort in conforming to rules of priestly celibacy, which from childhood they knew to be part of the vocation.

- Marriage was attractive. Parenting was not imperative. I'm at peace with the choice for celibacy. . . . I'm at peace about having a *family* in spiritual leadership. . . . My choice was for the priesthood and celibacy was part of the package. I never thought of it as a choice for celibacy. If I had the option I would like to be married. I see people with whom the type of marriage I envision would be attractive to develop.
- I would like to be a husband. I think I could have been a good husband to someone . . . though I couldn't pastor the same way I pastor now, with sixty-hour work weeks.

The wives who had years with their husbands before shifts were made to religious ministries are said to have had some difficulty adjusting to the role of minister's wife. One husband says,

- [My wife] . . . has had much more of an adjustment period than I have, because she's trying to adjust to a new role of being in the background. . . . She's a music person and she's used to . . . being more in front of people and being in a leadership role . . . where I was kind of in the congregation taking care of the kids. . . . This has . . . been a role reversal in some sense and so she's still not sure all of what it means to be a pastor's wife. I think I settled in easier than she did.

Several clergymen in the study married women with religious commitments in groups other than the ones the husbands entered as professional leaders. With one exception these men report that their wives have affiliated with the husband's denomination willingly and comfortably, even though the new affiliation may not represent wholly the wife's religious views.

The exception involves a man who was considering a Protestant ministry vocation and dating a devout Roman Catholic woman. He didn't think that, as a Protestant minister, he could have a Catholic wife. He remembers that at one point during the courtship she commented, "How can I say 'yes' to marrying you unless you ask; and how can you ask unless you're ready to take me as I am?" He continues:

- [It] made a lot of sense. . . . Finally, one of the few times in my life the Lord really spoke to me, and said, "Look! her faith is her faith; don't worry about it!" I went ahead and married her. My decision to go into the ministry was all right with her. My feeling is that if I were a plumber our relationship would be exactly the same; and I have both good and bad feelings about that. On the one hand I want her to be [like] my mother [a woman described as a quintessential minister's wife]; on the other hand I don't want her to be like my mother . . . obsessed with appearances. . . . This church is very accepting. It's nice . . . in many ways: the night my wife's brother was killed by a drunk driver . . . I had the privilege of being able to call the priest and say, "Look, she needs pastoral care."

A plus from this different affiliation is that the couple is freed from a common dilemma of clergy spouses; namely, the potential loss of professional pastoral care through marriage to the pastor of one's own spiritual community; and the attendant inhibition on seeking care elsewhere lest that be seen by the spouse and others as a sign of broken confidence in the marital or professional trustworthiness of the clergy spouse. This informant says that, for him and his wife, the lines are very clear; neither expects that he will function as her professional pastor.

Several informants describe the first stages of marital adjustment as upsetting and disorienting to them because they had never experienced overt confrontations in family disagreements and were totally unprepared for dealing with on-the-table arguments. (One was the man who spoke of his college years in terms of wildness and rebellion; he says all that defiance was conducted with a very controlled personal presentation.) These men found direct engagement in disagreements very threatening initially, but learned to deal with it and now sometimes idealize it as a more honest and productive way to negotiate mutually satisfactory resolutions. Even when they speak appreciatively of directness as a contributor to intimacy, they tend to retain a language of demand and control for it; for example, "She won't let me get by with . . . ," "She makes me . . . ," "She insists . . ."

One man recalls an incident from early in his marriage.

- I had this silly notion that I was an intelligent person and I was going to marry an intelligent person and, being intelligent people, we would never argue. (Laugh) I grew up thinking that; I really believed that; and when [my wife] and I argued on our honeymoon, I was devastated. I *never* expected that to happen. Well, you know, her family was different than my family. They used to argue and it meant nothing to them; it was an intellectual discussion and everybody loved each other. In my family . . . if you argued you were punished and love was withheld. . . . I had to learn to communicate feelings; I had to learn to argue. Ministry is not so different. Argument in marriage served a positive function.

Others, too, talk of early surprises and problems in marital adjustment.

- I think the aspect that was not . . . expected was the way in which I would have to . . give up aspects of my life to make a go of it. A lot of that for me was spontaneity—doing crazy things on the spur of the moment . . . things that for me in my early years were a great part of who I was. . . . I think I've regained a lot of that in my present marriage. For me that's what makes a lot of my happiness—the creative stuff that comes out of me . . . that I can go do with nobody ever caring about . . . or . . . I can bring other people along with me.

- One of the things that I experienced—that we experienced—in our first year of marriage was a difficult adjustment time. I'm very orderly and systematic . . . I'm a left-brained person; and so I like to have everything all decent and in order and when I had to deal with somebody else that didn't do things just the way I did that was a cause of some conflict. . . . We were able to work through it. We just had some real rocky times where I felt that our marriage was ordained by God; my wife . . . wasn't so sure that was the case. . . . Moving . . . near her folks was important because she was feeling lonely and when we got back to her turf she was more relaxed in our relationship. So I see that as part of God's providence for our marriage as well as my job career.

A man who entered his second marriage while in seminary (both partners having been previously married and divorced) says, "We both liked the idea of marriage but were scared of the actuality." In their long marriage they have worked hard, according to him, to deal with marital and parental problems in a healthy way and to develop their relationship commitment as a true friendship. His own parents (now in their ninth decade of life) provide for him an appealing model of a relationship in which the mutual enjoyment and "sparks" are still evident.

Another man, also, speaks of using his parents' marriage as a personal criterion for truly healthy intimacy. As he tells it, he always assessed his own relationships with girlfriends in terms of potential for growing into the kind of marriage his parents had.

Seven of these ministers' wives are employed full time in public-sector work. They include a university professor, an elementary teaching specialist, a clinical social worker, and several administrative specialists with business, financial, technical, and human-service organizations. Five wives have part-time employment in types of work that are similar to those of the full-time workers. Four wives work primarily in home- and church-related activities. One of these women is so heavily invested in church-acknowledged ministries that she has her own office space in the building complex and is there half of most days.

Each of the sixteen clergy couples has at least two children. The largest number is six, and the median is three. These numbers include various combinations of biological offspring, stepchildren, and adoptive children. The four informants whose first marriages were terminated by death or divorce have at least one child, each, from the earlier marriage. After the divorces, one man was the primary custodial parent, two were not.

The man whose first wife died told about the attention-getting family that came with his second marriage. Through mutual friends, he had met the woman who became his second wife. Each had suddenly lost a spouse close to the time of the youngest child's birth. Each had one other child, a couple of years older. At the time of their marriage they had, between them, two three-year-olds and two one-year-olds. With three infant seats in the back of the car and another in the front, he says, they turned a lot of heads.

Overall, the statements about parenting, as well as marriage, were focused strongly on positive rewards such as ministry enhancement and personal expansion of life perspectives.

- It's remarkable how much bigger I am in the same body. I can't believe what capacities I have for compassion, patience, joy, admiration. . . . I didn't know . . . any of that about myself. I have thought (and I mean no offense to anybody) . . . but if you haven't had children you haven't lived. If you've chosen not to have children there's an element of existence that you just don't know. . . . I feel sorry for people who make that choice. [With people who choose helping professions but who do not have children of their own] the stuff [those] people do is convenient for them; [your own] children are inconvenient. It's convenient to work out your schedule and say "goodbye." But this arbitrariness of children expands your capacity for enjoying life . . . [It's] an explosion of development.

A clergyman who was engaged two weeks after he met the woman he married said that during the first years of their marriage having children was an unresolved issue between them.

- She got married assuming we were going to have kids. We'd never talked about it. I couldn't picture working on a sermon and being bothered by kids. . . . We were on a hike . . . backpacking and we really had it out. . . . She made it clear that we either have kids or she was leaving.

I asked if the children, in fact, had been a negative experience and he quickly answered,

Oh, no! . . . It's been wonderful. I'm overjoyed—very glad. . . . They really are a delight. It's kinda silly to think that I was resistant.

While talking about his meditation and prayer experiences a minister includes comments about his relationship with his children.

- Now having two young children . . . when they come up and hug me . . . with their love and their trust . . . that's an affirmation of my life . . . that I don't know if you can duplicate. . . . Watching them grow and develop is a wonderful affirmation of the nurture of love—what it can do . . . and the discipline of love.

Where marriages had occurred before or during seminary education, wives tended to contribute employment earnings to the couple's income through those years. In one case a pregnancy precipitated a crisis. The couple "wrestled and fussed" about the implications, feeling that perhaps seminary would have to be dropped. A friend questioned whether God wanted the baby and the education to conflict. They decided to stay and the baby was born at the end of that school year. According to the informant, support came from the most unlikely places and the baby became the darling of both the seminary and the congregation he was serving as part of his ministerial preparation. Not only was material assistance of clothing and baby equipment given, but he was encouraged to bring the infant to class with him, and professors as well as professors' wives often volunteered childcare when he needed relief for required seminary activities. He claims that experience changed his consciousness about "what all could be in life and not sacrifice family life."

A healthy balance between demands of family and congregation remains a struggle for this minister, but he reports increasing comfort in preserving time for family things. The night before our interview he needed to move some church appointments to attend a daughter's track meet. He says he doesn't want his children to remember Daddy as not being around. As he has become more protective of family time he maintains that the congregation has been respectful and flexible, so that the balancing is much more manageable for him as time goes by.

In connection with his description of family births, one clergyman mentioned the importance to him of a child's sex. If this was an issue for others, there were no statements to that effect; I did not specifically ask them about the matter. Several of the men, however, did share their awareness, in families of origin, of the importance of being male. In terms of his own fathering experience, an informant says,

- Our second daughter was born and I went through a disappointment . . . because I was hoping and praying for a son . . . and so I didn't get as excited about child number two; and I think that was picked up on by her early in her . . . development. [Later] my son was born and I was excited about that. It was neat because my wife was involved in fellowship groups where the gifts of the Holy Spirit were being manifested (words of knowledge, prophecy, etc.) and someone had a word of knowledge for her as she was pregnant: that this would be a boy. . . . He was a blessing, and still is, in our lives, and we believe that God has an extra special . . . purpose for his life.

There are occasional descriptions of young adult or teen children with serious developmental problems of a psychological, emotional, or relational nature. A father whose family includes both biological and adoptive children says that he and his wife are comfortable getting professional help when it is necessary, as it has been occasionally. By and large, the descriptions of children are heavily tilted toward high academic performance, multiple interests, and appropriate social maturation.

One man compares current marital and parental satisfactions.

- Marriage becomes more and more fulfilling every year. It just grows deeper . . . not routine but gratifying. . . . We just know one another and how we operate. . . . Parenting, on the other hand, as we are faced with the monster called adolescence for the first time, there are some real heartaches. . . . we wonder whether we're getting through or not . . . attempting to set values for our children.

Ideally, the informants value family life, marriage, and parenting, believing that there should be an integrative balance of personal investments in family and ministry. Operationally, all of the married men talk of serious conflicts in the use of time. Some are minimally vexed, but most describe quality family time as a persistent issue with spouse and children. The families are frequently reported as convinced that the congregation gets priority status and they themselves come low on the list of items for the pastor's attention.

One minister says that congregations can consume a pastor, but they also want the pastor to have a perfect family. In his estimation, this inevitably creates much tension. He expects the increasing prevalence of two-career families like his own to help provide better understanding and more realistic expectations for "preacher's families." However, another says,

- A minister has a lot more control over that than perhaps they're willing to take responsibility for exercising. If their personal life is very much in flux then it becomes an issue, but not because the church is making an issue; it's because *you're* making an issue.

In general, wives are said to be the major household and childcare organizers, though the informants often credit themselves and others with making important contributions. During the early years of children's development many wives are described as preferring to move to the greater flexibility of volunteer or part-time work (rather than full-time employment) so they can have more time for family. Whatever arrangements are struck by the couple, most of the men seem unable to escape at least some ambivalence about conflicting expectations from traditional and equalitarian ideals.

Since I was mostly hearing such steady expressions of appreciation and satisfaction about marriage and parenting, I was especially interested in how the men see their professional and domestic responsibilities fitting together. Several voices are clear on the matter of integrating personal and professional concerns as a single ministry—a single caring. One talks about balanced caring for self and others throughout life. He thinks that people who pretend they don't need time for themselves are self-deceptive—running away from something. He sees care for self and care for others as necessary to each other and jointly required in family caring as well as pastoral caring in the congregation.

Another claims he doesn't experience stress and thinks that stress is simply a failure to approach ministry objectively. He values his family; family time is important, he says, and he makes the necessary scheduling shifts to see that family and congregation are both tended responsibly.

Both rabbis appear fairly free of stress about work/home conflicts. I suspect that this can, in part, be explained by the traditional centering of Jewish religious observance in the family context. Such a religious perspective may foster an integrative orientation more naturally flowing from the institutional affiliations. Nonetheless, both also comment on the extraordinary contributions from their wives toward reduction of possible tension. One says,

- My wife . . . "puts the best face" and helps . . . create less of a conflict than I think there would otherwise be. She is fully supportive . . . and I think she trusts that I would rather be home than out.

Others also report that wives assist them substantially in their ministries and help shield them from problems connected with work/home time allocation.

- [My wife] grew up in the church. She is extremely supportive. I've met many clergy and spouses and seen lots of lack of support.

I asked him to tell me more about what the word "support" means to him in this context. He responds,

That's complex; because she's also demanding of my time for her and for family. *Demanding*. I am a workaholic, but if I can make appointments with other people, why can't I make time for family? And she's very strong about that . . . [while] still understanding the importance of church, the emergency call, the Sunday morning pressure, the Saturday sermon preparation pressure. . . . you know, she gives me that space that I need.

He also describes a number of ways she has assisted him in the ministry directly. He says she will not take jobs by default—just because no one else is there to do them, but she selectively accepts tasks on her own terms. He claims she has built up programs that were in disarray, leaving them in good shape for her successors. Another man says,

- Our relationship, from my perspective, is wonderful. . . . We have seen our ministry as a team effort right from the beginning. I'd say she supports me but, in very real ways, she has separate ministries of her own . . . the moms' morning group . . . writing occasional articles . . . devoting herself to staying at home with the kids (a conviction I share, but was expecting I would marry someone more feminist). She's significantly more conservative than I am. I probably married "Tipper Gore" and . . . a year before . . . thought I'd marry "Hillary Clinton." I've been delighted . . . in ways I had not anticipated, given the demanding nature of the ministry. She's actively interested and concerned and working toward seeing that that's *our* church. It eliminates so many pressures that I see in other staff marriages. . . . I stated clearly to the congregation . . . that I see the primary spiritual role that I have [as] being a good father and husband. That means I limit my time away; I . . . work hard not to work too long; and I try to reserve *good* time as well as *lots* of time for the kids so I can be a factor in their lives.

It is precisely the *non*engagement of his wife in his ministry that one informant credits with providing stress relief.

- My wife is Roman Catholic and she is not enmeshed in my ministry. . . . I've seen other spouses completely involved in the church. . . . [For me] they're two separate worlds. . . . My home is a refuge, a very good place to me. My children are very loving children, due to the modeling of their mother.

From three to five, on weekday afternoons, this minister takes care of his children while his wife is still at work. He says he finds the time alone with them very enjoyable.

Still, many of the men seem considerably more troubled than the afore-mentioned ones about what they see as inescapable conflicting "demands" (a *very* frequently used word) from congregational and familial commit-ments. During an interview in which a clergyman rues the fact that pastoring takes *so* much time and the family loses out, he mentions that his wife calls the church "his other wife."

I asked another clergyman whether ministry and family life seemed well integrated or in conflict for him. He replies,

- It's the greatest conflict of my life. They're not integrated at all, although I'm getting healthier about it. The most difficult problems in our married life have been around the demands of my job that I seemingly always have chosen when there's a choice between family and [congregation]. That's changed . . . now since my wife went back to work outside the home. I'm probably at the healthiest point I've been in my public ministry now in terms of when I am at home I am at home. . . . We're working to put a system in place in the congregation here where we have a minister on call for the week . . . and people have accepted that. Every time you ask me what's the biggest tension in my life it's between being responsible parent, responsible spouse, responsible pastor and still finding time for [me] in all that. . . . My ten-year-old daughter just sobbed a couple months ago, "Why do you have to be a pastor? Here all my friends' parents have ordinary jobs. I'm so embarrassed . . . you're never home."

It is clear from many statements in the interviews that this man values and enjoys his family and considers his marriage healthy and equalitarian. He talks both admiringly and lovingly of his wife. When I asked about leisure and fun he said his greatest contentment is in grabbing twenty minutes to take a walk with his wife and talk with her. Still the scheduling conflicts—finding enough time for everything and everyone—produce the greatest tension for him. He interprets this as partly due to internalized traditional ideas of marriage and parenting in which the husband/father "helps out a little" from time to time "to relieve the wife." He's consciously committed to an equalitarian spousal relationship and cooperative parent-ing, but thinks that residual traditional assumptions about family make him feel pushed around by all these "additional" responsibilities.

Another informant also refers to ways that traditional and equalitarian expectations affect him and his wife (engaged in full-time professional work).

- She [does] two-thirds of the child care; I [do] a third of the child care; I get a lot more strokes because people think it's wonderful when men do *anything*. . . . Both of our careers, in some ways, have suffered.

The language is telling. The men often see careers as potentially "suffering," families as potentially "suffering," personal happiness and freedom of choice as "suffering." The consternation around "sacrificing" so much they deem important shows strongly in the narratives. Does this simply represent a "failure to approach ministry objectively," as the one informant stated? Is it unrealistic expectations of parishioners, families, and denominations? Is it failure to assess adequately the burdens intrinsic to freely chosen commitments? Are traditional "zero-sum rules" for assessing the tending of alternatives preventing resolutions? These and related questions cannot be answered from the data, though some light may be shed. What comes through loud and clear from the stories is a great deal of discomfort (I'm inclined to say "pain") connected with balancing need-claims from the two life realms they say they most value.

Several clergymen speak eloquently and at considerable length about their struggle over this constellation of issues. They also talk about growth in seeing what's at stake, as well as in dealing more satisfactorily with choices. Some refer to times when they set themselves up for personal crises by refusing in advance to make room on calendars for anticipatable family requirements around such family events as births, special celebrations, and moving times.

- [Early in ministry] I was havin' a ball—I really was! I got a little carried away. . . . When my first . . . was born . . . in the morning . . . that afternoon I was takin' a busload of kids [out of state] backpacking. That was just stupid. I don't know why in the world I ever allowed it to happen but I was so caught up in what I was doing. . . . One week later I took another group.

During that absence his wife became ill and his father-in-law had unexpected major surgery; he was out of touch and unaware of her needs.

I share this very painfully because I was not a good father and I was not a good role model to families in the parish. I really failed to take my family seriously. . . . But I was getting *all* this affirmation from the people: "He's so wonderful and he's takin' the kids here and there. We like him so much. . . ." And there was just total disregard for my family. (Long pause) Now if that were to happen today my wife . . . would not put up with that kind of nonsense. I think back then we were kinda programmed to comply and to please and to make our mark. She harbored a lot of resentment over that. When we left [a former parish] I was not around to help with the packing . . . yaknow, just off "doin' the work of the Lord"!

Now he and his wife are providing leadership in a program for first-location clergy couples.

We deal with conflict management; we deal with taking care of yourself in the parish . . . clergy family issues . . . my wife has a whole section for spouses. . . . I share this account at . . . pastors' meetings to let them know that, yaknow, I've made some *big* mistakes and I hope that they don't get so caught up with their work in the church.

The following is a less dramatic account of the conflicting responsibilities bind, but with similar implications.

• My son was born . . . six weeks premature . . . and spent about the first forty days of his life in the hospital. That was quite a stressful time for me. . . . I was responsible for our [regional] annual meeting so I was trying to organize that; I was training camp staff people the same week he was born; so I was running between three different places trying to keep everything juggled.

It is not always apparent in the stories whether the expression "personal time" refers to family time or alone time.

• One of the things that has been most frustrating to me is a lack of personal time. Because of that lack of personal time I don't feel I have as much to give . . . my spiritual batteries are being drained. . . . . Sometimes there's some resentment when I get called the first thing at home after leaving here. . . . I don't feel that *any* of my time is my own. They know where to get me and I feel that sometimes I want to say, "Hey! Back off! Give me some time to myself." . . . My family is beginning to have resentment toward the time that I have to spend [at church] and my son said, "Dad, we never see you any more." . . . I am going to start taking some quality time for myself and my family.

Just as it is not always evident to me whether distinctions are being made between "alone" and "family" time, so also the time allocation and privacy issues blur into each other. In quotations already displayed the overlap can be seen. Several others speak to the matter of how decisions about use of time can become decisions to give up needed privacy.

One informant says he "chooses to be a transparent person" and feels he can generally "manage privacy issues OK." But he's aware that his use of time is a critical factor. He claims he has little trouble with the pastoral "fish bowl" now; he had much more difficulty being in the public eye as a pastor's son, growing up in the parsonage.

Another, who says he's been clear in discouraging drop-by visiting (and the congregation has cooperated), is nevertheless aware of constant community reviewal of goings and comings at his home. He understands that this is the way rural towns operate, and it's not a major irritant for him, but he would prefer not to have to make small talk around their observations about his activities or enter into all the expected pastoral "schmoozing" when he runs out to a store or the post office.

According to a third man, privacy is a matter of being very clear about your needs, your availability schedule, and the vocation's requirement that you be reasonably flexible. He says, "People don't want your privacy; they want *you*," so you have to let them know how and when it works best to get to you.

By and large, the men indicate they don't have big issues around privacy. They've elected to be public people, and they appear to savor, rather than resent, the high visibility of the vocation. Mostly they say they've been able to set boundaries that are comfortable for themselves, and their congregations have used good judgment (about calling them at home, for example).

A pastor with small children comments that privacy issues for him are not so much related to the congregation as to his own life stage. As a parent of little ones, he finds he goes from availability at church to availability at home; and that turns out to be more availability than he'd like to deal with on a regular basis. However, he thinks that will change in a very few years.

With regard to friendships, there are only a few exceptions to the decision *not* to have special friendships with people in the congregation. Most informants think that close friendships with certain members of the local religious community would invite confusions of roles and likely jealousies. Some say they develop no close friendships at all apart from family. Two of these say they sometimes feel isolated and lonely. Most who do have close friends other than their own family develop these relationships with other clergy, clergy couples, or people engaged in other kinds of work (sometimes wives' work associates).

In four interviews, clergymen speak of deep and satisfying friendships *within* the congregations they serve. One of these is a priest who spends much of his leisure time enjoying the company of several parish families with whom he's especially close. He's comfortable with this and says that the value to him and his congregation far outweighs the problems. He does mention an instance in which an intrafamily court action caused him to back off from a close association. However, it had no serious repercussions as he sees it. The others who talk of friendships with couples within their churches seem to feel that the closeness is a humanizing factor in their ministries. One says that discovering this new vulnerability and closeness with members (against the conventional wisdom) has been a real breakthrough for him and his wife. They also have friendships outside their parish.

A man who says he has not developed close friendships inside or outside his congregation seemed rather pensive after telling me that. In the pause I asked the tag question, "Would you like to?" He replied,

- I don't know that about myself. I feel that I would, but I ask myself, "Why haven't I?" Maybe I want things just the way they are.

Leisure activities that were listed for me in the interviews were wide-ranging. Some of the men are very athletic and say they have regular workout or sports schedules. Common leisure activities across the nineteen are walking, running, biking, watching TV programs, going to the movies, reading, playing musical instruments, listening to music, visiting with friends, gardening, and eating out. Often these things are done with wives and/or children. Less frequently mentioned are basketball, woodworking, going to plays, cross-country skiing, and using various kinds of exercise machines. The following activities are each mentioned only once; playing cards, roller-blading, camping, canoeing, sailing, telephoning friends at a distance, maintaining the car, restoring old cars, and playing golf, racquetball, tennis, and baseball. The baseball item is not contributed by the former professional player (who, incidentally says he does no sports now). Rather it is mentioned by one of two other men who, as youths, aspired to big league careers but came to realize that they were not that good. One says the love remains very strong. He plays whenever he can, reads about baseball, watches, and listens—a very big interest.

For quite a few of the men the activities mentioned are plainly a sometime thing. Faced with hectic and unpredictable schedules, they indicate there's often time and energy for little more than relaxing with family, a bit of walking, and maybe a little reading or a movie.

Perhaps, now, this is sufficient information to give a sense of the group of men that delivered their views. I have tried to present a representative assemblage of items for indicating the real people whose perspectives form the heart of the study. Additional biographical bits will appear attached to material selected in specific thematic areas.

Chapter 4

Theological Views

Simply put, theology is the study of God. Any presence identified as God-presence, however, does not submit to ordinary direct examination or rational inquiry. Though not all persons of any time and place have been religious, all societies have produced religions. It seems that human collectivities are irrevocably disposed to seek, ponder, and ritually embody mystical experiences of connection with the spirit center of life and meaning.

Thought and talk about what this God-presence is like, and how one can describe the experience of being touched by or enveloped in universal spiritual truth, tend to separate into first-person testimony and third-person reports; that is, witness to one's own breakthrough experiences and the passing on of others' experiences or commentary. Over time, these may settle into stable canons of religious lore—generally revered foundations of a group's religious identity and tenets.

A residual question in the canonization process is whether (and how) the traditional religious base may be open to further illuminating additions from a later religious literature or instead may be formalized officially as unalterable. This is a version of the core issue that emerges from the epistemological stances described in Chapter 2, and we shall see echoes in the quotations used throughout this chapter.

Judaism, Islam, and Christianity have been intensely "heady" religions—encouraging much rational inquiry and sophisticated argumentation about God and religious truth, heavily focused on authoritative texts. Christianity, for example, has a history of multiple sectarian splits originating in correctness disputes over theological interpretations. There still is a strong expectation among many Christians that the clergy leader be responsible for delivering the correct thinking about God—for being the professional God-defining expert. Few present-day Christian clergy (if this study is any indication) are prepared to fulfill that sort of expectation or even think of it as legitimate. Yet they do intend to meet the perceived expectation that they think about and talk about God, that they ponder and discuss their own and others' experiences of faith and moral choice. An important part of examining clergy worldviews, therefore, is looking at how clergy image God-presence and to what source or sources they attribute their perspectives.

THEOLOGICAL BASES

In talking about theological bases some informants refer to the elements of the Wesley Quadrilateral (as they do, in discussing moral bases). Those who mention it are not limited to the Methodists, though it lies in their tradition; and many who cite its elements of Scripture, tradition, reason, and experience as their theological sources do not cite John Wesley. I am not implying that the latter are "closet Wesleyans." I think, rather, that the Wesley Quadrilateral somehow captures very widely trusted headstreams for religious beliefs and theological reflection. The strongest emphasis among the nineteen, overall, is on the Scripture foundation. They talk variously about Scripture, tradition, reason, and experience as being mediated through mentor-models, discussions, seminary training, reading, humor, contemplation, introspection, liturgy, sacrament, and myriad mundane events.

The selected quotations reveal much of the content of the men's theologies, though they are focused explicitly on a discussion of sources. The excerpts reflect the huge difference in the sheer volume of thinking delivered on the subject by different clergymen.

In response to my question about theological sources one informant comments,

- Well, obviously, I believe that all theology is a matter of the Bible, the word of God. . . . I don't put any weight on tradition at all.

Having described his theological foundation in this unitary way, as did several other clergymen, he shifted the narrative immediately to the meaning of the Bible for him. Perspectives on the Bible are a very important part of the views on theology, throughout this group, and will be dealt with specifically, later in the chapter.

One of the rabbis says he got into the congregational rabbinate through some quirks of life experience that also shaped his theology. He was an observant Jew from late childhood but entered seminary with neither scholarly nor pastoral goals. He was more attracted to Jewish agency work, he thought, and to the perspectives of the Jewish Reconstructionist Movement of Mordecai Kaplan.

Kaplan's distinguishing emphases, the informant recalls, were "a nontheological, nonsupernatural approach to God and a widely broadened sense of what constitutes Jewish life." The rabbi found himself drawn to Kaplan's modern scientific and sociological thinking and his Jewish Center Movement, incorporating religious, cultural, and social interests of Jews.

Later the rabbi came under the influence of Protestant teacher John Fletcher, who came to his seminary as a lecturer and was advocating an experimental, integrative approach to theological studies—training built around the dialectical interplay of textual interpretations and relationships with congregations. The rabbi claims he was never much interested in orthodoxy, as such, and this approach made great good sense to him, though at his seminary it was largely ignored.

- Understand that I come to this as somewhat of a moderate, by definition. The Conservative movement by its self-definition and by its history . . . has worked to avoid extremes. One of the things that we say, perhaps a little bit unfairly but, I think, with some justice, is that our concern with Orthodoxy is that it is too concerned with the commandments between man and God and not enough concerned with commandments between man and his fellow man; and the Reform movement is the opposite. We're trying for that balance that says you can be concerned with both—not . . . one against the other. . . . Both are very important. [Scripture and traditions] really go together . . . because . . . we say there are two kinds of Torah: there is the written Torah, which is the five books of Moses, and there is the oral Torah, which is, at least theoretically, the tradition that God gave to Moses on Mt. Sinai, unwritten. That which is expounded upon in the Talmud and in the teaching of sages fits into the oral Torah; that is, it continues to be as if it came from Sinai, as well. The authority of both is largely equal. Now, that's not entirely true. We certainly do give higher priority to that which is written, but they're *all* considered to be Torah.

Other informants talk about the sources of their theology in quite different terms.

- [My theological resources are] biblical and experiential. I do very little literature. I do very little of long theological conversations with academicians or even colleagues. I don't do much study. Most of my theology is based on reading the Bible and living the life that I do.

- An image comes to mind immediately when you talk about [theological bases]. . . . John Wesley had what is known as the Wesley Quadrilateral. . . . I use that as my grid for running my theological/biblical perspectives through. . . . Scripture . . . [has] primacy over all the others. The others are tradition, reason, and experience. I . . . try to bounce those things that I hear off my own experience but also off of those experiences that I read about that are coming from a trusted author. . . . I say, well, this person is solid and if that experience was theirs then I don't put it down as fanaticism. I also am, I guess, much interested in and committed to tradition, especially when it comes to worship and framing the liturgy. . . . I try to utilize a lot of the traditional approaches to worship, not being stifled by them, but inspired. I also employ reason, to a large extent, perhaps because of my background in data processing. Logic is a key to computer programming, so I see reason as a very important part of my doing theology. . . . It, along with the other three elements, helps to legitimize, and I guess solidify, what my theological position is. I have to think things through and I'm very methodical. . . . I'm not a jack rabbit; I don't jump into things very quickly. . . . God does honor our personalities and our preferences for how we relate to things and respond. So that's kind of my broad-brush perspective on theological-biblical processing.

The man whose statement you just read, and the one whose statement you are about to read, both emphasize their heavy reliance on reason. Yet in many respects their ideas about how reasoning will serve to clarify and strengthen their beliefs are different indeed. Relative to matters of spirituality, religion, text interpretation, ethics, or politics, the two are as widely separated in their views as any two men among the nineteen.

- You understand that I belong to a religious movement that has no creed. The central . . . principle is freedom. It's the right and responsibility of individual persons to make up their own minds about religious questions. Consequently, I have a congregation . . . whose beliefs range all over the place . . . from people who . . . very proudly call themselves Christians . . . to people who are . . . goddess worshipers . . . to people who are very militant atheists. . . . My own belief system, I suppose, derives, to a large extent from [Benedict de] Spinoza and [L. A.] Feuerbach. Spinoza's idea of the universe, and all that is, being what God is . . . that this is the ultimate . . . the natural is the ultimate—I accept that. . . . I do not see any evidence of an intentional deity involving itself in the affairs of human beings. And so I follow the Feuerbachian understanding that when we talk about God what we're talking about is a projection of qualities within human beings, out away from us so that we don't have to be as responsible for them. . . . So one does not truthfully say that God is love; the truth is that love is God . . . that [love] is the highest attainment of human beings and that that is the best process by which we can function. . . .

I believe that to be true; I believe that it is imperative that we operate with a sense of respect for others; I think tolerance is fundamental . . . and I mean it in both the negative and positive senses. The negative sense of "You're wrong but I'm gonna let you go on being wrong . . . I'm not gonna get in your way" . . . the more positive sense that "I have something to learn from you." . . . We each have some light. The only foolish person is the one who thinks "My light is the only light." The point is that there is light. . . . And I'd like to share; well what is *your* light . . . and . . . *your* light? I know I can't hear from everybody, but within reasonable, practical bounds I'd like to hear from a lot of people. . . .

I think we must use our reason. It's the best gift we have. It's not a perfect gift. It's not an ultimate gift, but it is the best gift we have for trying to puzzle out what it is we need to do. I'm more mistrustful of emotions than I am of reason, although both are clearly flawed. *We* are flawed. . . . I think it's important to use the mental faculties we have as best we can, but they must, in some sense, be informed by love [or] they will fail. When it comes to the final choice I think we have to go with our faculties of reason.

Based on those ideas, what I would say is: I draw on the Scriptures of the world for wisdom, for insight, and for richness. I find a great deal in religious writings. I am intrigued, in particular, by the Hebrew Bible. That is the source that most interests me. . . . I think that there are many . . . sources that are of great value. I'm slowly trying to work my way into a better understanding of Eastern texts . . . the Tao Te Ching. . . . I see much that is powerful there.

He cites Nils Bor as somewhere making the point that the opposite of a false statement is a true statement; but the opposite of a profound truth is sometimes another profound truth.

Other truth sources for this informant are contemporary writers such as Joseph Campbell, Mircea Eliade, Doris Lessing, Elie Wiesel, Isaac Singer, Rollo May, and a long list of other thinkers he cites during the interviews. Wherever one finds the elements of tradition, ritual, mythical narrative, and ethical concerns, he thinks one can look for how the human spirit is being revealed and touched. He also keeps humor books around, believing that much rich truth about the human condition emerges in humor.

- The life of Christ would be the source [of my theology], . . . understood in the context of what Christ was for the Israelites. . . . Into that we can add whatever "old testament" each of us brings. . . . I think we need to understand the Israelite nation's . . . old covenant with God but then to look at *all* of our old testaments. The Native American people have *their* old covenant with God; each of us brings our own old testament . . . the way we were with God, or Christ, . . . claiming our own story, . . . *my* personal experience of faith. . . . I'm steeped in a lot of real traditional theology, but when I interpret it in the light of my own personal experience, then it becomes real radical—real different. The doctrine of the Trinity *is* core, although I've struggled and at times rejected that. It's core in its relational aspect. It defines God as a relational God. . . . I have a strong . . . belief that all people come to God through Christ. . . . See, the people of my congregation are probably much more liberal or broad in their theology than I am here. I find the people in my church say, "Well, whether you're Jewish or Buddhist or Christian it's all the same God." Yes . . . but we all come to that God, or are able to, because of Jesus Christ. That's where I would be very traditional, very conservative. . . . I think that God has a strong enough ego to handle people being saved through Christ without really naming the name. That wouldn't be offensive to God. . . . I am a universalist, in that I believe the whole creation has been saved through Christ; and I also believe that a majority of creation doesn't know that. . . . I know that Old Testament scholars dislike this approach, but I have to approach Scripture this way to see its truths most clearly.

- I was in seminary for a *long* time, through high school, college, graduate school . . . thirteen years in seminary. So that's my major input. . . . As far as basic theological beliefs, I'm very straight . . . [I hold] official Catholic doctrinal beliefs. . . . The things that are present in the Creed and part of Catholic theology I don't have any disagreement with, doctrinally. I disagree with certain elements of ecclesiastical directives, but that's separate from doctrinal [pronouncements].

- Let me keep in tension the process of how I get [my theology] and the sources from whence I get it. . . . There are kind of four ways that I continually shape my theological perspective. One is to be engaged in conversation with others who think theologically. That's a very important piece for me. For several years I was in a theological discussion group of ten clergy. We would read together . . . we would try to meet with seminary faculty and read things that they were seeking to have published . . . new thoughts. . . . They'd come and dialogue with us before submitting it to publication. So that's one part of the process. A second is reading. I'm shaped by what I read but I also tend to read . . . in the progression of how I'm thinking. A third is the text of Scripture, and a fourth is the context of our life today. I see those four [ways] as all pieces of what . . . undergirds my theological understanding. [Traditions and statements of church and denomination are] *in* what I read.

  In my own . . . theological journey I was heavily influenced for about ten years by liberation theology because I found it very contextually rooted. It fit also the context of my life, in terms of the events of the '60s and '70s and how it was being shaped by social-justice issues globally and nationally and locally. I found liberation theologians were . . . doing theology in a way that . . . got myself out of my head; and [they] also said there was a praxis—a way of uniting reflection and action . . . that had never been united for me very well in the way that I was raised or . . . the way I had seen my church do theology and mission. . . . I also, then, began to read feminist theologians who were stretching me to think in terms of images of God and theological language and metaphors in a different kind of way. Probably in the last five years I've now gone back to reading more of what I would call orthodox [denominational] dialogue. I've come to be more comfortable with the tradition as I now understand it. Maybe I never did understand it as clearly before. So I don't think I've left the influence of liberation and feminist theology. I don't need it as much now as I did. One of the challenges is simply finding the time . . . to do extensive reading.

My greatest disappointment, in the job I have right now, is [that] my week gets filled with appointments. During the Persian Gulf War, I joined a group of five and we sat with [an Islamic] man. I realized I knew almost nothing about Islam. And so we said, "Will you meet with us for three months and just get us up to speed on the basics of Islam?" That's an important way that I need to learn. . . . I didn't put my theology together in seminary; I think that's a lifelong task. I've certainly grown more theologically and intellectually in the . . . years since I left seminary . . . and boy! I hope that doesn't ever change. Seminary just kind of . . . got me headed in the right direction and helped me to frame the questions . . . and now every time I write a sermon I'm growing theologically. . . . People tell me that I am very attentive to theology in my preaching, over against a lot of popular preaching today, which just tries to be kind of advice for living . . . and yet I also weave the contemporary experience very much into my sermons, as well.

- Currently I probably would say [my major resource is] what I call "periodical theology." I subscribe to a lot of magazines . . . newspapers . . . homily helps. Obviously, I don't read them all well, but in skimming through twenty to thirty religious periodicals a month you get a sense of what're the hot issues and what's some of the kind of . . . current thinking. Then, occasionally, if a topic continues, and I need to know it better, I'll pick up a short course, back at the seminary . . . take a seminar, . . . buy a more in-depth book. . . . Some of the periodicals . . . are pretty thoughtful.

At that point I asked, "Now if we can get underneath that into *how* you make the selection of *which* periodicals . . . papers . . . books . . . seminars, would the root resources for your theology be more scriptural? More the traditions of the church? More the experiences you yourself are involved in? Some combination?"

I would say two of those would be prime attractions. One would be Scriptural and the second would be the lived experience of the church. If I [were] going to a seminar and they were offering ten different things . . . but two of them would be . . . a Scripture scholar and . . . a liberation theologian, I wouldn't even look at what some of the others were. . . . If there [were] a liturgical or history expert, [experts in] patristics . . . or ecclesiology, . . . those would attract me but not as heavy as the lived experience and somebody who's still struggling to reinterpret Scripture. . . . I would say Scripture first, lived experience second, and tradition third. . . . [Tradition is] the one I'm more skeptical of, because sometimes what has come through the tradition is just one group's interpretation.

- My theology is grounded in formal theology, in the Scholastic tradition, in historical-critical methods, in the . . . confessions, and . . . the use of the means of grace. I'm very much tuned in to the role of sacraments in building our community, and the identity that we derive from baptism and eucharist. I also have come to recognize that the symbols of the church and the primary themes of the faith . . . have fluid meanings for me. . . . I'm able to articulate the formal theology; I'm also able to move beyond the traditional expressions . . . and to recognize that there are new categories, . . . other ways in which the language of theology can sometimes give way to other kinds of dialogue. I have benefited from going through a formal Jewish-Christian dialogue experience . . . and that helped me to recognize the open-endedness of some of our key words, such as salvation and righteousness, and even justice. I've grown to appreciate the ways in which the traditions of Scripture itself had a history that is really pertinent to how we read it now. . . . We are better equipped to preach the gospel when we recognize the history . . . of Scripture and its usage, and the various contexts and layers . . . the various genres . . . in Scripture. . . . So I'm able, as a pastor, to . . . recognize that I am called into the body of Jesus Christ; and also that I carry Christ into the dialogue where Christ is actively loving enemies and reaching out to people who are different and outside of the recognized covenant and whose own understanding of God . . . may lead me well outside the parameters of the . . . secured places that the church represents.

     Maybe that is . . . another aspect of my theology: the church represents a place secured by Jesus where . . . the child in us (the part that is defenseless or needs a defender) can find that kind of safety. It's something . . . we don't give up at all or surrender—this identity in Christ—but we don't use it, I feel, as triumphalists to . . . designate other people as determined to be doomed, worthless . . . and not sharing our human experience. I try to recognize when [theology and ministry] have diverged. My theology is enhanced as I recognize it in what we're doing. My intention is that they would be interwoven; I don't want to do theology, and *then* do ministry. I see what is at stake in theology as I do ministry. . . . This idea of *praxis* . . . is very real; you do find growth and meaning in doing theology and seeing it reflected in your ministry.

SCRIPTURES

All of the clergymen speak of biblical texts as central or somehow important in their theologies; so, added to what you've already seen of their references to Scripture, I'd like to share quotations that show the variety in their views.

- "The Bible is always more than meets the eye." I think that's true. I find it substantively different than any other text I use. I have no problem saying I believe that it's inspired; I'm not sure I can qualify what that means. I'm confident that in the Bible God has expressed the truths that are there to change our lives. I like [the quotation] "The main points and the plain points coincide, and it's more than enough." I would insist . . . that the original intent to the original audience is the primary message. We must not take from that some principles that are at variance with the original intention.

A small number of informants are comfortable labeling themselves as conservatives, and they appear much less disposed than others to employ critical-analytical or dialectical interpretive approaches in seeking insight from biblical texts.

- The Bible is the standard for all of life. It's a bureau of weights and measures for mankind . . . alive . . . sharper than a two-edge sword. It evokes creative purposes in people. It brings conviction, encouragement. It gives lasting impact because it, alone, has life in itself. I believe in the literal translation of the Word of God. The Bible was inspired to be written, *entirely*. . . . Often it is about people who were *not* inspired at all; . . . often *un*inspired people are quoted. Higher criticism is not very important. Let the Bible interpret itself from different passages. Don't take just one statement; look other places, too.
- I believe Scripture is infallible for all generations and applications and walks of life, . . . not inerrant; that's an important distinction to me. I *have* encountered conflicts in Scripture. . . . Apparent contradictions need to be acknowledged so that one can see the emphases that show through louder than the contradictions. . . . I don't want to insult people in saying, "This one says this and that one says that." Both of them can't be right. . . . I back away from that, saying "This gospel writer came from this perspective; that one came from that perspective." . . . . When I remember that, I hear emphases coming through more loudly than the apparent contradiction. That's why I prefer not to use "inerrant." It feels too restrictive and cramped. [From Scripture] I expect instruction for daily living. I also expect to draw insight into some of the issues I'm dealing with—not only in my own life, but in . . . pastoral care. I expect God to speak to me. . . . To narrow that down would be difficult. . . . I want to have a method by which I work through Scripture to understand it more clearly, in its totality—not just bits and pieces here and there. I need to fit things together.

This minister says his first seminary year really shook him up in that he came to see his faith pretty much as "blind faith" and felt he needed to develop more awareness of trustworthy grounding. The experience proved fruitful for him, he claims, and resulted in a "foundation more solidly in place, theologically." He proceeded to review for me the central tenets of his faith. It was a concise credal version of a traditionally Christian under-standing of the biblical text's main points, and was delivered in a formal teaching style.

> I feel that the crucial issue, theologically, for me, is that Jesus Christ is the only son of God and that he is our savior and that through faith in him we gain access to God the father and eternal life. That's first and foremost in my belief system. Secondly . . . all have sinned; . . . the doctrine of original sin is definitely a tenet of my faith. All need the savior and Jesus Christ is the only way that we find the cleansing for our sins that we need to be restored to a relationship with God. . . . The Trinity is a key doctrine . . . that God the Father, God the Son, and God the Spirit are three in one . . . that it was not a progression of hierarchical proportions but a gradual manifestation of the one true God. As Jesus came he showed us, in human form, what God was like. Jesus was both divine and human and through him we have a clear picture of who God is and what God expects of his children. I believe that the role of the Holy Spirit was, and continues to be, vital in the life of Christian believers, in that there is nothing that we can do of ourselves without the empowering presence of the Spirit. To live a holy life we must have God's Holy Spirit within us. If we seek to be faithful witnesses of our Lord, we need to have the Holy Spirit going through our words and going before us to prepare hearts to receive that message. I think that the virgin birth is a key doctrine, because without that the origin of Christ begins to get shaky, and the foundations it's built on. From there, my faith is weakened . . . starts to deteriorate.

Others, also, talk about having changed perspectives in seminary and after, as their faith positions and ministries have evolved.

- I feel Scripture is truly inspired. I bring a childlike simplicity about interpreta-tion. I'm not a chapter-and-verse person who expects direct guidance on specific situations. . . . [I am] not a literalist, but I see the power of God evident through the accounts. My D.Min. program challenged my simple approach. . . . it "blew me out of the water" on biblical interpretation. . . . I had chosen it precisely because I wanted a different kind of seminary influence . . . but I still get excited about miracles, for example, in spite of higher criticism and knowledge of context. . . . I like helping people relate to Scriptures as something they can use in daily life. . . . I draw strength from people in the Bible like David and Noah, who are pictured *with* glaring faults. We share weaknesses; it's a comfort that God can redeem and use our weaknesses.

- The Bible is the record of God's story for us to study and figure out for our own lives . . . how it is that we relate to God. We can't expect to find answers to all our questions. . . . We need to be open to meaning because God is not yet finished shedding light.

Most of the informants think that they honor the biblical texts best, and open themselves most fully to the truth these texts carry by paying attention to dialectical critical methods of interpretation; though some would not refer to them with such terminology. Seminaries tended to familiarize them with such approaches and now the men regularly examine contextual elements of passages and connections with current experiences of faith in seeking illumination. They do not see intellectual inquiry as either insulting God or somehow compromising inspiration. In the next quotations, as well as in some of the previous ones, you see instances of this widespread interpretive stance.

- I want the nuances probed. . . . Proof-texting doesn't work. The Bible says essentially one thing: God is love. We can see the human concept of God growing as we read the Bible through. It moves from an awesome, fearsome God to God one can argue with, to God who can be trusted, to God who can be rested in. God gives up life and power for us. I love the Bible; I am fascinated increasingly by it. We can't worship the words; we must worship God. The context is important.

- In parochial school there was Bible study every day . . . and Bible history. In sixth grade, I *memorized* the Gospel of Matthew; I thought *every* Catholic kid did this. . . . So when I want to church on Sundays the texts were already familiar literature and reinforced Scripture that was in me. . . . The charismatic movement renewed the significance of the Scriptures for me. I took every possible Scripture course at the seminary. . . . I am not a literalist, I can't logically understand how people could have a literal interpretation of Scripture. It was written first for particular needs; people addressed particular questions that they needed clarified. . . . I like to put myself into the setting of the question . . . with societal and culture things . . . and ask, "Why was this written? To whom? What was the question?" . . . Matthew's and Luke's genealogies are different; did one have a bad list? The names, as such, were not central to what was being said. They felt free to rearrange details to emphasize the intended theological points about God and Jesus. . . . I see these guys as being different from us twentieth-century people; they didn't have our strong need to be historically and scientifically accurate in particulars.

- The cliché is old but [the Bible is] the Living Word . . . an experience I can go back to with different life experiences and it tells me something different each time. [With regard to interpretation of a passage:] my first instinct is, "What does this say to me right now?" My second level is, "What is the original context of this passage?" The third is, "What is the mystical mystery message here; where's this old dynamite gonna blow open what I traditionally thought it meant and what my first reaction was?"

- The key word in describing the Bible, for me, is *inspired* . . . the God-breathed word. . . . [It is] such a rich image . . . the wind of the Holy Spirit. . . . It must live in the life of the community and must be continually read, studied . . . struggled with. You know, there are a lot of things in Scripture that I find are not particularly helpful. Many times I just—God! *why* is this in your book for us? . . . We have to understand that this is the story of how the people of God have struggled to understand God . . . and then that same passage that can be so difficult can be so freeing. . . . This [understanding] gives great power and validity to Scripture. It also says Scripture is to call us into these same questions and struggles that the people of God have always had . . . and to seek our own answers . . . and it validates our own experience. I saw a bumper sticker last week: "God said it. I believe it. That settles it." OK, to me, that's *not* a living power of God in their life; that's worshiping the Bible and making it a dead-end word. To me, the Bible's not yet finished. *We're* writing it each day. It should be extended within each community of faith.

- The Bible is the rule of faith for me. It's not perfect science or history or literature. It's the record of struggle with God over a long time, . . . the life of Christ, . . . the beginnings of the church. My complaint is that the canon is closed. I favor a hermaneutic of suspicion. That's a fascinating concept—what's missing? what's *not* said here? . . . I'm not a literalist. I'm very free with interpretation. . . . I *love* the parables!

- I try to share with this congregation its need to line up its decision-making process with what the Bible has to say for our lives, and about our lives. . . . The word ought to be open to the world. And the world ought to be open to what the word has to say for it. . . . When something is said, what is the context it was said in? Who was the audience? What is the background of the speaker, or the author? I think you have to have an understanding of that before you can say what these words mean. For us, it's not just a historical document but it takes on a life of its own. It oughta have something to say about our life. . . . It becomes a road map that . . . leads us and guides us and makes sense of life, no matter where we find ourselves.

- The cultural context existing at the time of the writer is important because, although clearly the Bible's messages have spiritual implications, they also are to be taken and practiced in our daily living. . . . So I think it's important to understand the context out of which something is written . . . and then to also understand the culture that I work . . . and serve in.

- The Bible, to me, is the written record of human beings' understanding of how the God of Abraham, Isaac, and Jacob has interacted in human history. In that sense, for me, Scripture—just alone Scripture—is a kind of secondary experience. It speaks the truth, as a whole. . . . Actually, when I was in seminary and read Orthodox theology, it helped: Scripture is . . . the "second icon" after Christ. . . . The whole thing is a picture . . . (not any particular part) . . . of an active, living God. We do not enter into the life of Scripture without the help of the gift of the Holy Spirit. . . . Somehow the distance between us here on the verge of the twenty-first century and the people in all those years prior . . . is . . . bridged. We enter into a living experience that enters into us. . . . You gotta work to understand the truth of this. I try, first of all, just to trust . . . my own experience of the first encounter in reading. And then I try to be brutally honest: "This doesn't make any sense to me; I don't like this; this really moves me; I like this." . . . Then there is an effort to try to understand what this particular part of Scripture is saying in the context of Scripture itself, . . . applying all the literary and textual techniques that are being used today to try to understand what might be going on and to try to understand what it meant back then, . . . dialoguing with myself [about the text and about myself]. And then I try to read it again . . . with a second naivete, recognizing that, for me, I am ultimately *under* the authority of Scripture, not *over*. Some academics who study Scripture are able to put Scripture at a distance, with all their rational tools, and to leave it at that; whereas, a coal miner or farmer might be able to just comprehend the kernel of truth there and integrate that into their lives in a way that it becomes a part of their very being, and speaks more to the truth than all of the rational, intellectual work. . . . The strange thing is that . . . people . . . who work intellectually, rationally, academically . . . still contribute . . . to the living faith of others, even when it's not possible for *them*.

- There is a liberating effect in acknowledging . . . that there is not a clear directive in Scripture for every question that we find ourselves confronted with and challenged by. . . . This idea of the righteousness of God . . . manifest *apart* from the law—. . . to find that . . . is to take the risk of choice and exercising judgment, and of really letting your spirit and your heart direct you. We are called to take part in history and to give ourselves to the critical issues of our history in the making, to expend ourselves in the making of history, and to do all that that requires . . . suffering . . . making mistakes.

- When I hear the expression "word of God"—the speech of God—I hear reference to God's self-revelatory activity. . . . The creation story is "and God *said*, and God *said*." So God's speech there is described as God's creating word. When the people of Israel were in bondage, Moses came to Pharaoh. Moses said, "Let my people go." There, the activity of God was through God's liberating speech. When God came to Abraham to establish a covenant . . . it was God's binding speech. John speaks of Jesus as the *logos* made flesh—the word of God now incarnate. . . . So when I hear the expression "word of God" I am first imaging God's liberating, creating, binding incarnate speech; and the event of that speech isn't just a historic document, but it is present reality every time that word is spoken—in Scripture, . . . through it's proclamation in preaching, . . . in Jesus, the Christ, . . . and when people tell the story through their own lives.

I separate "word of God" and Scripture, . . . written by human beings and human communities but *holding* the living word. The Bible is our norm for that living word . . . and Jesus is the "norming norm." . . . Where I have trouble then . . . is [when] Christology becomes the "norming norm" for the whole Old

Testament . . . and I have trouble with kind of having to interpret everything in the Old Testament Christologically. . . . I battle between being "Jewish," which I understand raises all the *questions* necessary for faith and life, where Christians tend to say the Bible *answers* all the questions necessary for faith and life. There's a lot of me [that] is more "Jewish"—that says, "Gol, I wish *we* had a history of *Midrash.* . . .

I use Biblical critical methods in reading; I mean, I still ask, you know, what was going on in the mind of the person who put this passage together with the passage that precedes it. I also read it in terms of literary criticism; what does its literary form say to us? . . . I also try to understand . . . context . . . when it was first spoken . . . and today. The problem is that those are tools on the way to that piece of Scripture now becoming transforming . . . in our life today. . . . The question gets to be 'How does that word shape our life of faith today, intellectually and experientially?' I work with a group of university graduate students here that . . . say [Genesis] is archaic, . . . and [I] begin to show them that the first chapter of Genesis was written in the context of exile. It was not seeking to explain when the world began or how the world began; but it was a piece of liturgy written in the context of God's people being in Babylon and wondering if the God of the covenant had now abandoned them. And they looked to the heavens and they sang a hymn of praise to the creator and said, "If God has created all of this, certainly God will remember God's promises to us and bring us back to the promised land." When people can begin to see that the first chapter of Genesis is worship . . . and that the *how* of the creation and the *when* . . . can be filled in by what we understand in our classes at the university, . . . you give permission to people to see a whole different way. . . . My problem is I tend to be such a rationalist that I kinda wanta explain everything away critically, which I don't think you can do. The part I have most difficulty doing is *praying* the Scriptures. The Scriptures also exist to be prayed. . . . That's something I would like to learn to do again.

The final quotation on this theme comes from a rabbi and brings an especially interesting slant on Scripture.

• Jews traditionally talk to each other . . . using Bible verses, . . . [and they] usually talk about God with traditional words and patterns. In earlier times people were even better at it. Every kid went to school and had the Bible hammered into his head. . . . Christian kids did, as well. . . . I enjoy, at times when I teach, pulling out examples of that—both in Jewish life and in Christian life. . . . Some of the great speakers of all time have expressed themselves magnificently by pulling out a verse at the right time. . . . Things like that can be very powerful self-expression, even though they are drawing on a traditional text. It *can* sound very mechanical and it really isn't. It's like someone saying, "To have to speak with grammatical rules is artificial" . . . Look, I don't feel that using traditional forms and traditional prayers is straitjacketing my self-expression. . . . [They] are just like part of my vocabulary.

GOD-IMAGERY

Typically, I began the second interview session by asking the men to share the images of God they comfortably use in their thinking and talking about God.

One man immediately separated himself from the term "image" I had used. He responded, "God is spirit. I'm very careful to keep the understanding of God away from any *image*." I failed to ask a question that might have been helpful here: Did he perhaps think that by "image" I meant concrete pictures or statuary?

Many men spoke of quite dramatic shifts in God-imagery, over time. One says he "probably began with an old man sitting on a throne, holding a book and recording all actions in two columns." While he claims that such an image "still lurks in the background" for him, his present idea is an inclusively loving God; and the picture of God as "mother hen gathering chicks" is now "central" for him—"a wonderful image."

Another says that he was raised in a church that personified *everything* in Jesus language. He was an adult before God-ness, as such, was first contemplated by him. Now he is convinced that language can never capture the full sense of the experience with God; no concept is more than partially revealing. He credits his wife's spirituality with having expanded his concepts of God tremendously.

Relational action terms dominate the statements—words such as balancing, harmonizing, loving, forgiving, supporting, restoring, listening, caring, ordering, controlling, judging, helping, consoling, inspiring, challenging, giving companionship, bringing possibility, sacrificing, cherishing, nurturing, understanding, freeing, all-embracing.

Some informants speak more in terms of qualities, seeing God as just, righteous, severe, gentle, awesome, powerful, merciful, compassionate, kind, sensitive, personal, wise, benevolent, distant, transcendent or familiar. Only one informant includes the classical descriptions of God as "omnipotent" and "omniscient" in his statement, though he does so in discussing the problems attached to thinking of God as having both qualities. "All-loving" is used frequently, along with God *as* love. Some of the ministers add qualifying statements. Some seem to fear a too soft image of God—a deity who requires no real responsibility from humans. Others seem to fear a too sentimental idea of love—equated with good feelings and lacking firm resolve in the face of conflict or suffering.

- Judgment is certainly an element of my image of God. . . . We often get a little too comfortable with our concept of God and forget that the judgment and severity element is certainly a part of God.

- God is love is *true* for me, but needs constant explanation and identification of implications.

Among the Christians, Jesus (often referred to as "the Christ") emerges in most of the responses as the ultimate image of God, the most comprehensive and accessible metaphor—what theologian Sallie McFague captures in her phrase "Jesus as *parable* of God." In the stories of Jesus, many say they find immensely evocative images of God's ways among people, God's ability to touch people's hearts and lives in ordinary situations. Some of these episodes from the recorded Jesus events form meditational mantras and life-sustaining images for certain informants. One of these ministers finds himself drawn, as well, toward images of God as sea, energy, penetrating light.

"Father" was not mentioned much in connection with my request for God imagery. However, I suspect this absence may be an oversight due to its being taken-for-granted; most of the men express comfort with the term in other parts of the interviews, though many report that they are no longer comfortable with it as the only, or ultimate, term. Quite a few list "mother" as an increasingly natural and helpful image for them, and one adds "sister" and "brother."

A single interview includes references to visual symbols such as the cross ("a powerful image of life shaped by suffering and conflict that reflect God's blessing and presence") and the circle ("used especially among Africans and Native Americans to speak of oneness, of unifying presence"). In addition to his discussion of imaging through symbols, this man is one of several who find animal and nature tales to be fruitful bearers of God-imaging characters and motifs. They cite biblical parables, as well as traditional and contemporary tales, as examples. One is especially fond of some "trickster" images. He comments,

- One of the major elements of survival is a good sense of humor. If that's essential for us, by inference you say that had to be part of God. You start reading Scriptures with that view, you see just a lot of tongue-in-cheek stuff. I relish that side of God, because it's so relational. Many times it's so tender, and it also gives me the ability to kinda laugh at myself.

Occasionally, a minister mentions augmentation or expansion of childhood God-images through the presence in his life of some memorable person or persons who came to symbolize, for him, what God-presence means. It may or may not be some family member. One man says his early "loving father" image for God has grown into an image of a black woman he's known who lives out a "radically free-spirited" life in the midst of "very much bound" social realities.

The three explicitly non-Christian ministers—the two rabbis and the Unitarian Universalist clergyman—maintain that they have little or no interest in trying to image or define God, as such. Since some traditionally religious folk find it hard to comprehend how anyone might be religious without a clear idea of a God entity, excerpts from these men's statements may be helpful.

- I'm someone who uses "predicate theology"—"such is godly," "this is godly," "that is godly." What *God is* I'm not sure, but what *is godly* I have some ideas about. . . . Most of the time my God-language is that of . . . the ultimate arbiter of balance and justice in the world. Now that's not "God is love" stuff. . . . The one who makes peace in the high heavens: may that one also make peace here on earth. But the word "peace," or *shalom*, in that sense, means harmony. . . . And that model, and the possibility of human beings participating in that harmony, . . . is what, in a sense, God would have us do. . . . In matters of social justice I think of God in me. When I'm in need of help I think of God as separate and helping.

He talks about the "spark of the divine" in humans as an image of God that may come to be recognized in persons as originating beyond themselves—as a sort of implantation from outside that one can relate to from within. (Incidentally, among the Christian ministers who speak of imaging God as within oneself, one observes, "God *in* me is not mere vanity.") The rabbi continues,

In rhythm with God . . . in harmony, in sync . . . you have an awareness of God. . . . I relate to the echoes of God . . . the tracings of God . . . what I sense as the will of God. . . . The fact that we live in this world and not another, and that certain things are possible and that certain things aren't . . . I assume that there's a Limiter with a capital "L."

- The focus is on what is ordered, not so much on who does the ordering. The word we use, for example, for creator . . . means artist . . who fashions . . . shapes. . . . not one who sets in motion but one who really puts a lot of things in place and makes them fit and makes them work and makes them beautiful. There's very little focus in Judaism on what God really is. . . . Some people complain [about] that. . . . I understand that; but a lot of what we say about God comes down to "Gee, we don't really know."

- I tend to avoid God language because I think God language is imprecise. . . . In our twentieth-century Western culture, "God" comes with so much baggage attached to it that it is virtually impossible to speak clearly and deeply meaningfully about it. I did a sermon a few months ago, though, in which I talked about *intimations* of God. . . . I suggest that we need to remember that to say the word "God" is not to describe the thing itself, whatever that is, but merely to use a word or concept—a kind of mask . . . that points in the direction and no more than that. . . . One of my concerns about the use of God language is that people forget. . . . that and begin associating the language itself as being absolute even though it's only language *about* the absolute. . . .

We do have intimations of what . . . this God-force may be. I suggested several points; first of all, *mystery*. There are literally tens of thousands of religions that humanity has bodied forth. . . . No religion has ever gotten the fullness of it. It seems to me that what remains eternal are the questions: Where do we come from? Where are we going? What does it all mean? . . . And so I think that the first thing that one could say, when one discusses that which is most fundamental . . . absolute . . . abiding, is mystery.

The second thing, I think, is found in much of what Jewish history has been about and much of what is found in the Hebrew bible, namely, *argument* with God . . . beginning with Abraham . . . and his wonderful negotiation . . . with God. . . . What that suggests to me is that it is human responsibility, at least as much as whatever creative force generated the universe . . . to take care of the universe and to make things right—even to challenge the universe itself when the universe is not doing things right. . .

A third thing that I think is important has to do with the idea of *connection*, or to use the more common word, *love*. We tie into things. . . . in tying into things—in relating to things . . . people . . . institutions . . . systems . . . ideas . . . causes—we find a sense of meaningfulness in our lives. Perhaps the deepest sense is found in the generations of our families; but whatever the ties are, this is the way that we discover a sense of meaningfulness. . . . It's the connections that count. I'm not prepared to say much more about God than that. . . .

I'm always bothered by preachers who talk about the will of God; how on earth does a person know that? And why would you be trying to tell somebody else? . . . One of the things that always disturbed me when I was a Christian was the ease with which Christians presumed to know what the will of God was for the world. Maybe I'm just not a worthy candidate or something, but I don't know that . . . and I think we should be more modest in our claims and more humble before the mystery and the magnificence of the universe constantly surprising us. . . . When I'm in a hospital room or at a home with somebody who's very sick or terribly depressed, if God language is what they need, and the language they talk, I talk it. That's not the place to discuss theology or linguistics and I don't pretend to do that. My primary concern as a minister is essentially pastoral . . . to love people so that they can love themselves and love others, which is the way, I think, that you create community.

Ironically, this man observes that he probably appreciates and makes use of Christian insights more now than he did when he was an identified Christian.

The non-Christian clergy are not the only ones deeply concerned about the potential for God language becoming religious imprisonment, stifling spiritual growth. Scattered through the interviews are numerous comments about the need to make room for experiences of God and new insights by being clear about the status of language as metaphorical approximation—a view through a darkened glass. Following are statements from Christian informants serving in denominations that are often stereotyped as theologically formalistic. The first man had listed "all-embracing" among his images of God. I asked him to tell me a bit more about what that means for him.

- I would accept that Jesus is a way to the heart of God, but not merely the historical Jesus. So I would see God and Jesus working through Buddha . . . Hindu tradition . . . Native American spirituality. . . . It would be God breaking beyond denominational lines . . . beyond Christian lines, as traditionally defined. . . . Some of the Scriptural basis for me would be the first chapter of John: "In the beginning was the word and the word was God." Definitely you can only deal with it in a poetic sense, not in a logical [one]. . . . I sense what a lot of the "new age" hunger is for, and yet I'm really uncomfortable with their *limiting* in saying "God is all we can imagine." It keeps it still within *us*. Essential to my image of God is a relationship.

- I free-associate when you speak the word "God." I don't image visually as much as I focus on activity. In my theological understanding, God is known primarily and essentially in terms of God's activity as revealed in Scripture and as revealed in the life of the church. . . . I've been strong on inclusive language. . . . Certainly I do not view God as male or female. I think the church has willfully stepped aside from the metaphors for God that tend to be more historically what we would equate with being feminine metaphors. . . . I also think we're in a trap if we take historically stereotypical feminine . . . traits (for instance, God as nurturer . . .) lifting them up . . . saying, "Now we're accenting the feminine traits of God." That precludes men from being nurturers. In each congregation [where I've been] we've spent a *lot* of time tending this issue, though I know people who . . . see that as a luxury of the middle class—to sit around and worry about God language. But I know that language defines reality; that's a premise of my understanding. And certainly our language about God defines the reality that we know God to be in our lives.

People who do not see God-language concerns as mere frivolities of the middle class but who are seriously concerned about the biasing of feminist thought from its white, middle-class origins, have developed "womanist" social critique, incorporating racial and economic class sensibilities. I did not use the term "womanist" in asking for views, and only one man used it spontaneously in identifying important dimensions of his theological formation. His opinion will follow shortly, among the comments on feminist theologies.

In strong contrast with the last quotation, the following statement comes from a minister who finds only one image for God ultimately true to his understanding of who God is.

- For me [the most comfortable image] would be father God, heavenly father. I am not at all shy about saying that I'm not buying into the elimination of male God language. . . . That is where I see Jesus pointing us . . . and how he best related to the creator. As long as I keep creator-sustainer in mind as an attribute of God and not a substitution for father God, I have no problem. . . . I try to be sensitive . . . in light of many people's struggles to understand God if he is imaged like an earthly father . . . in view of all the abuse . . . connected with parent-child relationships, and how that may be a very terrifying image; but I still feel that would be a compromise for me to eliminate "father God." . . . I would never say "mother God." That is totally uncomfortable.

I asked this man whether he made a distinction between eliminating father language and augmenting it with other metaphors. He says he would not object to other descriptions as long as it is made plain that they are only metaphors. This points up one of the hazards of all communication: discrepant meanings between communicators. In this case, he is using "metaphor" in the sense of being only peripheral to essential meaning; whereas I understand it as intrinsic to all language use and meaning construction. Nevertheless, the thrust of his response is clear.

Two or three interviewees appeared to interpret my request for their most common and comfortable ways of talking about God as a probe into what they are doing about gender-inclusive language. They immediately launched reflections on feminist language issues, after which I attempted to broaden the God-language discussion by asking additional questions. It may be that these responses were triggered by assumptions about what the interviewer's focus as an academic or a woman would be. It may be that the responses actually do represent these men's main or only conscious considerations of the options in God language. Overall, many men speak of language inclusivity challenges as raising complicated issues, creating language self-consciousness, and involving much transitional awkwardness of expression. Still, most say they are committed to gender-inclusive people language and at least are thinking about how God language works. Many informants credit women associates with helping them to expand their imaging of God and their speech metaphor, as well as their general understanding of language function in forming conscious- ness. One says he especially appreciates the seriousness with which feminist theology takes images of God as freeing—something he claims he hadn't thought of before.

DIALECTICAL AND FEMINIST THEOLOGIES

As they talked about theological and biblical perspectives, many of the informants spontaneously introduced discussion of dialectical or existential approaches. When they did not, I asked whether they were familiar with such perspectives (especially liberationist and feminist versions) and whether they had found such thinking helpful in their ministries. If they had not already given me some good indicators of basic familiarity, I tried to incorporate simple interpretations into the question so that the person was not left groping for my meaning.

Some claimed little knowledge, interest, or opinion, and were relatively silent on the subject. Some claimed little knowledge or interest but shared opinions. Some are well informed and personally invested. Occasionally the perspectives emerged in delightfully nonscholarly ways.

- For me it's the newspaper in one hand and the Bible in the other. . . . It's not just me holding the Bible and the newspaper; it's the other person also holding the Bible and the newspaper, and we need to talk about it. Liberation theology has opened up that dialogue . . . to include others and others' thinking—things I haven't thought about . . . another image of God or another, . . . nonmale, nonwhite perspective. It has opened up for me new models and new thinking in relation to theology.

Not a lot is said about liberation theology, though a number of references to it appear in earlier sections. Where it is seen as a positive influence, the focus is on its faith-reflection-action praxis and its "option for the poor"— concern for the oppressed. Where it is dismissed in negative terms, the focus tends to be on its "political agenda." Mixed responses tend to split along these same lines, with some saying that they like the social criticism and the emphasis on integrated, experience-based theology but are uncomfort- able with what they see as a narrowly doctrinaire political thrust.

In the following selections about feminist theologies, striking contrasts appear in both evaluative judgments and supportive rationale.

- I couldn't really tell you what a feminist theology is. I do read in the paper . . . of some things feminists say . . . they want to call God a "she"; they obviously do not affect me at all. I am not feminist; I don't know that anybody in ministry should be.

In response to my query about whether he'd share his impressions of what feminism is, this minister comments,

Most of the people who take leadership in that movement are almost anti-God. They kind of believe that the Bible is part of the problem . . . is outdated. They are also usually anti-male . . . and most of those take an extremely liberal view—whether it's politics or theology or anything. . . . I think the ones we would call the feminist leaders do not represent the women of America, or even those who have been oppressed to some degree. . . . [In the congregation] I meet people who I would consider almost a feminist in their attitude; but I must admit that my interpretation of a feminist is primarily a left-wing group.

- It's fair to say this [feminism] is not a hotly debated topic in this congregation. I can't remember an instance where this issue really came up and was batted around by a group of people. I have personal feelings in regard to the feminist movement being . . . a self-interest group. . . . I try not to use male pronouns when talking about people, . . . trying to include all people in what I'm saying, and not just the male population. From a theological point of view I think the feminist theologians are *way* off base in interpreting not only Scripture but experience and tradition; and a lot of times they don't even make sense. So it's an issue for me. . . . I don't think the feminist movement has been totally bad; they've moved us away from such a narrow-minded, patriarchal language . . . really examining how the woman fits in. . . . But that's one of the very few redeeming values, in my way of thinking.

- I've not done a lot of reading in [feminist theologies]. . . . I tend to shy away from . . . extremists in any kind of position. I'm more comfortable in the middle of the road. But they've been helpful . . . to challenge my thinking . . . and open up some avenues for me. I work hard at being inclusive in my language and my imageries and in my models. In general, I'd say that the older members of the congregation accept that from me with no outward, verbal, visible resistance.

- I'm somewhat familiar with feminist theology. I see it as a mixed blessing. It has helped me have greater sensitivity to the person of God and to needs of women in the congregation. There are many shades of feminism; I'm much more comfortable with some points than others. But I and the congregation respond much more to the style of presentation than the idea itself. I think the congregation is favorable to . . . encouraging equal development . . . to enlargement of views of God to include the feminine side, but there's real resistance to what is perceived as a militant, angry feminism that also is in the church. . . . Language issues are touchy in the congregation and they're slow to accept female authority.

- I was bludgeoned into submission, very early on in seminary, as to inclusivity—very reluctantly so at first . . . but discovering after a while that it came natural. . . . In a small church such as I'm serving, to refer to God as "her" is startling, but to refer to God as one who gives to us the motherly embrace, the nurture of motherhood, the sensitivity of what's generally referred to as the feminine, is a lot less jarring and very natural to people. . . . I freely change Scripture to reflect a more inclusive understanding of God, but . . . I'm not zealous; I don't back up or correct myself if a male pronoun slips through. . . .

   Feminist theology is part of the American church. No matter what your opinion of it, it's here . . . and that's good. Half of that which God created has never had a voice . . . until recent generations. . . . When we consider what we have cheated ourselves out of . . . by putting down women, . . . ignoring their voices, . . . their opinions, their hopes and dreams, . . . in its simplest, selfish form, we men owe it to *ourselves* to listen, whether we like it or not. . . . For the most part, it's not mine to agree or disagree, but to listen to. I believe that the long-term, overall experience of the church will dictate what is good and what is useless. The voice has come forth from the very painful lives of many women and will never be silenced, and it's good. Where it will lead I don't know; there's still latent bastions of opposition to listening to God's women. That's too bad. For myself . . . I take what I can use, what makes sense to me, and the rest I try not to get too upset about.

- I think one of the central revolutions of our time, and perhaps *the* most important one, is the feminist revolution of the late twentieth century. . . . I look to what women have to say about what it means to be a woman in our kind of society. . . . Our congregation is what I would call liberal on such issues. . . . We made a commitment eleven years ago, as a congregation, to the use of inclusive language, after we had done an intensive one-year study recommended by our associational office. . . . We also began very slowly (and I don't think we did as good a job with this) to try and recognize that it's not just male/female, but it's also nuclear family and singles. . . . The issue of inclusiveness has broadened out . . . in terms of gay, lesbian, and bisexual individuals. We're trying to discover language . . . that will be welcoming and affirming of them, as well. . . . The intern minister for next year is a man who has worked in the men's movement. That's not something I've done; I don't personally have a lot of interest in it, but he does and I'm hoping that one of the things he will do is get a men's group going. . . . The women are interested in that. . . . One of the things I have loved about the women in this church, who have worked in this movement, is that they have genuinely brought a sense of lovingness to it. They do not chastise; they do not criticize; they simply say, "Here's a position we'd appreciate if you would help us with."

At another point in the interview, speaking of women ministers in his denomination, the informant says that a very powerful thing women have done as ministers is "to bring some juice, some life, some spirit to what, in our ministry, had been a rather tiresome intellectualism."

A minister whose regional supervisors are currently female clergy mentions that he occasionally has women preachers as guests, to get his congregation used to the idea of women in professional ministry. He reports a memorable occasion when a bishop preached at a special service.

- We've got a bishop who's an incredibly gifted administrator. . . . She preached here once and people just loved her. I was very proud; it was a very proud night. We made leaps and bounds in the name of women in leadership and all of those issues. . . . There's a whole element—a dynamic—that's been missing for years and it needs to be heard because, you know, a high percentage of our churches are made up of women.

With great admiration he told of another guest preacher who very effectively used a graphic domestic illustration to make a spiritual point. Paraphrasing her words, he continues:

"My baby was sick and puked all over my manuscript at breakfast." I thought, "That's great! How many women in that congregation are going to say, 'This person is real!' or 'Wow! That happened to *me* this week—and yet they're still talking about *faith*.' " I like that.

This same minister reports that at a regional meeting he regularly sees a clergywoman who is outspokenly concerned about women's representation at all levels in the church. He says she makes people nervous and there is criticism behind her back but that he has really appreciated her contributions. According to him, she "shows lots of courage" and he feels he has never before been around someone so clear about the issues. Still, when we were dealing with God language, he indicated he remains troubled and ambivalent.

[My God images are] primarily masculine. . . . I'm experiencing considerable ambivalence because I'm very sensitive to feminine issues and I've become very close to some female clergy and their concerns are very real about masculine language. They've held my toes to the fire and I do appreciate [that], but I'm struggling, at that point. Part of me wants to hold onto that masculine side of God; it's very reassuring to me. Change is hard. . . . I don't wanna see God just neutered, OK? I'm trying to introduce female concepts of God, but it hasn't been easy; it's letting go of years and years and years. . . . I work with a number of recent graduates from seminary. For them it's natural.

- I'm bound into a church that is male dominated. . . . I perceive the ordination of women as running into a brick wall, so I don't get involved with that issue. We try to be inclusive in our language. I'm not comfortable replacing Father, Son, and Holy Spirit in public prayer like I am in private prayer. . . . At the same time, I'm irritated at scriptural translations where the background of certain words is inclusive and the translation is noninclusive; so we revise that in our scriptural readings here.

- I've not read a lot of feminist theology but kindof have gotten it by osmosis. There's a pattern I'm noticing among our leadership. . . . At least four women who have been at that center of leadership here in the parish have . . . chosen to leave the Catholic Church. It's too painful to stay. I'm real aware that my reaction at first was, "I gotta show them it's OK to stay." Right now my thought is, "I'd like us, as a faith community, to find a way of blessing these people and sending them on ahead so they can create some structures that maybe the whole church can move towards". . . . There's a lot of wisdom there, . . . a lot of lived reality that's gonna be of value to the church. I hope the church doesn't shut its ears.

Recently this priest happened to meet one of the women who left, and they had a conversation, which she ended with the statement, "I'm not a fickle lover; I *love* the Catholic Church; I just can't live with it now." He is convinced that she loves the church even more than he does.

One clergyman, who says he spends much time tending the issue, thinks the church has plateaued, maybe even stalled, in the matter of God language. He thinks there's much support for using inclusive *people* language but that there's been a tendency to walk away from the subtle and complex implications of how we talk about God. Since he believes that language is an important shaper in our definitions of reality, this tendency greatly concerns him.

Other voices follow:

- I realize the image of God that has come out strongest for me is a feminine image . . . of a being that makes room in itself for other being to be, and to be free. . . . I think [feminist theology] is profoundly helpful. . . . But if it refuses to put itself in dialogue with others it reminds me too much of experiences with "true believer" orthodoxies. . . . There's no doubt in my mind that feminist theologians' contribution is central to the future of theology and must be integrated into any theology that doesn't take account of it.

- I'm enjoying new metaphor in my female associate's imaging, as a preacher and teacher. Feminist theologians are good when they stimulate new thinking about who God is . . . growth . . . and love. I find "goddess" talk offensive; yet I don't want my words to be a barrier to faith. I don't want a male or female god to worship, but a *whole* god—beyond our limited experience and thought. I think women have been done a *terrible* disservice by Judaic-Christian religion. Women's second-place status is offensive; it *must* be changed. Many disciples were women but they're not listed among the twelve because the culture couldn't tolerate this idea. Where would the church be today without women's concerns and activities?

- I continued to have to step into the role of spokesperson for the black community . . . to recognize that this would be a part of my ministry, . . . and I've grown in that role, I think, through the years. It continued to develop for me in seminary, as well as my own . . . interests in feminist and womanist thought, . . . the issues, . . . the perspectives, . . . the critique. . . . All this is something I developed an interest in and studied formally and also tried to integrate into my own style and understanding of the ministry. . . . Seminary was a good, growing period for me. . . . I found the environment stimulating and very much an equipping experience. . . . It gave me a lot of tools for doing theology and for my own development as a Christian leader.

- I think what feminist theology has done for me is it really takes seriously images of God. That's something I had not thought a lot about before I was introduced to feminist theology. I am a feminist in that I believe we were created human first of all. I do not believe that God is male or female . . . but can embody qualities of both. . . . What it has done for me is to help me to love that which is feminine in me, and that is very hard for men to do. One of the greatest insults for a boy is for another boy to call you a girl: "You girl!" . . . We have lost so much. We have psychologists telling us that . . . everybody's inner child is neglected and suffering, and, you know, this all relates to the fact that we have had no Mother God to tend us. Our own mothers we devalue; their care for us was something to be pushed away and rebelled against because it would make us soft and needy. So feminist theology comes with a very prophetic voice to this situation. . . . As we affirm both femininity and masculinity the whole set of concepts begins to break down. . . . The concern [among antifeminist persons] seems to be . . . "Now *this* [male imaging for God] is a *core* belief; if you change *this* then the whole world breaks apart for me and I don't know where to go with that."

He struggles with how to keep his own inclusiveness commitments in the midst of a congregation some of whose women declare they do not feel excluded by male language and imagery or by conventional sex roles. He wants to respect their life perspectives and also to challenge what he sees as hurtful injustices they've likely suffered unconsciously.

DEVOTIONAL PRACTICES

Part of religious life is ritual performance of shared beliefs, sentiments, and attitudes around the perceived spiritual reality. From the most elaborate and formal high-religion traditions to the most simple and informal low-religion traditions, communities, over time, develop relatively stable routines of worship and spiritual replenishment.

Communities of religious faith have special needs for gathering around symbols and rituals that embody the spiritual realities believers seek to affirm. The symbol system informs and evokes, both conserving the religious community's historic legacy and offering itself for new appropriations in new contexts.

Symbol systems vary widely as to concrete elements. Vocal and instrumental music, dance, sculpture, drama, stained glass, special lighting, wood carving, garments, furnishings, architecture, processions, perfumes, gestures, postures, jewelry, texts, scrolls, books, address forms (sermons, meditations), litanies, sacred days and seasons, greetings, blessings, ceremonies of eating, washing, and life transition—these and many more items constitute the pool of possibilities from which distinctive clusters of observance are drawn, the ritual reenactments of "our story" of being with God.

Who, in the process of self-review, has not noticed that by the second or third time one has recounted an important event or insight, the choices of words, inflections, and sequences have evolved from *a* telling about it to *the* telling about it? A formula has emerged. It happens this way in movements and communities as well.

Conducting worship services and doing liturgy are high on the lists of things that informants enjoy most about their work. Overall, they also "love" the preaching part, though not necessarily the preparation. It is clear that, in all cases, the nineteen could see themselves in terms of this public ceremonial performance as they moved into ministry, and they indicate comfort in this aspect of their work. Most appear to savor presiding at worship services as one of the most highly rewarding parts of their professional lives.

Apart from information they volunteered, I did not seek to have them talk about their specific orders of worship and devotional practices, as congregations. (They range from highly formalized liturgical patterns to exceedingly informal routines that leave much leeway for individual testimonials, spontaneous prayers, and emotional/vocal congregational participation.) I did, however, ask each person what he does for his own spiritual nurture and development. Over and over I heard words like the wistful plaint, "It's so *hard* to find the time to do what I think I should—or think I want—in my devotional life." Nevertheless, they describe a wide range of activities that they say help them stay in touch with God, selves, and commitments.

A priest who comments that he's not as good at devotional practices as he'd like to be, or as he thinks some others are, still describes what, from my data, is one of the steadiest and most extensive personal devotional disciplines in the group: daily physical exercise, mass, and morning and evening prayer offices for priests; sporadic prayer in many different forms; and occasional rosaries, retreats, and meetings with a spiritual director. One of the rabbis participates in a similar set of daily observances. A pastor in a less liturgically structured tradition says he devotes a minimum of an hour a day to prayer and also reads Scripture daily.

Some others speak of shifting from a time when they thought of devotional life more as specific practices to a time when prayer and devotion came to be an "abiding experience, a way of thinking, a constant awareness of and communion with God's presence." One informant thinks that this is what the biblical admonition to "pray without ceasing" means, though he continues to retain certain "prescribed acts" as important and helpful in spiritual development.

Many of the men say they try to take fifteen or twenty minutes at the beginning of each work day for a brief meditation and prayer time—often reading from a book of meditational selections that include a Scripture verse, small commentary, and prayer for each day. Other sorts of reading are mentioned as well: Scripture, other people's sermons, stories of faith, and a wide variety of choices from religious and secular writings.

Frequently mentioned are "alone times"—quiet times of prayer, thoughtful reflection, introspection, and meditation on some event or passage. Several people include just listening for what God might be saying. Some report that they feel especially open to God's leading when they are engaged in physical exercise, such as walking, running, biking, or rollerblading.

One says that occasionally his private prayer time is carried out at the altar in his church. Another says his prayers are much more consistently relational than private—offered in the course of the events at hand. Still another speaks of "crying prayers" that have emerged in his life as a very healing experience. Every few months he feels a need to unburden himself of overwhelming concerns and frustrations with personal, congregational, and worldwide problems. He has discovered that if he allows himself to cry while praying, the emotional outpouring becomes, he thinks, something like the experience of speaking in tongues. It results, for him, in an aftermath of ecstasy and spiritual renewal.

Two report a day of fasting each week and several days in times of special need. In at least one of these cases the whole congregation observes the weekly fast day. The pastor claims spiritual gains, in the group, of purification, sanctification, sacrifice, discipline, insight, growth, healing, and intercessory help.

A man who labels himself as "too compulsive" says he studiously avoids adding more disciplines to his life. He moves among different modes, such as meditation, journaling, retreats, spending a half day in prayer at home, listening to impulses to stop reading and go to the chapel, and pondering the symbolic meanings of things on his shelf of devotional objects (an old rosary, an icon, a Tibetan prayer wheel, a crystal, a Celtic cross, a sandal-wood Buddha, an Indian prayer shawl, and a Native American feather).

Another man echoes this free-format idea. He says he has "no special, regular routine, but can tell right away when it's neglected." In addition to spiritual growth weekends and regular meetings with a clergy support group, he says he relies mostly on simple prayer times, introspection, and physical exercise for spiritual replenishment.

Several clergymen list each of the following as aspects of their own spiritual sustenance: conversations with others, caring for others, journaling, meetings with "spiritual directors" (though one says he *hates* that term), and retreat weekends (one does occasional Cursillo weekends). There are many references to recreational and relaxation times as *spiritually* refreshing, even the reading of mysteries and going to different sorts of entertainment. Sermon preparation is devotional and spiritually nurturing for one informant (contrasted with another who says sermon preparation is as close to hell as he ever wants to get).

About a third of the ministers say they participate in local clergy support groups that they find enjoyable. In one case, the group is very informal. The denominational affiliations, ages, and tenures of the members are very different, and they frequently meet for coffee at a local eatery. It's a rural-small-town setting where "everyone knows everyone," so the group provides the informant with not only a rich set of friendship and spiritual growth experiences, but also an opportunity to model the ecumenical respect he considers important. The ministers do some cross-referrals for counseling, according to their perceived strengths. They encourage their congregants to go for pastoral help where they're most comfortable in a given matter, knowing their own pastor won't be insulted or angry.

- A lot of visiting and . . . joking goes on. That's really, to me, where the heart of ecumenical activity is because the people could[n't] care less about their denominational theological identity. They just like the church family and they also love their friends and neighbors that go to the other churches. And when *we* are seen together . . . that's just so powerful for them and so that's been really important that we remain friends. . . . And it's helpful for *us* and we do it for ourselves, but yet it's good for the ministry of the churches. . . . I've noticed how I minister to the whole town, not just to *my* church. . . . I think I have more people now going to [a long-tenure clergyman, compared to the informant who is relatively short tenure]. . . . That's fine. Once they're given that permission, they know I'm not threatened with it.

Almost half the clergymen express doubt that they "know what works" for them, are "doing enough," or dependably know how to get the self-renewal they need. Yet that means, of course, that about half do *not* express such misgivings. Given the nature of ministerial work, with its large "on-call" component and its wide-ranging responsibilities, they know that they cannot count on "leftover" time for spiritual self-tending; they need to be focused and intentional about it. Part of the perceived problematic time pressure that many mention may stem from the personality configurations common among the informants (and possibly common among those drawn to congregational ministry or "successful" in it). With few exceptions the men are more disposed to be professionally active than to be with self, family, or friends in an intentionally free, open, and receptive mode. Some have made peace with the activist types they see themselves to be and have learned to integrate self-renewal with multiple associations and tasks. Others see professional activities and spiritual replenishment as needing to be tended differently, and they are uncomfortable with seeming to give priority to the former, as they think they do.

One man talks about how easily distracted he is from any quiet time for meditation or reading in his office. He says he's too "people-attracted"; if he's sitting quietly in his office and hears people in the hall he inevitably goes out to be with them. Another confesses that he does not know how to use "alone time" fruitfully.

It is clear that the two Catholic priest informants had a formal preparation for spiritual feeding that was qualitatively different from that of the others, though some others seem to have arrived at a similar level of appreciation for disciplines of spiritual receptiveness. In the long years of seminary, starting from early adolescence, these future priests had been presented with models, instructions, techniques, and special daily times for learning the worshipful, mystical, contemplative aspects of ministerial vocation. They both say this emphasis and the years of "rehearsal" time have been rich experiences for them.

SIN

Requesting an interpretation of the concept "sin" was not on my interview schedule, originally. However, ideas about sin sometimes were included as the men shared their thinking with me. If the term turned up, but little explanation was offered as to how it was being used, I asked the man to tell me more about what the word means to him. Following a common practice in this type of data gathering (allowing what spontaneously emerges to inform the process), I began adding "sin" to the interview schedule in later sessions. More than two thirds of the clergy say something about sin at some point.

Sin is an important category of traditional Christian theology, with a substantial history in Western public thought, as well. It is a concept often said to be out of fashion, though it figures heavily in both everyday and professional humor; and letters to the editor in various publications reveal that dead earnest statements about sin are no rarity. Hence, in selecting themes to be included in the chapter, I felt this one might have special interest.

- [Sin is] the choice to turn inward . . . the choice to more and more center all of reality in yourself. When I say turn inward, it's not the contemplative life but . . . seeing everything in terms of how it affects *you*. To me that choice is essentially to cut yourself off from the opportunity for God to get in or for you to get into the heart of God. . . . We used to be able to list sins . . . and count the number of times you've committed sin—which in some ways makes sin a very easy thing to deal with; you can count 'em up and say I'm sorry and not deal with it in terms of relationship, those patterns you have to change and risks you have to take.

- To me sin is a state of being a slave in the process of being freed. . . . Where I've struggled with it is naming specific things as sin . . . confessing sins. . . . [Naming specific sins] leads to moralisms and legalisms, and that's just exactly what Christ stood against. . . . Sin [as alienating social processes and belief systems] is our oppressor and the challenge we have is to name our oppressor. . . . Where the oppressor can be easily named and rejected there is real life. You find this in churches of South Africa, inner-city congregations, gay and lesbian congregations. . . . But, see, for most of us in middle-class America we love our sin—we love our oppressor so much and we don't even recognize that we're being oppressed. The oppressor is that which we think is freeing us and it's all messed up in our heads. Jesus Christ has even become synonymous with this oppressor. . . . We have made prosperity . . . the "American Dream," . . . made *that* freedom, . . . but it's oppressing us. In the pursuit of that we're harming one another, . . . we're driving more and more people into poverty, . . . we're perpetuating all the "isms." . . . If you'd start naming *that* [the conventional American Dream] as evil, . . . you'd lose a *lot* of members!

- I preached a sermon on sin that is still having repercussions in this congregation, . . . still being talked about. . . . now has been dubbed "the infamous sermon" because it cut through the niceties that often surround sin, . . . the sugar coating, . . . the dressing up of some of the things that God calls sin; and [it] penetrated to the heart of some people to the point that it made changes in their life-styles. Looking back on that and reflecting on what a struggle I had about

how I would deal with such a volatile issue, . . . the turmoil that was within me,
I understand, I think, somewhat what the prophets of old were referring to . . .
that there's a "burning in my bones" to tell this. But I also recognize the risk that
I face in doing this.

- Sin means, to me, literally missing the mark—being cut off in our relationship
with God. For me it is singular . . . not plural. It is an aspect of everybody's
life . . . that needs to be recognized and dealt with . . . [if one is] to go on. . . . I
believe that's an important aspect of our worshiping together . . . to recognize
our estrangement from God, to name that, and then to seek wholeness. . . . For
me it is particularly important to name and to recognize the sin but also to name
and to recognize that God still loves us even though we sin and we do not come
close to what God wants us to be.

- In seminary I tended to use more psychological images . . . alienation . . . separation. . . . Then, as I got exposed to liberation theology, it was more comfortable to
image sin as oppression . . . bondage. . . . Now as I've kind of gone back to more of
my Lutheran roots (but not in the sense I was raised . . .) Luther says sin is unbelief;
and sin, which is unbelief, is manifested in sin*s*, which can be the sin of being
separated—from oneself, interiorly; from those around you; from the creation; from
God the creator. . . . I think we've tended to very much individualize the notion of
sin, . . . but it's also corporate. . . . I tip much more to the corporate [view]. . . . I
mean, when you talk about original sin and everybody gets to arguing about "How
can babies be born with sin" and "How can babies, beautiful as they are, sin?" . . .
I think we're talking much more about the created order into which a child is
born. . . . No matter what a child can do, the child cannot escape the bondage, the
brokenness, the oppression of systems . . . institutions, . . . the fabric of the society
in which we as human beings live.

- I really perceive sin, first off, from a relational perspective—whatever hurts my
relationship with God, in small ways or greater ways. Objectively, there can be
acts or omissions that are the setting, so to speak, of my making choices that are
hurting the relationship with God. . . . The seriousness of sin can't be reflected,
primarily, with the objective [elements]; it's gotta be primarily reflected in the
subjective elements.

A priest concludes an extensive explanation of the traditional. Catholic
categories of venial and mortal sin and a description of some of the common
fears of his parents' generation about inadvertent commission of a mortal
sin with the following observation:

God's pretty doggone loving. As long as a person has the intent of trying to
follow God . . . *honest* intent, . . . it's gonna be . . . rare, if ever, that a person is
at that kind of degree of breaking off the relationship with God.

- To me, to speak of sin in a sense is to speak of my humanity. . . . The distinction
that's drawn between humankind and God, . . . the qualities that are considered

"by nature" or of "original sin," . . . these are really theological categories that are . . . talking about the human experience. . . . Being reconciled to our identity as humans is important in the church. The church, I think, has to offer some kind of reconciliation with who we are. Theology must be true to anthropology as well as to any . . . spiritual and divine reality.

- Sin is a haughtiness that disposes a person to reject or deny the centrality of God.

- Sin is a wonderful thing! . . . an absolutely wonderful thing, for the simple and crystal clear reason that sin is that thing, however you describe it, that puts us all on the same level . . . pope or politician, beggar or banker. . . . We are told through Scripture, both the Old and New Testament, the historical books, the prophets, the epistles . . . that we are sinners before the Lord. The message is not . . . we're awful, terrible people. The message is . . . we all start on the same foot. I choose not to focus on sin, per se, because all it is is a starting point. . . . We're told . . . we continue to sin, no matter who we are, and that really kinda takes the pressure off. No one can live a sinless life. . . . The greatest danger in the concept of sin is when we start making lists and consume ourselves by focusing on sin instead of focusing on love. I've been associated with many people, over the years, who just get all worked up . . . over not sinning, and, in doing so, ignore the life . . . we can give. I don't know how else to describe it. Sin is a diversion from God, turning our eyes from that which God would intend for us.

As a theological concept, sin does not have the centrality for the Jewish rabbis that it does for the Christian ministers. About good and evil, as categories, one rabbi says,

- It is a question of faith for me. I can't say that something's good or evil unless I call on a faith statement [about what I believe, from experience and available wisdom, may show the presence of evil or good at work in the world]. I will say, . . . this would *appear* to be evil in an ultimate sense; and that would *appear* to be good in an ultimate sense. . . . *God knows*. It's not simply a throwaway line, because when I use that I mean . . . the sequence of circumstances and relations which . . . result from this . . . in their infinite variety God *knows* because that's what God *is*.

The other rabbi had made a reference to heaven and hell. When I asked for some sense of the meaning of those terms for him he commented that they have very little significance for him. He says he probably doesn't believe in life after death. The focus he has on why we do things "is not to get to a place in heaven, but to make the world a better place. . . . Fixing up the world is an old Jewish concern."

Ultimate truth and ultimate goodness beliefs are so inter-developed that it is difficult to tease them apart for separate presentation of data. Ideas of God and goodness are not just connected to each other; they are intrinsic to each other in religious thought.

So, mindful of overlaps and interpenetrations, we now turn from theological perspectives to moral. As the transition is made to a new set of themes and quotations, a reminder is in order: to look for additional comments on subjects already addressed and to carry the knowledge from this chapter into consideration of the quotations to come.

In the broad areas of theology, morality, and community formation, it is apparent that much of the difference among the informants derives from the epistemological issues I've already identified. Through the words they use, some of the men can be seen to think of truth as objectively based in authoritative traditional texts and teachings. Others appear to regard cognitive, moral, and procedural religious knowledge as socially constructed and emerging from a dialectical interplay of traditional beliefs and direct experience. Important consequences for imaging and conducting life flow from whether one sees truth, including God-truth, in more absolute or more intersubjective terms.

Chapter 5

Moral Leadership

Moral theologian Daniel Maguire speaks of the moral act as "that which is worthy of humans in all their preciousness." Such a statement resonates as distilled wisdom from years of moral struggling, observing, and pondering. It refers to concrete life situations where one strains to see how, and with what consequences, human beliefs and intentions become action choices in networks of human relations. Such a statement may also be hopelessly obscure to persons just starting to find a way of life that will be satisfying, responsible, good, and perhaps even noble; or to persons who have seen little worth, let alone preciousness, in humans, including themselves.

Traditionally, the clergy vocation entails the social expectation that ordained religious professionals should be trustworthy moral guides. Since ministers are supposed to have and teach spiritual integrity, they tend to be judged deficient if they do not speak clearly, credibly, and consistently about the nature of goodness, or comport themselves as embodiments of their stated ideals.

MORAL MODELING

Some of the informants simply take it for granted that moral modeling is part of their chosen vocation; they know and accept the "public eye" as a legitimate and important arena for clarifying their teachings and showing what faith in God looks like in day-to-day living.

Other informants experience more discomfort and burden from congregants' expectation that clergy ought to lead exemplary lives. Part of the difference in attitude may lie in how the men understand "moral modeling." Those with greater comfort seem to think of it more as making their authentic faith journey visible among the people they serve. Those with lesser comfort are reacting more to an idea of moral model as "perfected human"—an ideal they resent as illegitimate, pretentious, and impossible.

- I think that [a minister] *should* have to be a moral model. I don't find it difficult or conflicting. I think also our President needs to be a moral model. I think a university staff needs to be a moral model for those they're shaping. Our society has run so much from that work of modeling because we want people to do what we say without any responsibility of us acting it out ourselves. . . . If someone is cheating on his income taxes I'm not going to let him . . . sit on a committee that's establishing income tax for the rest of us. It just doesn't make sense. Practicing what we preach is essential in all stratas of society, and especially ministry. I don't find it an undue pressure. I'd quit preaching if I didn't want to live that way.

- You try to be honest in your life. When you fail you're willing to accept that. A few years ago the archbishop was arrested on a drunk driving charge and spent a night in jail. In my estimation he's been a much more effective bishop since then. I don't try to fall into the pattern of being unhuman or above being human. . . . . I think that would be the expectation of some people—that the clergyperson can't be angry and can't even get a speeding ticket or can't have prejudices. . . . When I preach I try to talk sometimes from my own experiences so they know I'm not sitting in the chapel all day. I think the modeling experience is to be as human as you can be, which means laughter and humor and sometimes the anger and frustration and the doubts. . . . I think faith calls me to struggle to be real; to ask myself time and time again, "As an American white male, am I avoiding the real challenge of the Gospel and just watering it down so that we're all nice and happy?" . . . Do I need, at times, to be willing to be more radical, in terms of the radicalness that's in the Gospel?

- [Moral modeling] is not burdensome to me. It's been working out well. I do not play a pastor's role other than who I am. I am who I am. I think the people here are very accepting of that and have, in fact, told me, you know, about my relationship with the congregation . . . that I am just [own name]. I kind of welcome that aspect of it. I find that many of the young people and many of the kids look up to me, and I think part of that is [being] a moral model. I'm not afraid to discuss with them issues of importance, issues of morality, issues that affect them and their lives. . . . I seek not to give them *the* answer but to get them to talk about what are the options and what do they want to do with their life. The important content [of the moral model] for me is to show God's love with what I say and who I am. I seek to live that out in a way that will be understandable.

- We as clergy debate this issue [of moral modeling] vociferously when we're together. I take the stand that . . . there are two standards in our culture, one for public office holders and one for private citizens. By virtue of being in a public office one is held up to a moral modeling that goes with the office . . . (that we tend to equate with perfection, which I think is a trap—that you're going to be the perfect spouse, perfect parent, perfect pastor, perfect citizen). The challenge is to accept the moral modeling that goes with the public office but to also acknowledge one's humanity. . . . Moral modeling permeates my life in the sense that, well, that I take seriously my parenting role because I model that for other fathers. . . . Sometimes my failure as a parent comes [out] in my preaching . . . simply being called to the task of *being* a parent comes [out] in my preaching. People see me sitting in the pews; I take some Sundays where I don't publicly preside and I sit with my family and struggle with my kids making chaos in church and disrupting the worship and I have to take my crying kid out. Part of the public modeling is that I'm attentive to my marriage. Part . . . is that I set boundaries in relationships. . . . Sexuality, for instance, is a part of every human relationship. . . . [and there is] the power that goes with the pastoral office . . . and how I acknowledge that sexuality. . . . There have been times the boundary is blurred . . . so I've named the fact that I'm primarily committed to my relationship with my wife . . . so we can redefine the boundaries in the relationship with the parishioner.

  I . . . model . . . life-style, economics, use of resources, and my own stewardship, through my political involvements in my own community . . . in what some would probably call secular issues. A part of moral modeling for me is acknowledging failure. That's a harder one . . . to be able to stand up publicly and ask for forgiveness. . . . We blame and we scapegoat, . . . but rare is the person who publicly says, "I am at fault." . . . I need to invite the congregation into my own struggles. . . . The sermons I do that are kind of the passionate "doubting Thomas" sermons get lots of positive response 'cause it's a real permission giver.

- I certainly don't expect *preaching* to be a model, . . . but stopping and listening to someone when they have a need—I would hope that that could be a model. . . . Justice. Equality. I'm appalled at the racism in this . . . area; I've never *seen* it to this extent, and I want to model love and acceptance across racial, ethnic, sexual boundaries . . . to be seen having lunch with a black person, working on a project together, giving power in a church to a woman . . . I would hope I could be a good minister but also be a good father and husband, and sometimes that's a difficult balance; but if I'm gonna be honest . . . not hypocritical . . . I'm gonna spend time and energy with my family. Well, that's a model. I'm glad, proud, to be able to say to someone who wants to meet at five o'clock, "I'm sorry, five to seven is my family hour." I want to be home between five and seven for dinner and to catch up on the day. I think that's an important statement.

Most of the informants say that how they behave as husbands and fathers is seen by both them and their congregants as important aspects of ministerial functioning. However, awareness of this importance among the black clergymen appears especially keen. The black ministers are also among the most highly involved in community health and solidarity projects outside their own congregations.

- In our community, and specifically in this church—like most African American churches—I have a great deal of responsibility for the children and the young people. For many of them I am the father figure. I am also an adviser to a lot of our members in terms of life situations, specifically young adults who may not . . . have a close relationship with a father; a lot of single mothers who may not have a man in the household . . . want a male perspective. . . . So shepherding, for me, means that caring kind of interaction with the congregation. We do a lot of hugging around here, especially with the children . . . a lot of embracing and touching. That's a kind of therapy, in many times of need and times of crisis. I take two hours every Wednesday and my younger brother and I go to a local high school here . . . and work with a group of twenty ninth- and tenth-grade black males on what it means to assume their responsibility.

This man describes other programs in the community where his high profile, plus his athletic and health-care experiences, serve to make him a frequent choice for teaching/modeling roles with local institutions, especially those dealing with African American youth.

I take a tough stand on our being responsible for our own communities and our own welfare. I take a hard line about premarital sex, babies havin' babies, drugs in our community, the responsibility of the middle class for those who have not been as fortunate, and our need to really invest in ourselves and empower ourselves. . . . They know my family means a lot to me.

Part of what one man would like to model openly is how to be a responsible gay Christian. He comments,

- To me [being "out"] would be very helpful, ideally. . . . I think I could work very well (with people who experience that pain) . . . in a specialized ministry where my gifts could be more fully used. I try to see this whole thing as a special talent . . . [as] gifts for ministry. . . . I'm very proud of the relationship we [he and his committed partner] have with one another . . . and I think we could model something for others.

People do come to this man for counseling—sometimes gay and lesbian people struggling with various problems and issues, and sometimes parents with same-sex-oriented children. He says that often he has been curious about why they trust him with these conversations and whether they identify him as gay. None has voiced such an assumption; what they *have* said is that they sense they will find acceptance and caring sensitivity. These qualities apparently are being modeled effectively.

- I try to be the best person I can, personally. At the same time, I don't want to project an image that I'm perfect, . . . so . . . my difficulty in keeping consistent in prayer or the fact that I'll have low tolerance or patience with people who have low tolerance or patience with people, . . . those things I'll bring into homilies quite a bit. . . . My perspective on being a role model is to say, "This is a real challenge for me and maybe it's a challenge for you." . . . I'll tend to use myself more as a model of . . . trying to work through these challenges, not as a model of "I've reached this plateau, and be like me." . . . One of the things here . . . [is that] people let me be the person I am. They accept that I'm trying to work hard at it. They accept that I'm real. It gives me a freedom to . . . accept the struggles and share with people.

- I think that it is appropriate . . . to expect clergy to be good. . . . It's not always comfortable. I'm a human being and that's not always as attuned to God's will as I'd like to be . . . so there are times when I'd like to do things that might not be the most helpful. So there is tension. . . . Baptism says that all of us are supposed to live a qualitatively different life. . . . I think that the clergy person's job is to model that, morally, as perfectly as we can; but I think to hold somebody up to being perfect . . . would be sick. . . . People can get upset when a clergyman is having a good time or . . . wears certain clothes, or drives a sports car, or drinks, or smokes, or plays the lottery. . . . It really has to do with a diminished understanding of God's desire for us to celebrate and nurture life, to really enjoy life. So I don't like that. . . . Frankly, I'm in this [denomination] because I thought there was more room for clergy to be more embracing of life than I had felt in the [former affiliation].

- [Part of what should be modeled is] fidelity and faithfulness to both wife or husband and children . . . fidelity and faithfulness in relationships with others. . . . If I were single, . . . I would expect that I would not engage in . . . relationships that step beyond the bounds of a pastor-parishioner relationship. . . . One of the areas that I think is a moral issue is materialism and comfort . . . to live a life not obsessed with the perfect lawn, the perfect car . . . with appearances. That includes not "marrying the church"; that includes saying no to [an event] they want me to do on Monday, because I'm going on vacation on Sunday. I will do [the event] Sunday afternoon and postpone leaving a few hours, but I will not stay Monday. . . . I'd get somebody else to do it, . . . saying, "Look, I love you. You are my parishioners. But my family takes priority."

In some regards I believe that a minister *ought* to be a moral model but by those same standards I fail; I'm not as moral as I should be. So I have a personal battle with myself over that. I resist being held up as an example. Not a lot of people *do* it, that I'm aware of—hold me up as an example of moral fortitude of any sort. It says in James, "The teacher shall be held accountable for *more* than others." It says in the prophets, "To whom much is given much is expected." I guess what I'm saying is I expect more of myself than some ministers who say, "Aah, it's the same as being a UPS driver." My guess is that the majority of the people in my church have no idea what I'm like inside. There's a small handful that do . . . who have a good feel for who I am . . . and [with them] I feel genuinely accepted. . . . The rest of the church knows that I'm "different"; they generally like me but I don't think they give it a lot of thought: I'm the *pastor.* . . . *Pastor* is one of those very rigid expectations.

Along with his opinion that, mostly, people have pretty rigid ideas of what ministers should be like, this informant says he also is aware of a public perception that clergy are silly, ineffectual sorts. The following "postscript" from him, plus the next full quotation, from another man, show how imagined public condescension and/or a fear that people will become inauthentic in their presence can cause clergy discomfort and reticence about revealing clergy identity.

I believe the media reflects public opinion . . . and the reason we like to bash the media is because we don't like to see our reflections. But if you look at . . . clergy in the media you find an absolute line of buffoons . . . gentle, kind-hearted buffoons.

- [Moral modeling is] a responsibility that, at times, I find to be a burden. I guess there are times that I like to get away and out of the context of ministry, and when I'm on vacation or traveling I just go to great lengths to avoid revealing my career. On an airplane . . . traveling, often times I lie and tell people that I'm a fireman [Actually he *is* a volunteer fireman.] . . . [It's] not that I want to do dishonest things or devious things, but . . . it can be a burden constantly having people look to you as full of virtue. Now I've shared that with the congregation and I've told them there have been situations where I've not wanted to be in the role of minister, and they appreciate that, and I think they understood that for the first time. I think they saw that . . . you're set up . . . and people approach you differently. Their language changes, they stop telling you the things that they were telling you, or they set you up as someone they're confessing to. I don't like that; there's times I want to get out from under that and just be a person. I share human failings with the folks. You obviously have to use discretion, but I share with them times I lose patience or times that I don't live up to everything that might be perceived that a minister should be.

I remember one summer we were in Canada and [there was] a play-off game and the only place in this little burg that had a TV happened to be a bar. I went to the bar and was watching this game and . . . the fellow next to me was a plumber from Cleveland (he had no idea, of course, who I was or what I was doing) and he got into a discussion with an Indian fishing guide, . . . who offered to take him to where all the fish were biting. It was interesting (their dialogue) and I was kind of in between them, and at the conclusion the man, who was inebriated, made some racial comments to this Native American and I thought, "Am I gonna play the role of minister and intervene here and tell him that's inappropriate?" I just kind of tried to divert some things and get him to talk more about himself, but, again, there's times that I would like to escape that role and responsibility.

- [Moral modeling] has [been burdensome] on occasion, particularly with the use of alcohol. . . . I found when I first came here that people wanted me to drink with them. I do drink and so I did that, and then discovered that what that meant to them was that I was giving a stamp of approval to their abuse of alcohol. So . . . I discovered I *can't* drink with them. I do feel the need to be a moral model. For me personally [it's] challenging . . . [to be] what they may have thought was the moral model and trying to present a new one. I've tried to strip away some of the surfacy things. I talk in my sermons . . . publicly . . . where I feel I've failed. I try to model that I care for myself. . . . I try to model that men and women can be close (and men and men) . . . without it being a romantic thing. I try to model unbiased pastoral care for all the members to see one another in a gracious light, forgiving pasts.

- I think [ministerial moral modeling] is imperative, but I think it's imperative that it be properly understood. I think that the distinction needs to be made between common shared humanity, frailty, that all of us have and the legitimate expectation that the pastor will model what he or she preaches and teaches. And since I have been talking about holiness of life as well as grace, I see the need to flesh that out, at the same time that I feel a need to be vulnerable in my own life. . . . For instance, if I would be found in a pattern of sexual misconduct or if I were to be convicted of a felony I would expect that I would need to resign. We had a member of the staff that was involved in a pattern of affairs and tendered his resignation, and it was accepted, but the issue was whether we should go public or not . . . (we had not in the past). . . . We thought it was important to start to model dealing openly, especially since there was fear that [we] did not know all of the partners.

- In the last several years the ministers of [our denomination] have come into some very intensive discussions about [moral modeling] because several of our ministers, it has been learned, have really overstepped the bounds. [Name number 1] in his previous parish had been sleeping with women he counseled, . . . a large number . . . they stopped counting at twenty. [Name number 2] got into trouble; he left his wife for a [married] woman in the congregation and two marriages ended. [Name number 3] has been accused, so ministers have been discussing these issues. . . . My feeling is, very strongly, that I must never lose sight of the fact that I am the minister—that I am not just an individual person but I hold an office. . . . I do feel a sense that when I stand in front of people and I say, "Insofar as I am able to discern the good in this situation, and the path to follow, this is what we must do" (and I am *expected* to say things like that from time to time; that is part of what I am called to be as the spiritual leader of this congregation), then I feel a profound responsibility to honor that, in terms of my time and my voice and my money and whatever other dimensions of commitment are called for . . .

When the city . . . was deciding whether to pass a domestic partnership ordinance they met on Monday. Monday is my day off and . . . I regard that with as much seriousness as I do a Sunday. . . . Yet . . . how could I *not* go and speak on this issue, which was of tremendous importance in this congregation, . . . about which I had spoken, about which I had written a letter to the newspaper? It was hard because I was number 83 on a list of 105 speakers in a public forum. It was past eleven on a Monday night. Usually . . . I'd have been asleep. . . . Somehow I had myself together and was able to say something . . . I would not have done that, necessarily, as an ordinary citizen, but I *did* do it as a minister. . . . I feel it's important that I speak for people in this congregation who themselves find it hard to speak. Take the example of gay and lesbian couples: Many of them were afraid to go—even to show their faces there—even though they support it—because they are not "out" at their jobs; they're afraid of losing their jobs. It's important that I be one of the people who will be present to speak for them because of the very disability under which they must suffer because of society's attitudes. Sometimes I find that real onerous; I do not deny it.

I am a very typical American in many respects, in being very protective of my autonomy. I don't like to have expectations made of me; I want to decide for myself, but I'm more comfortable now than I was before. I also am watchful. . . . I do *not* sound off on every single issue. I just can't. I try to save my voice for those moments when I feel that I can really make some difference. . . . The burden of it is shown in a mediative piece I once did . . . titled "The Most Embarrassing Question I've Ever Been Asked." . . . It was this: "Do you practice what you preach?" The dilemma of responding is, of course, you *want* to practice what you preach because you don't want to be hypocritical. You don't want to just mouth words. But do you *only* want to preach what you're able to prac- tice? . . . By trying to proclaim the highest ideals, and the fact that I have to struggle with those and be conscious of them all the time, I'm deeply aware of the discrepancy between what I can imagine, what I know to be true and beautiful, and my own very weak efforts to try to live up to those things. . . . I think that's one of the deep pains of the kind of work ministers do.

The only man who claims he would welcome an administrative role in his denominational structure talks about it in modeling terms, that is, it would give him a chance to show democratic techniques of community governance.

In these words about moral modeling a number of the men allude to the modeling of healthy attitudes toward family, marriage, and sexuality as being important in ministry. Some of the men evidence high confidence that they can and should proceed with traditional pastoral-caring intimacies while "tending boundaries" in relationships, carefully, responsibly, and openly. This they see as the way the modeling ought to happen. Others appear to be withdrawing more and more from private consultations with women, ostensibly as a way of showing that they provide no opportunity for scandal.

Beyond the voices already heard, here are a few more, explicitly focused on managing impressions in these sexually charged times.

- Clergy and sexuality. It's like all of a sudden . . . the whole world discovered that the clergy are sexual. . . . It's frightening to be a clergyperson today. Last week I took a group of kids—the confirmation class from last year—on a summer trip.

He goes on to describe a situation in which the boys' tent was too crowded and one kid was not fitting in well, while he (the pastor) had extra room in his own two-person tent. In years past, he says, he would have invited the boy to come over with him, but now he does not feel comfortable with such a decision. He thinks the current social/sexual climate "stops persons from much ministry and caring that is necessary."

A man who now refers most of his counseling requests to specialized professional counselors says,

- I'm also, frankly, very very concerned with professional liability. . . . I used to encourage people to come in. The area of responsibility in the cases that have been . . . tried against ministers . . . has been growing. I don't have liability insurance for that type thing. . . . Seventy-five percent of the people that come to . . . you are women and I don't want to be in a room like this [a very small office] with a woman . . . alone.
- One issue that hasn't been a major issue for me but is a major issue with clergy . . . is the issue of sexuality in the ministry. . . . Increasingly there is an awareness of the kind of power relationships that ministers have with congregants and a potential for abuse that sometimes becomes reality, very sadly.

While this man claims that sexuality issues have presented him with no major pastoral dilemmas through the years, he nonetheless is not inclined to minimize the sticky negotiations that ministers often face in these matters, related to their work. Being outspoken about human rights and respectful acceptance for all people doubtless contributes to his being sought out for affirmation by those whose personal problems may be severe.

In my own instance here we've had a couple of issues that have been difficult. One has to do with a pedophile who somehow identified with me as a kind of father figure. . . . [He] wanted me to give a blessing to his pedophilia, to preach about that . . . to hail him for his courage in being a pedophile. . . . The danger was that he was potentially . . . violent and his identification with me as a father figure was because his own father . . . had not given him the paternal support he needed.

Another instance that comes to mind is a young woman who was sexually abused as a child by her alcoholic father. She has attached herself to me in very unhealthy ways, in my view. She's an extraordinarily bright person. She is coming to grips with this experience as a child in a fairly new way. . . . As she [does] that she keeps discovering new depths of difficulty and pain, . . . she has been suicidal . . . and she has confided in me. . . . Frankly, I've been nervous about it. I have talked with one place where she has been institutionalized. . . . They were cautious about confidentiality but did give me some advice which I followed, namely, to distance myself very clearly. . . . She wants me to be her friend. I tried to tell her I can't be her friend; I can be her minister. That's been difficult. . . . I am tense about it. I sat down at the congregational meeting . . . and she sat directly behind me. Fortunately, my wife came and sat right next to me. . . . I made certain . . . that there was a very strong show of affection between us. . . .

These issues of sexuality and ministry and power are very, very difficult issues; I'll make no bones about it. I am a very deeply committed monogamist and I am *appalled* at what some of my colleagues do. I do not agree at all with their actions even though I hear them try to justify them. . . . I do a lot of *this* [turning his hand to make his wedding ring obvious]. . . . I talk about [my wife]. . . . I'm careful about the language I use lest there be *any* kind of misunderstanding. . . . But I think this is a very, very difficult issue. I really do.

I asked if he thought this situation had changed during his ministry.

Yes. It has changed dramatically. The major reason it has changed . . . is because of the number of women who have come into the ministry. . . . The "old boys' network," the "old boys' club," just isn't there any more. I can remember in the early years of my ministry . . . there were a couple of ministers [who] liked to brag about sleeping with congregants and they thought it was clever. I never thought it was clever. . . . I thought it was a dreadful abuse of a minister's power and position. I didn't say so as strongly as I should have. I was new to the ministry and wanting to be liked; I didn't speak up. But I did ask some questions. I think that's changed because now you have ministers' meetings where there are men and women. Indeed in our group . . . it's about evenly balanced.

GOOD PERSONS AND HEALTHY RELATIONSHIPS

With ideas of moral modeling fresh in mind, the reader may find it helpful to see what was said about good persons and healthy relationships. Throughout these considerations of moral modeling, human goodness indicators, and healthy relationship characteristics, the rabbis speak distinctively, with more dialogical views of both God and good persons. There is a necessary shift in the terms of the discourse, compared to the Christian ministers. The metaphor of the Unitarian Universalist minister constitutes something of a bridge between Jewish and Christian thinking about moral leadership.

Conclusions about what it means to be a responsible human are often quite indistinguishable among the informants, in concrete, practical terms. However, ideas come to be referenced, explained, or justified using different rationales. When I asked the ministers to tell me what a truly good person might be like (not a person who was trying merely to give an impression of goodness) they responded in several ways. Most commonly, they simply list qualities such a person would have. Some of the men add a bit of commentary. Some describe "the truly good person" by way of personal vignettes of people they have known. I have gathered together, in no particular order, a list of the qualities mentioned among the nineteen men.

kindness	compassion
unselfishness	courage
capacity for caring	understanding
genuine interest in others' real experiences	acceptance of others (and of others' views and choices)
sensitivity to others	empathy
balance	joy
humor	service-orientation
uncomplainingness	self-awareness
honesty	dedication
spiritual aliveness, struggle, growth	tolerance
confidence	nonjudgmental attitudes
hope	justice
purpose	fairness
open-mindedness	steadiness
sincerity	consistency
practical agreement with the Ten Commandments most of the time	faithfulness in commitments

The list is by no means exhaustive; a careful sifting of interview data, apart from this direct focus, would turn up many other references to the perceived nature of human goodness. Only one of the men interviewed describes the good person entirely in terms of theological tenets of salvation, though in other places he talks in more mundane terms about what should be expected from responsible humans.

Goodness, however framed, is not a static quality. It implies intentions, choices, acts—set in complicated relationship networks. Hence, what the ministers say about healthy relationships extends our view of what they think a good person is like. Again, descriptions tend to take the form of listings—qualities said to be characteristic of a healthy relationship. Though I took care to introduce the theme by saying I was not seeking responses in terms of sexual/marital relationships only, some items do suggest that focus. Generally, it can be assumed that mutuality is intended for the qualities named as contributing to relationship health, whether or not it is stated. I have allowed some redundancy in the list because I think the variants indicate slightly different slants.

trust

honesty

understanding that diversity is
   in the nature of individuality

refusal to be a doormat

willingness to repent, forgive, con-
   fess, give—in a regenerative way

alertness to needs

affirmation

giving to other's well-being

challenge

truthfulness

joint projects, such as house,
   children, garden, trips, drama

personal validation

respect

support

non-controlling

honoring of differences

understanding that individuals
   contribute unique values to a
   relationship

constant, active love, even when
   there are disagreements

mutual affection

sensitivity

freedom within mutually agreed upon,
   clear boundaries

common direction in spite of differences

agreement about "the big picture" in
   life

sharing of thoughts

helpfulness

no seeking of revenge

protective of the other's freedom

enjoyment

willingness to engage in conflict responsibility—working it through to reconciliation

room for development

clarity of role understanding

loving in criticism

lack of rejection, fear

communication health

behavior managed so that
   nothing obscures joint
   dream

openness to speaking truth, honestly,
   even if it might hurt another's feelings

eagerness to meet other's needs	active give and take
cooperation	no harboring of resentments
desire to be together, share interests, preferences, focuses	interest in and curiosity about the other
seeing the other "as Jesus"	God's grace at work in acceptance
authentic emotional display	ability to show strengths and weaknesses
exploration of possibilities	no discounting of other's worth or weight in relationship
freedom to be	

In well-designed survey research, the questionnaires and interview schedules often return to the same issues with questions couched in different terms. This precaution clarifies intentions of participants and enhances validity of findings. So also, in reporting narrative data, gathered under less tightly controlled circumstances, informants' views take on more robust and precise definition as alternative, "filters" are used to address a broad theme.

Thus far the filters for viewing moral perspectives have been the topics "moral modeling," "good persons," and "healthy relationships." Several other small arrays of response follow. Then I shall proceed to quotations regarding moral foundations and resources and, finally, clergy statements about selected specific moral issues.

SALIENT MORAL CONCERNS AND SOCIAL CONCERN LEVELS

As we talked about matters of morality during the interviews, I asked the men to tick off for me their salient moral concerns. I suggested that they not try to rank them but just share the handful of issues that are uppermost in their minds. Those they mention are included in the following list (some of them framed as negatives, some as positives).

environmental degradation	materialism
homosexuality	budget deficit
1. equal rights	child and spouse abuse
2. elimination or life change	drugs
abortion	consumerism
1. rights of choice	AIDS
2. elimination or outlawing	honesty in all human relations

violence	war and images of war
sexual responsibility	capital punishment
loss of community vision	political oppression in the world
authoritarian fanaticism	generational tension
racial conflict	sexual misconduct, especially by clergy
"family values" used as political weapon	dearth of real struggle to make marriage and family work well for people
leadership integrity	gap between rich and poor
economic justice and poverty	STDs
multicultural acceptance	greed
community and international selfishness	Muslim-Jewish-Christian dialogue for understanding
adversarial relations as "normal"	medical ethics
birth control	nuclear disarmament
secularism	city health issues
safety and survival of Jews in the world	economic oppression in the world

The list of salient concerns is tilted heavily toward problems that require social-structural solutions, though, of course, there is always the individual, personal dimension as well. Yet many of the ministers indicate that they avoid taking sides in political debates and say they do not have time to involve themselves, symbolically or organizationally, in community or interest-group affairs. Most of the men describe their ministerial activity as connected almost entirely with the local congregation. To some degree the preaching, teaching, and conversational functions are reportedly used to raise moral questions, but several men express wariness about offending congregants.

About a third of the ministers describe high-profile community activism in and beyond their congregations. In at least two cases, the congregations are said to have well-established reputations for political involvement, from neighborhood to international levels of concern; and candidates who show potential for continuing such involvement are sought out for the senior minister position. In two other cases, city congregations that were very small when the informants came to them have grown prodigiously and now carry on a multitude of community services available to a wide range of people who are not necessarily members.

A very small number of ministers say their concern is primarily for the spiritual health and salvation of individual persons, whom they then expect to be responsible morally, in terms of their own situations, perspectives, and possibilities.

Several of the men directly address the matter of connections between personal and corporate morality. The following seven statements show leaning and struggling, but also the keen awareness that human experience is neither a wholly individual, nor a merely collective, matter.

- People's hearts are changed every day they're alive. That is more of a constant process. . . . Working with structures is where we have an arena to exercise, in an orderly way, power . . . and to relate to where power is. I also don't think that people who are in the "right" camp . . . are always necessarily reflecting hearts in the right places. . . . There's such a variety of factors that pertain to how I feel about what I'm doing, and what I should be doing, that I don't think we should overstate how that's operating in building our community life together. . . . We're starting to pull out space for dialogue and for people to question . . . and say more. . . . But some people are conditioned that that [questioning] is absolutely *not* what church is for: . . . . The church has an answer. Jesus is the answer, so all you do is say you agree or you don't, or you're brought into that anxiety of "Oh, I don't know if I can form this position."

- I try to create for myself as broad a spectrum of possibility for positive living as I can. That doesn't mean I'm not focused on certain things. . . . Somehow my search is to incrementally see where I can stretch myself . . . increase the mitzvah base [good-deed base] in whatever areas [I] can possibly see to do that. . . . Let me give you the issue of . . . what's now known as communitarianism. . . . The fact that my salvation is through the *community* in Jewish life and that other popular traditions of salvation are *personal* . . . hey, listen! I personally *like* Judaism for that reason. What I do *may* be good for me. That doesn't matter; what matters is what's good for the community. That's the thing that will, in a sense, in formal Jewish life, *save* me.

Throughout his interview the following man often describes social/moral issues in systems terms. Yet, in the quotation, he tilts toward a solution perspective focused on individual change. He believes that individuals must have patience with the slow movement of institutions and that institutions must help reconcile differences among individuals. He observes that whenever he uses the gospel to evaluate social structure he gets complaints that he's being "so political." Still, though he is convinced that institutional structure must be addressed, he says he tends to fall back on more characterological considerations of action principles and personal consequences.

- Even though I would favor the ordination of practicing homosexuals, if I cannot persuade the church that that is in continuity with tradition, then that's not the fault of the church; that means I just have to do more work in terms of being able to persuade people to decide to do that. Intellectual impatience must not make one unfaithful to the *community* of faith and its understanding of church orders.

An informant who begins his statement focused on individuals, nevertheless comes down solidly for structural change as a priority, where choices must be made.

- Social action is living out Christian community. . . . I think the heart and soul of it is in the one-on-one. . . . That's where it begins. . . . I think there are times when the church clearly needs to just simply act . . . in what we know is right, even though the hearts of the people might not be ready to follow. . . . Later on we'll work at catching people up to it. . . . It might take time, but we don't just . . . wait around because somebody might be offended . . . while people's lives . . . [and] worth are at stake. . . . The bad thing with that is there's always the conservative backlash, but I think the conservative backlash usually helps the cause in the long run, anyway, because they confront people with how ridiculous their own prejudice is.

My sense is that in the last two statements we see examples of ministers struggling on many levels to discern how moral interventions may be simultaneously most helpful and hopeful, least alienating, most timely, least confusing, most true to one's own commitments, least problematic in one's affiliations, most plain, least simplistic, most bold, least disrespectful. All people trying to be responsible in a diverse and complex society face similar dilemmas, but the clergy position heightens expectations from self and others that a moral way of life can be imagined, embraced, and articulated in concrete circumstances, regardless of the amount of life complication.

Directly related to this modern need for a dependable moral compass in an increasingly complex arena of moral decision making is a renewed interest in the story form—the well-told tale—as a vehicle for conveying God-truth or moral vision. Though this thrust emerges in schools of theology, sociology of religion writings, and church publications, only one informant says he relies heavily on his skills as a professional story teller to deliver the accessible moral insight in the artistic construction of, for example, "the noble act," "the wasted gift," or "the saving grace." He is also concerned about pointing to needs for structural reform.

- My tendency would be to put more emphasis on the structural part. . . . I personally don't run into a lot of inherently evil people. I find a lot of people, including myself, who at times do very evil things because we haven't learned how, or are too afraid, to challenge the structure.

- I tip much more to the corporate [perspective on social issues] because I'm fighting the culture, I'm fighting years and years of [individualistic denominational] piety. . . . I will not do private baptisms because that's an oxymoron . . . no, that's not the word; what's the word for two things that can't stand together? To me, when we are baptized we are grafted into a community and we become part of a corporate entity. We're not simply joined to God individually. The meal of communion is a corporate meal. There are very personal moments of faith but there's no such thing as individualized faith. I always get nervous with the pronoun "my" as descriptive of faith: my faith, my God, my Jesus. None of us come to faith on our own, . . . somehow the corporateness of the church has reached us. It may be individuals belonging to that community that have told us the stories or invited us to worship. . . . So in that community I believe strongly that we need to be attentive to personal needs, but I also think we need to move the community to tend to those needs, rather than professionalize clergy. . . . It is one of the toughest things to buck as a pastor because of the [individualistic] culture we live in.

- I would use the phrase "dynamic tension." . . . One of the things I have clearly learned is that both [attention to individuals and institutions] matter. It is not just a case of saving individuals who will then save the world. It's not merely a case, on the other hand, of creating perfect institutions that will then create perfect people. It is an endless interchange between the institution and the individual. Both of them demand our attention. I think, for example, at this moment, we are confronting a massive crisis in our institutions, and I think . . . there is a profound need to address American public institutions, not the least of which is the American governing system. . . . We have allowed a deterioration in that system.

EPITAPH FANTASIES

In most of the interviews, I asked the informant to imagine an epitaph for himself—one that pleased him to think about as true for his life. Among the descriptions, we can perhaps discern the outline of intended moral leadership values. In some cases a given clergyman offered more than one statement.

He helped to create mitzvah [good-deed] makers.

He really loved and cared about people.

He gave his life for God and church as he understood it.

He is appreciated for the thought and energy he put into it.

He tried to help people enjoy life and be good Christians as well.

He brought seekers toward fullness in Christ.

He brought peace.

He loved people, Jews, Judaism, the twentieth century, and bringing them all
together.

His role didn't get in the way of being a real person.

He was there with help when we needed him.

He was a good friend and enjoyable companion.

He had integrity in all areas of endeavor.

He was someone that, when we saw him and heard him, we knew that we were with
someone who had spent time with God.

He lived his life striving to follow the teachings and example of Jesus Christ.

God is not finished with you yet.

God loves you.

God wants to make your life better.

He cared enough to make a difference.

He was a good preacher who knew when to quit. Timing is all; with preaching, with
Jesus, with ministers.

Integrity and laughter.

I have finished the fight; I have fought the good course; a crown is laid up for me
in heaven.

He helped someone when he passed this way.

He was not afraid to ask new questions.

He enjoyed the years of life.

He cared, he laughed, he really lived.

One man, who did not deliver an "epitaph," does talk earnestly, and at
length, about wanting to develop the qualities he saw in his father-in-law.
He speaks admiringly of the man as being radically grace-centered; full of
a sense of the mystery of humanness; committed to growth and critical
thinking; tending others personally, even when disagreeing; poetic about
creation, ministry, Bible stories; curious; well integrated; a good listener;
humble; unwilling to massage the church for self-gain; never afraid of new
ideas. During their shared years the father-in-law was a treasured mentor
and friend, as well as relative, to the informant, who now savors the memory.
I thought it was a description worth including.

MORAL FOUNDATIONS AND RESOURCES

A question about bedrock foundations and resources for moral judgments
brought forth a great deal of information. I asked each man to tell me where
he gets his moral criteria, where he searches for help when struggling

through some knotty moral issue. The following statements reveal a varied set of reported "basics."

Several ministers again mention the Wesley Quadrilateral (Scripture, religious tradition, reason, and experience) as a summary of their central resources for moral judgments. All nineteen indicate respect for all four of these bases for moral insights. However, there are major differences in how weight is assigned to the four sources, and whether they are thought of additively or dialectically; that is, as compoundings of information or as embedded in each other's development and interpretive force. The epistemological distinctions discussed in Chapter 2 will emerge here, sometimes clearly and sometimes veiled. The quotations do not lend themselves to easy categorization. The sequence, very roughly, moves from the more traditional to the more dialectical, with many interesting mixes.

- [My primary resource is] the moral theology background . . . developed in the context of how the church has taken Scripture and tradition. Our effective understanding is that God has a moral order . . . for us to discover, and not to invent. . . . I buy that, very much. It's not a matter of: Is it popular now? or Should we change it now? I have a firm acceptance, for example, on the abortion issue; you know, our church is clear on that. It's never gonna change with 99 percent of the people. . . . The church tradition has wrestled with these issues in the past; they looked to Scripture for answers, they looked to other things, they looked to natural law and divine order in nature for direction in that, and then tried to logically see what is the order for our moral lives. I accept that.

- The Bible is, to me, the absolute authority. . . . I think the Word is the absolute in any given situation. . . . I try to find a basis or an answer that would fit the particular situation. I don't think there's anything really in life that is new under the sun, according to Scripture—that you can't find an answer, or some direction, for. If I really can't find Scripture that is knowledgeable I always use that proverb, "In all thy ways acknowledge him and he shall direct thy path." I believe that there is divine direction, . . . divine intervention. . . . I think that if a person comes to me with a problem and we take it to God in prayer, I believe there is that divine connection . . . we're on the same wave . . . and direction as to how you should go. . . . If there is not an agreement I feel that one of us . . . somebody's not on the right wave length.

- [My resources are] one, life experience; two, counsel of those whom I respect; and three, my perspective on the biblical message. . . . I'd be closer to the view of Scripture that sees it as objective truth that is transcendent to experience [and] which we then apply to our own situation.

- [My bedrock moral resource] is the Bible. I would have to say I'm looking [in the Bible] more for an orientation in life than a specific incident because, again, situations . . . conditions that exist at a certain time . . . may not exist today. God speaks through situations that are recorded in Scripture. . . . I do not believe that we are called to mirror it . . . but . . . there are implicit in those messages, truths that can be identified. . . . There may be other Scripture passages that will help to identify [those truths]. . . . It's a complex matter, but I think that in the Bible there's often all that we need.

- First and foremost [my moral resource] is talkin' to the Boss—prayer. Secondarily . . . ideally, it probably would be Scripture . . . but . . . it's probably other people that I trust and talk to. Scripture and study are somewhere down the line. [What kinds of things I study] depends on what I'm working through.

This man says he has not found denominational social statements very helpful. He considers them jargon-laden, political, and often out of touch with real people.

The Jewish traditions include a steady stream of rabbinical commentary, integrating the sense of ancient texts with contemporary questions in many eras and situations. Thus dialectical criticism has been incorporated into the traditional literature as part of how the tradition functions.

- The bedrock is Jewish literature—what we call the teaching of our sages, which involves the Talmud and its commentaries, [and] current . . . literature of response. . . . There's a great deal of literature being written . . . coming out of a great deal of scholarship on . . . [e.g.,] death and dying, . . . homosexuality, . . . concerning what's required . . . and what Jewish tradition requires.

A Christian who is an avid reader of religious and secular scholarship and who associates regularly with professionals in human-services agencies in his city speaks as follows:

- For me [the bedrock is] a combination of a lot of different things. I have a mental-health background, so for me, people's situation and circumstance have a lot to do with the prescription; and what may be good medicine for one member may be bad medicine for another, based upon where a member is at, and what they've gone through, and what situation they're dealing with. . . . There have been times, with some of them, I've encouraged them to stay home on Sunday, because their house may be in turmoil . . . their husband or wife may not be in church and if every time they turn around they're down here, then church becomes a hideaway. And in some of those situations I . . . believe they're here too much. They need to spend some quality time at home. It's been interesting that when they've gone home and told the spouse what I have said . . . maybe I'm not the big bad boogieman that they think, and they say, "Well this guy is really sensitive to our home situation and is concerned about that."

I'm not opposed to meeting folk on their turf. I've met folks at jobs. I've met folks at poolrooms, basketball courts, whatever else the case may be. I have to be comfortable with where they're at and not always expect them to come through my doors if, in fact, I want to be relevant. There aren't any mute issues here. We basically deal with all of them as they impact this community. We have to, because I've got a very diverse congregation. I take the philosophy . . . [It is my business] to not only comfort the afflicted but afflict the comfortable also. I have all of that sitting here on Sunday morning.

While this man addresses the question primarily in terms of assessing personal needs for specific types of caring, he had already made clear in other parts of the interview that the "combination of things" mentioned in the first sentence of the quotation includes heavy reliance on biblical mandates for caring, and on prayer.

Having earlier identified his moral grounding as the emphases of the Wesley Quadrilateral, one man proceeds to talk about experience more in terms of eroding beliefs and ideals than in terms of illuminating and embodying traditional truths in life.

- Experience certainly has tempered my scriptural understanding and some of the other factors, because I guess I realized that I could literally sell my soul to the church, and be all the things that my background had taught me, and become very bitter. . . . Particularly when I got to this area . . . it was very disillusioning to realize that a high percentage of the folks this weekend will be up north at their cottages . . . and . . . travel there in luxury automobiles. I've had to accept that and work with it and meet people where they are.

   Then, I guess, it was also disillusioning to bring that evangelical enthusiasm and zeal and then to meet the experience of . . . you know, I've got a doctorate, and to realize that somebody is making three and four times as much money as I! I wasn't at all aware of that [in the beginning]; I was very naive. At first I thought, "So what! I'm here to serve." Then when my children got older and they wanted tennis shoes just like the other kids and they wanted to attend the same camps . . . those are the realities that can temper your former experience and also Scripture and tradition and all of that. And . . . that sounds very materialistic, but it's something that seminary had not prepared me for.

The next informant's words reflect a conceptual framework taken from a respected teacher. Within each category the dialectical-existential approach is expected to operate and the four forms of discourse are understood to be interactive in their contributions to moral insight.

- I've been most shaped by James Gustafson in Chicago. . . . Gustafson contends there are four forms of moral discourse. One is the prophetic, which . . . names evil evil and names just as just. It's visceral. It sees things in black and white. . . . It's the discourse of righteous indignation . . . of Martin Luther King, and the Berrigans, and the liberation theologians, . . . and of Amos. There's much of me that still calls the church to that kind of passion. The second form of moral discourse is narrative. It's the story . . . of the victims of injustice . . . the parables . . . the people of God in bondage, in exile, in the wilderness. . . . It's the victim of abuse telling what it's like to live in a dysfunctional family with a batterer. It's the story of a doubting Thomas. . . . The third form is . . . metaphysical. It's the distinctions of the philosophers. The fourth form is policy, which is . . . those who take the righteous indignation of the prophet and the stories of the victims and the distinctions of the philosophers and have to somehow make those all into policy. It's the person who is elected to office . . . or runs an agency or has to allocate a budget at a college or is gonna make decisions about hirings and firings and priorities for expending funds, or it's the person who's gonna work on organizing a neighborhood. It seems to me that when a church is at its best doing ethics, it's got all four of those forms of moral discourse operative.

- What I try to do is to look to other people who have encountered situations not totally dissimilar. I look to human beings, human situations, because I do not regard any text as ultimate. . . . I might look to something in the Hebrew Bible because I think there's a lot there, but I'm just as likely to look to Martin Luther King. . . . I also look . . . for the past ten to twelve years to . . . the voice of feminists. . . . At the time of the Gulf War starting, I knew that something was going to happen and I would have to address this at some point. I looked back to the work of William Ellery Channing and Theodore Parker and John Haynes Holmes in my own movement. I looked to the writings of Dr. Martin Luther King. . . . I looked to various feminist authors (Gloria Steinem was one of them) and tried to imagine . . . how she might have responded. . . . What was Patricia Schroeder . . . saying? What would a woman like Sojourner Truth have said . . . Harriet Tubman? I was trying to reflect on this . . . trying to get a better understanding of what . . . I thought . . . and of what the truth was, . . . what the moral good was in this situation.

- First [I look for moral direction by] listening to the stories of people who are involved. With the case of abortion I need to listen to women who have struggled with that and decided to have abortions and what that was like for them. I need to listen to women who struggled with that and decided to keep their children and what that's been like. Gay and lesbian people need to tell their own story, and we need to listen to it and see that as being one valid expression of God's word. . . . More broad are things like war and poverty. . . . We have to put the face on it.

    Scripture often, for me, is not particularly helpful except in that it proclaims God's radical acceptance of us all in Jesus Christ. And then it talks about themes of community, of caring for other, as much as you care for yourself. . . . Within our community of faith it's a matter of listening and discerning what's helpful and what's not . . . and to name those things which are not. . . . In individuals' lives I really feel that people do the best they can. . . . One thing we don't understand very well in our society is community and what it means to live in community. . . . We have an ethic of "What's good for me is good for everybody; God helps those who help themselves." So as Christians we need to develop a sense of . . . mutual responsibility to one another. . . . I think we need to listen to the stories of Jesus. . . . The weekend of the Los Angeles riots I preached about casting our nets on the other side. . . . It was so easy for us to place moral judgments against whoever we did. . . . How can we try to . . . step back and cast our net on the other side and see the whole thing from a different angle? I feel that I'm sounding more nebulous . . . than I really am. I think that Christianity offers some very clear guides for moral and ethical decision making, but I just don't think it offers specific answers.

The final selection in this group comes from a man who says he is continuing to move toward accenting broad values, ideals, and intentions and then offering an array of stories and cases that show how such abstractions may be embodied in concrete relationships and situations. He claims there has not been much resistance from congregants to what they see as a very liberal ministerial approach.

- When people join this parish we try to be real clear in our orientation what are our guiding principles and . . . what we are about. . . . And . . . I am real sensitive in the way I preach, not to fall into the dogmatic "this *is*." . . . More and more we preach with images and say, "Here's a gospel value we just heard . . . today; let me play out some scenarios for you." I give them a lot of room. . . . I try to go back to gospel values; I try to see what are some . . . that seem to be important in Jesus' teachings. . . . When I was first ordained I think I would try to have an absolute *answer* for every situation. Now I more and more am trying to say I'd like to have a *value* for each situation, knowing that I probably won't be able to apply it completely to every situation. I'm more willing to accept the complexity. Moral answers that fit even a hundred years ago in what seemed a simpler context cannot just be laid over on very complex [situations]. . . . I guess [I'm thinking] especially of medical/moral issues. . . . When do you pull the plug? . . . I've given up trying to have an absolute answer for . . . people.

  On sexual issues I find that I'm much more liberal in counseling others than I am in my own life. . . . Jesus seemed to be very comfortable with people struggling through their sexuality. That did not seem to be the bedrock of his judging of them. . . . There's a value here that says sexuality is extremely important, but God seems to know that we might make more than the normal amount of mistakes that way, because it's so much a part of our struggle for relationships. So the value is honesty in relationships. . . . When a couple comes in that're having an affair or something, rather than trying to say it's right or wrong, I try and say "What's the quality of the relationship? What's your commitment to the relationship? How honest are you with that relationship?"

HOMOSEXUALITY

In discussing moral issues, many of the men, as we have seen, included views on sexual morality, sometimes offering comments about homosexuality. If they did not, I specifically asked if they wished to share observations about same-sex orientation. A few take the position that homosexual behavior is an immoral choice. A few say that the matter is not discussed in their congregations; but they believe they have homosexual members. The majority declare full and open acceptance of same-sex-oriented people (sometimes referred to as SSOs) into their congregations; but they differ as to whether homosexual physical intimacy, even in committed relationships, is morally acceptable. As the men talked about homosexuality I heard evidence that they reflect the general tendency in the United States to focus on males. One man is aware of this and comments that the idea of lesbianism doesn't bother him in the same way.

Many of the ministers are actively seeking to elevate levels of knowledge and of sensitivity about life struggle issues relative to homosexuality. These tend to emphasize a single standard of personal commitment for all sexual relationships and focus on such values as honesty, clarification of intentions, and trust building, regardless of a couple's sexual orientation. In quite a few cases, the men express views incongruent with the official or dominant positions of their professional affiliations—sometimes more conservative, sometimes more liberal. For example, a Catholic priest wants people with same-sex orientation to feel welcome in the congregation and has a full committee in the parish to make gay and lesbian rights a matter of growing sensitivity in the church. They struggle with how to respond to the Vatican's latest document, he says: "The committee and I feel that the document is *so* off target." To say that homosexual people are "loved by God" but ought not have the same rights seems "so contradictory" to him. A question, he adds, that haunts him continually in his later years, is whether God calls some people simply to continue to say things that need to be said.

Several of the ministers mention that they were explicit about their support for gay and lesbian rights when they were being considered for their positions; so they have met little resistance in developing ministries consistent with their stated views.

Here is a sampling of further statements about homosexuality.

- I'd be very opposed to gay and lesbian rights because I find it to be anti-scriptural and, I think, very detrimental to society. I consider homosexuality . . . to be a sin . . . clearly a choice. I don't believe anyone is born gay or lesbian. . . . If people who advocate gay and lesbian rights had their way, they would like that if you were hiring someone as a pastor on a staff you couldn't even [broach] the question. I'd be violently opposed to such a position. I consider homosexual-ity . . . to be a sin. I don't, on the other hand, think that because somebody takes that position and is committing sin in those areas that you should not give them their ordinary freedoms. . . . For somebody to be mistreated because they are a homosexual is certainly not right. . . . I don't think that you take advantage of someone because they're sinful.

- While I want to make it clear that I'm not condemning people who have AIDS, I am condemning the life-style that potentially brought them to that point, whether . . . drug use or homosexual . . . encounters with people who are HIV positive. The big issue from a moral/ethical perspective in the whole AIDS arena, for me, is the life-style of the homosexual that perpetuates that virus and the desire to have approval from society for that life-style, which I see as *totally* outside scriptural approval, even though it's a big issue in our church. I feel very strongly that homosexuals should be helped to leave that life-style and that it should be viewed by the church as an unacceptable life-style, not to be condoned or affirmed in any way, most specifically not in ordination. The camp opposite mine see homosexuality as a genetic weakness, . . . something that can't be helped and something that we just have to accept as a legitimate option for people's lives. . . . They see it as a disease that is not at all sin-related. . . . It's very clearly a sin issue for me. It would be interesting for me to know where people in our congregation stand. I have no idea where everybody lines up; but by and large, the congregation is on the conservative side, not supporting homosexuality at all.

- The fairly orthodox, evangelical view of Scripture that I have makes the view of gay and lesbian activity problematic. The congregation would mostly approve of concern for social-political rights but would likely approve gay and lesbian *activities* less than other congregations in the conference. While I think that sexual orientation can be changed through the power of the Gospel, I'm not hopeful or dogmatic about that; but I do think that sexual activity is limited to fidelity in heterosexual marriage.

- We've been confronted with this problem [of known homosexual members]. . . . We love the individual. We don't condone his [life-style]. . . . We do believe that it is not the norm; and we do believe that God is able to change that life-style.

- [In my congregation] it's not a concern. . . . I'm sure that I have . . . Oh, I *know* that we have those with homosexual tendency here. . . . It would probably not be an issue talked about or discussed. It would be more of a taboo issue. I think they would be accepted on their personhood. There would be some folk who would be uncomfortable with their practices.

In response to a question about whether he thought his congregation would be accepting of a known homosexual couple as members, another informant says,

- Not at this time. No, they wouldn't. No. . . . I have friends who are gay. The people that I know that are gay I have accepted, and we're friends. I get uncomfortable when they talk about their lovers. . . . I had a horrible experience in high school that . . . left me with a real negative view of gays. I was assaulted by a gay man. Now I realize that's not characteristic. . . . The thing that *really* hurt: . . . a boy . . . was baby-sitting and . . . sodomized my son. That has flavored things for me. Our denomination has struggled for years over ordination of homosexuals. I am not supportive . . . and, again, my experiences have flavored that opinion, I'm sure. . . . Most of these gay folks are very responsible and would never, never hurt a child . . . and would probably be *less* likely to . . . inflict pain on a young person than a heterosexual person [would]. I know that.

A young man struggling with ambivalence says, "My jury is still out." But he claims to be working hard on the issue—reading, discussing, listening. He is bothered by the silence of the church over Dachau, the ignorance and parochialism of the church in so many areas. He comments, "The church is a very imperfect tool . . . a 'broken body,' Scripture would say." He believes that homosexual orientation is OK, but the *activity* is wrong; yet he says he's very uncomfortable with this position and "half doesn't believe" what he's saying. The idea of gay males is more troubling to him than the idea of lesbians.

- I know that I'm responding, in part, from homophobia . . . in part from a limited biblical understanding. . . . I try to be honest about it. I tell gays and lesbians I'm not comfortable. . . . It comes from my own stuff and I'm sorry. I'm in my own process of figuring it all out.

The congregation this man serves has seemed to him surprisingly liberal. They say they've known gay people all their lives and they're very noncondemning.

- I see an order that I believe is very scriptural, directed by God, for where sexuality comes into play and where it should not be exercised. Appropriate sexual intercourse is limited by the church to the [heterosexual] marriage relationship. We say there's a difference between orientation and action. . . . Morally, it makes no difference whether I'm *attracted* to a female or male. . . . Our challenge is to help people have respect for people as individuals, regardless of what their sexual orientation is, and to recognize that they have a right to basic human rights. It's easy for people in an area like this to have a prejudicial or judgmental image . . . because they don't know anybody [who is identified by them as homosexual].

Last year, he says, there was an AIDS-related death of a gay male in a prominent parish family. The informant conducted the funeral and nobody suggested he should have refused. People were pretty supportive to the mother of the deceased, he thinks.

- We're not doing a good job of dialoguing as a congregation on some of these issues. There are some homosexual members whose orientation remains "suspected." I imagine that's a burdensome existence. I think they feel that people tolerate them . . . not welcome them. . . . A good dialogue . . . would bring a lot of that out . . . and clarify.

A man whose affiliation is with a group that allows ordination of homosexual persons and whose congregation includes several known homosexual couples, says,

- I'm as active as the gay Jewish community will allow me to be in their affairs. When people are looking for support in the gay community they know who to talk to. The Jewish community is perhaps only slightly less homophobic than the balance of the American communities.
- I think generally the congregation is pretty tolerant of homosexuality . . . unless they make a big deal of it. I don't think the congregation would tolerate an openly gay priest [Episcopal]. An openly gay member wouldn't be a problem. . . . In our newsletter I asked people to vote against a repeal of gay-rights protection and I didn't get any flak at all on that. . . . *I* would have no problem with the ordination of an openly gay person because I happen to believe . . . that the majority of people who are homosexual are . . . predisposed that way. It's a part of God's creation . . . and as long as they're being responsible, decent, loving, caring people . . . that's OK.
- I've taken a strong stand that the church historically has alienated gay and lesbian persons and that it's time that we intentionally welcome gay and lesbian people back into the congregation. I think congregations need to have a significant number of gay and lesbian members before they face the issue about blessing gay and lesbian unions. . . . A couple of our most public gay members left to go to an all-gay congregation. . . . I think most people at this church hope that the issue is dead now—that we've done that issue and are going to do something else.
- I like to say I'm absolutely in the middle of the road . . . but I'm pretty much on the left of a lot of things . . . considering that my role is to find the compassionate, human, sensitive response . . . which isn't completely contradicted by requirements in Jewish law. We just had the first baby born in our congregation to a lesbian couple, . . . the mother artificially inseminated. There are some very complicated private and public issues. . . . I don't think it would be an issue [with the congregation] if the mothers come to services with the baby [as known

lesbians] but I think I *would* have a problem if I put . . . in my synagogue bulletin, congratulations to them as a couple. I was very hesitant about how to set up a certificate. . . . Normally when a baby girl is named . . . you call up her parents together . . . to name the baby. Fortunately, there are a lot of older traditions . . . where it is customary for one of the grandfathers to be asked. In this case I was lucky . . . the grandfather walked into the hospital while I was there visiting and said, "I'm in town just for a day. Can I come to services tomorrow morning and we'll name the baby?"

The gay minister I interviewed is in a life-partner relationship with a man in another community. He describes the commitment as monogamous and wants to trust his congregation with this information about his life; but so far has not told them. They appear to like him very much, but he fears they would not accept a gay pastor for their church, though he serves in a denomination that officially permits ordination of gay and lesbian candidates. Issues around homosexuality are frequently raised in his parish. He finds himself welcoming the opportunities for discussion and deals with the subject comfortably. Still, he hopes that one day his orientation and partner can be known openly in his local ministerial situation. Referring to his committed friendship, he says,

- It has been, to me, where God's grace has been most strong and known . . . in a very real way. . . . To be able to share that as a part of ministry would be very good, . . . to be able to tell my faith story, . . . the story of self-hatred, . . . coming into self-loving in God's love for me . . . struggling always to accept that love and believe it.

He is convinced that the biggest sin connected with homosexuality is the heterosexism and homophobia that those of same-sex orientation must endure.

ABORTION

Another controversial issue that has engaged the U.S. public in angry partisan politics is the issue of abortion rights. Surveys consistently show that the commonest stance in the U.S. population involves advocacy of thoughtful, intentional conceptions; nurture of and reverence for life from conception to death; *and* a protected legal option for abortion as a private, personal decision. The more articulate holders of this position tend to talk about honoring the sacredness of human life while preserving human freedom and responsibility for moral choices in a public forum of open moral discourse and compassionate caring. The dramatic public confrontations and political activities have been associated largely with "pro-life" interests that focus narrowly on bringing all biologically healthy conceptions through to birth; and "pro-choice" interests that focus narrowly on maintaining individual freedom to decide on a course of action. Absolutist approaches have characterized many of the high-profile leaders on both sides, and in this strong polarization of arguments, people who acknowledge the complexity of life issues often have found themselves shouted down by the purists. Apparently, from information I see, U.S. citizens have been inclined increasingly to disassociate themselves from the most extreme claims to moral righteousness, relative to abortion law, and are more disposed to formulate their opinions apart from "sides" at either edge of the discussion.

Insofar as the above accurately describes U.S. culture climate it may, in part, help to interpret the seeming quietism on this subject as evidenced in the interviews. Most of the informants indicate that there is little discussion of abortion issues in their congregations, as congregations. Some of these men are aware of different opinions held among members, but not voiced openly. Others claim they do not know what their congregants think about the matter.

Only three men identify themselves unambiguously as pro-life and against legal abortion expect in narrowly limited circumstances. One is Catholic and two are Protestant. None speaks of being involved in pro-life political activities; and one says he doesn't know what his members think.

Only one man describes himself as both overtly "pro-choice" and politically active (along with his congregation) in community attempts to secure the legality of choice. He emphasizes, however, that the congregation's commitment is to *choice*, not to abortion. They have congregational membership in a national religious coalition for abortion rights—a stance he says is common in the denomination. He claims that it "takes little courage" in his church to be in favor of abortion choice freedom. By his estimation, at least 90 percent of the membership are strong pro-choice people.

Most informants indicate that abortion is not a central concern in their ministries but they do share their views.

- This congregation . . . the message I've gotten is it's not worth public discourse anymore because everyone knows where they stand privately; and my subjective opinion is the majority is pro-choice in probably the kind of ratio that the culture is pro-choice. Personally I find it very hard . . . when women come to me who are pregnant and want to deal with what are their choices. The first thing I tell them is, intellectually, I'm pro-choice. Experientially, I am the father of . . . adopted children whose mothers chose to carry their pregnancy to term and place their children for adoption. . . . I have great difficulty integrating my emotional responses as [an] adoptive parent and my intellectual response as pro-choice. Therefore I'm not going to be helpful to their struggles 'cause I have too much of my own stuff involved. So I refer them to [other trusted local Christian counseling services]. . . . I say, "I will pastorally walk with you, but I can't [be] the primary person in the [decision] process; it's just not fair."

- Not knowing the ultimate answer to this question, as to who's going to be positively benefited, . . . I'm pro-choice; I'm also pro-procreation. I would counsel people to have the child if they can handle it emotionally.

- My sense is that . . . people in this congregation would be predominantly pro-choice but would believe . . . that abortion is morally wrong unless you can show why it isn't. But they don't wanna have the government determine that for them. . . . I don't have to [take a position] very often, but we're pretty congruent. I'm very pro-choice but I'm also very much concerned with molding the character of individuals in the community so that we will not have to have as many abortions.

- I was in the forefront of providing a forum for our congregation to unpack the abortion issue. We had a strong center here of pro-life folks and people who sit on the board of Planned Parenthood. It's a very volatile situation for our congregation. We think our service to the congregation this past spring was, for the second time, to run a six-week series on abortion, that climaxed a previous ten-week series on life-and-death issues. . . . In this last situation they were very polite. I have found that they become so emotional so quickly without those structures that they find it difficult to get any value from the other side.

From the pulpit, where "people can't argue back," he says he does not take a stand on either side. In teaching or in conversation he may reveal his own position, which is a "qualified pro-life position."

Philosophically I became more and more committed to a pro-life position . . . while at the same time, on a policy level, I became more and more confused as to how to bring that into the public arena.

- We don't really talk about [abortion] very much [in the congregation]. . . . I feel strongly that abortion is wrong . . . it's killing. . . . Even stronger still, I feel that I do not have the right, especially as a man, to tell a woman what to do with her body. That decision is between her and her maker and that which is created within her. Now there's a little middle ground in me; I believe that a husband has some say . . . in a committed Christian relationship. . . . I don't think a husband, even in that relationship, has the final say. . . . When I think of the amount of passion and the amount of money and the amount of time that is wasted in political circuses over the issue [of legality] it just makes me weep. The other thing that is lost on both sides, unfortunately, is compassion.

- [On abortion rights] we are split as a congregation and I'm torn as an individual. . . . I think the majority of people would say it needs to be legal but . . . we have a hard time with someone choosing it. Our denomination has taken a pro-choice stand.

- My personal stance is [that] we must have freedom for legal abortion. Women must be able to legally make that choice. It may not be the ideal, but we don't live in an ideal world. I said that publicly to the women's fellowship meeting last fall. I don't think anyone left because of it. . . . We cannot judge the situation that a woman may be in. I lived through the days when it was illegal and I think it was a terrible world. . . . We need to make people aware of the fact that when you are involved with an abortion you are taking a potential life. I do not think we're taking a person who has civil rights . . . but we are taking a potential life and we must deal with that reality. But we must minister to the woman who has to make that choice and we must give her, as a church, all the support we can . . . God is our judge; we can't judge one another. . . . We've gotta get off this kick of judging other people.

- I take a very strong position on abortion but primarily it would be to . . . encourage people to vote in a way to change things. . . . The way I interpret Scripture it's wrong to take a life. . . . But, as I said, there's some very ticklish issues. . . . Taking away someone's freedoms by using a bull horn out in public I would consider a wrong as well. . . . Picketing someone's private residence is not the kind of thing I would encourage someone to do or be in agreement with. . . . You can have strong opinions and not agree with [some of] the practices.

- It's interesting that really in our [African American] community you don't have a lot of dialogue about [abortion-rights issues]. . . . Our folks would do a lot before they would terminate a child. I think that's a . . . difference between our community and a lot of communities. . . . It's not usually our women saying we choose not to have this baby. If that choice is made, it's usually economic . . . [It] has nothing to do with "I want to be free to do other things." It's because "I can't afford it." . . . I have had members on both sides, in terms of those who have elected to keep their children and those who have had abortions. . . . I guess I'm blessed in a way; lots of times that choice has been discussed with me before . . . and in most cases we are able to encourage them to keep the child.

- The congregation is divided on abortion rights. Personally, I have a lot of ambivalence. I've counseled young women who have gotten abortions; and yet I have worked with so many adoptive parents (long sigh); so abortion as birth control I feel is wrong. However, the one fifteen-year-old I think of was not physically and emotionally, in any way shape or form, ready to have that baby.

- I am against abortion but, like Paul, I speak by permission and not by commandment. I believe there are certain instances where God judges the motive as well as the act. If you are raped I'm not so sure that I would say to you you have to have that baby. Incest. I think there are exceptions. . . . There are some things

God has not given me a direct "no" on. . . . I teach here that it is a matter of choice. . . . God has always given us a choice. Now, we suffer for our choices, but God has never taken away choice. Never.

- We have a "respect life" committee that tries to do a lot of information things in the parish. . . . I personally find abortion doing an easy solution in a very complex situation. I rarely speak . . . about abortion from the pulpit because my pastoral side knows how many women are extremely hurt and many times forced into that situation. I think I bow to that, not wanting to "guilt" one more person from the pulpit, and knowing that there'll be a voice within this parish community trying to raise that issue. I purposely haven't mentioned abortion in a sermon in ten years. That's not for lack of conviction. It's a sense that for so many people once they hear that from a voice of authority in any kind of condemning way it pushes them that much farther away. When I speak about that in education forums or . . . that kind of setting, I guess I really believe in that consistent life ethic. If we're gonna be strongly against abortion we gotta also be against war, euthanasia, death penalty . . . at least in my opinion, in terms of biblical values. If you're gonna be gung-ho on one, ya gotta be gung-ho all of 'em, or you really don't buy the value. My sense is [the congregation] would be divided. . . . The pro-choice—not pro-abortion!—might be stronger than the absolute no-discussion/no-option.

Throughout the quotations on abortion it is easy to see the emotional involvement and moral struggle lying close to the surface. This raises an important set of questions that cannot be settled through use of my data: Are the clergy reports of "not much discussion on the issue" related to lack of congregant interest in pursuing the topic? Or congregant fear that dialogue would be traumatically divisive in the community? Or clergy fear of stirring controversy? Or clergy lack of confidence that dialogue is necessary and beneficial? Or clergy discomfort with their own level of clarity? Or general unease among U.S. people in entering serious discussions of sexuality? Or is it widespread confidence among U.S. people (or members of a given congregation) that they already have enough trustworthy information for arriving at a personal position with which they can live?

These same questions apply to the discussion of same-sex orientation where again, with a very few exceptions, the men indicate little active community discussion around the subject. Though sexual problems were mentioned often in the narratives as being of great concern to the informants, none explicitly mentioned or implied pastoral or congregational involvement in ongoing comprehensive sex-education programs for children, youth, or adults.

ECONOMIC ISSUES

There seems to be even greater reluctance among the interviewees, and their congregations (as seen by the men) to enter open dialogue around economic issues such as poverty, materialism, greed, tax injustice, depersonalization of corporate economic structures, and systematic exploitation of labor forces.

In recent decades, social analysts have pointed out repeatedly that the high value put on individualism in the United States is quite remarkable in human history. Economic individualism, idealized as liberty, is widely promoted, and even indulged, at the expense of community well-being.

Many of the men interviewed went through college during years of student cynicism about capitalism, individual career success, and traditional values. Optimism about social change toward a nonracist, nonsexist, equalitarian society was running high. Hopes and ideals carried forward from that time blended with aspirations for ministerial careers, in the lives of some clergy, and were further shaped in seminary experiences. Several talk about the preference of their age cohort for inner-city or experimental ministries, which were romanticized as real, compared to "artificial" suburban life, which was the object of much youthful contempt. Two mention that in their seminaries, faculty made a conscious effort to counter this devaluing of suburban parishes. The students were asked to consider the fact that it is precisely in U.S. suburbs that the corporate economic power lives; so suburban ministries might be especially fruitful toward social structural change. They say the argument made sense to them at the time, but now they are much less sanguine about ministerial possibilities for influencing suburban economic power toward humanitarian reform.

Economic issues are salient for many clergy, as earlier statements have indicated. Yet most of them say economic policy issues are seldom addressed, as such, in their present ministries, and they express puzzled frustration about how to initiate helpful discussion. Not all are from the age cohort described, and not all are in suburban parishes; but among the informants it is clear that moral discourse about economic reform gnaws as an "oughta" that mostly doesn't happen.

All the men describe a wide range of charitable activities in their congregations. These include "food pantries," "clothes closets," "transportation pools," and "furniture warehouses" where poor people can receive supplemental assistance. Also included are various forms of disaster aid in emergencies, refugee assistance, and an assortment of denominational charities, as well as volunteer teaching and care giving. The clergymen say there is generally willing cooperation in projects that provide various types of relief for persons identified as needy. An international project born of systems-level critique and having social-policy implications, but appealing strongly to those who opt more for direct personal helping, is Habitat for Humanity. Quite a few ministers indicate that their congregations are involved in the construction of Habitat houses. Somehow this concept has been able to harness energies from both "systems reformers" and "doers of charitable acts."

The clergymen do not question their congregants' personal generosity. For whatever reasons—their own or their members' unease, their own or their members' disinterest—they do not, in their congregations, have vigorous moral questioning and discussing of socio-economic policy implications.

The African American clergy and their congregations constitute something of an exception to certain aspects of what I've said here and I will give attention to their situation after sharing some quotations from the others on economic justice.

- I get defensive when I'm speaking about justice issues. . . . People tend to go into a mode, "Well, this is just [name] speaking his own personal, private, political opinions now," and [they] don't see that I root that in my theological understanding and my understanding of Scripture. . . . I get both saddened and angered when people don't seem to see what I see [of] the connection between the two.

- As long as they wouldn't have to give up anything they'd be all *for* [economic justice]; when it hits close . . . *not* willing to significantly change life-styles. . . . I struggle. I would like to think that I would be willing . . . but I think only if *everybody* did. I am not willing to significantly alter my life-style as a symbolic protest, and . . . I'm disappointed with myself. . . . I would be 100 percent behind across-the-board-everybody-suffers kind of thing to create a more equal economic [situation].

- We are involved in Habitat for Humanity. . . . There are so many aspects to [economic concerns]. I think of trade with Latin America . . . rainforests. . . . It might come up in a Sunday school class, but we're not doing a lot about economic justice. . . . That's a very complex issue right now. . . . Everyone feels like they're poor; until they see figures of income, . . . until they rub shoulders . . . with someone who has a lot less, everybody feels strapped.

- Unlike the abortion issue, this congregation has never taken a stand as a congregation on [economic issues]. What we have is a diversity of opinion. There are Democrats, Republicans, Libertarians, Socialists. . . . Greens . . . all represented in this congregation. . . . I don't have any commitment to either of the major parties and I'm a little bit leery about some of the issues with the minor parties. Our congregation struggles with the question of economic justice. This particular congregation is a very well-to-do congregation. . . . more than 60 percent of [us] have graduate or professional degrees. I would say . . . probably 90 percent or better [have] college degrees. These are inordinately high numbers in churches. . . . Mostly these are people with a lot of brain power, with a lot of energy, with a lot of drive, with a lot of ambition; and they work very hard. . . . It's hard for these people to do more than to speak with some sense of the injustice of the gap between rich and poor. It's not an issue that inflames people here.

- When we started the parish we made a commitment to take a certain percentage [5 percent] of every Sunday's collection and that would go not just to the poor but to groups that challenge structures. Each year when those grants are made (and our justice committee . . . makes those) we lose several families. My fear was that, as we moved along, the tendency would be to start cutting into that and give less, but I was real proud that last year our council decided to raise that by $\frac{1}{2}$ percent a year, indefinitely. . . . Last year we did a . . . Habitat house from scratch. Those things go over better than the systems stuff.

RACIAL JUSTICE

Prior to the last data display I mentioned that the black pastors differ from the white, in some respects, when talking about moral concerns in the socioeconomic realm. As I begin this section on racial justice I want to deal first with those differences in attitude toward economic justice. They emerge from two sets of dynamics that impact the clergy and congregations differently, according to color lines.

I know of no responsible study in recent decades that has not concluded that, though there are numerous (and increasingly numerous) blacks who are famous, affluent, middle-class, professional, or otherwise visibly successful, African Americans are disproportionately represented among the poor, the unemployed, the illiterate, the victims and perpetrators of crime, substance abusers, the mentally ill, the ill-housed, and other categories of human need in U.S. society (when compared with European Americans). Along with well-documented studies of prejudice and discrimination patterns that systematically disadvantage black folks as a category, all the data showing differential social benefits indicate that U.S. society is objectively racist.

The legacy of racist history, stemming from chattel slavery times, might be expected to take generations to transcend under the best conditions of just laws and personal goodwill. And carefully gathered data, across the board, have not indicated that we, as a nation, have shown the best of goodwill.

Churches, schools, and neighborhoods remain dramatically segregated, with notable exceptions. All of the nineteen clergy interviewed minister to congregations dominated numerically by one racial group. The four black congregations are almost wholly black; the fifteen white congregations are either almost wholly white or somewhat integrated, largely due to university ties that yield a racial mix more international than intranational.

Given this picture, the black pastors and their congregations seldom have the options, exercised by many white groups, of ignoring economic/racial issues, dealing with them primarily as electives, or considering such issues mainly someone else's concern.

I spoke of two sets of dynamics affecting African American congregations. Apart from (but related to) the fact that they carry an especially heavy burden of consequences from racism built into the U.S. social structure, they live in a long and powerful tradition of church as major culture center. For decades after the Civil War, churches were the community gathering places that offered the greatest safety and solidarity for black people struggling to survive and thrive. Church was a place where people might consult with one another and organize intentions. Church incorporated entertainment and sociability. Church provided emotional release and personal support in times of grief, joy, hope, fear. Church networks became communication networks for political protest and economic assistance. The free-flowing, emotionally intense, hours-long, black church-service tradition has its origin in a time when one can easily imagine many African Americans' being reluctant to leave such a lifeline of affirmation, respite, and nurture. Even those of us who were not shaped in the twentieth-century version of that legacy find ourselves deeply touched by the richly evocative music of African American spirituality.

So, affected at some level by the residual problems of a racist social history, and also affected by the life-penetrating holism of black church culture in the United States, the four black ministers and congregations are doubtless more inclined than most of the white to be involved in economic, political, public educational, health, housing, and criminal-justice issues. There are, however, important differences among the four black informants also, and you will sense some of those differences in the tone of the statements they make. Two of them appear to be more highly aware of social-structural dimensions of problems and the need for correctives to address social processes. All see the need for constant encouragement and varied assistance delivered to persons as individuals, though one thinks his congregants are more comfortable handling such assistance according to their own initiative, rather than coordinating efforts within the congregation. Two lean toward a politically low profile in their communities. It is important at least to consider the possibility that their stated greater caution about stirring controversy might, in part, be affected by what they judged acceptable to me as a white interviewer.

The first and second quotations show the strongest contrasts among the four.

- My hope is the Lord will allow me to retire from [this congregation]. I think it has the ability to become a national model for ministry, especially in terms of team ministry and the impact that a church can have on the community. It would be my hope to develop a strong staff to deal with the social and spiritual issues of our community and our constituency. . . . When there are major issues in the community a lot of times I'm asked for input. . . . I mainly have been youth- and health-oriented [in the larger community outside his own congregation]. . . . A lot of educational issues are important for me. I also help with . . . a statewide adoption program . . . for hard-to-place youth. . . .

  If I could invent anything I'd invent self-esteem pills to make people feel better about themselves. . . . That impact so many of the issues that we find ourselves dealing with. Because if you don't feel good about yourself then maybe you think you deserve domestic violence. Maybe you don't have any problems puttin' drugs in your system . . . lettin' someone use you or abuse you sexually. . . . For me, that is a very key issue. . . . I don't believe the church can be the answer for every situation. . . . It may be other institutions will do that and do that as well, if not better, and maybe our role becomes to empower them. . . . There's all kinds of ways we can strengthen an agency. . . . I may have one of the most political congregations around. A young lady who coordinated the . . . Democratic mayoral campaign is in my congregation. And then one of the Republican City Council members is in this congregation. If there is a political race, you can bet an appearance will be made here by both candidates. They can't afford to ignore us politically. I place a very heavy emphasis on all our members being registered to vote. I very rarely will tell them who to vote for, but I definitely encourage them to vote.

- It seems that there's hesitancy, I think, on the part of many, to open up these issues [of racial justice]. They really don't want to get involved. . . . People realize that when these issues are addressed honestly that different views are going to surface and they have to be dealt with. I kinda get the feeling that people do things on a private, personal basis and don't necessarily look to the church to deal with it as a whole . . . as an institution. It's interesting because people want the church to counsel them in making decisions. . . . Once in a while an issue will come up, though, and some members . . . would encourage me to try to get the congregation behind community issues; . . . community revitalization is a big thing right now, for example.

- I try to teach our congregation that two wrongs don't make a right—that it's just as wrong for me to be prejudiced as it is for the white man to be prejudiced. It's just as wrong for me to dislike him as it is for him to dislike me. I'm not saying you put your head in the lion's mouth, but you seek to be law abiding, you seek to be trustworthy, you seek to be a good neighbor, . . . an honest employee. . . . No, we have not put on any active [political-action] campaign. I speak out against [racism]; I speak of the evils of it. . . . We've had workshops on how you should conduct yourself in the work place, how to take a test, even how to apply for a job. Sometimes we've had support groups if you feel like you were unjustly accused or fired. We have what we call a civic committee that will support and do as much investigating into the matter as we possibly can. I started a program here this year where I asked each member just to save five dollars a week . . . to cultivate that economic base that as a race I don't think we have. I try to encourage our members to support those members of our congregation who are in business . . . from the hairdressers to the morticians . . . to the little store operator . . . to the dry cleaner. . . . There is that need for us to become economi- cally independent.

- When *I* say "social action" I think it means people stepping out into the world that is the context in which they are living as a church. . . . It can mean a lot of things—pantries, advocacy in the state legislature, elections, school politics, supporting libraries, service clubs—all these kinds of things. . . . We are now looking at the idea of tutoring in the fall. We're doing a lot of outreach for our Bible school, to identify with some new people who aren't presently in the church. . . . I'm trying to maintain a trust level in putting [such things] before the church and to let it develop at a pace where it can really be truly what the church is doing, and not what one or two people are doing, or what I want to say the church is doing. . . .

  In the midst of situations we can have breakthroughs and hearts being turned, and we should always be appealing for people's hearts in the battle of ideas being waged and the battle for influence. All these things are going on, on a daily basis, for all of us. Given that, I think we have to ground ourselves in policy issues that will wield power effectively. Policy *does* change behavior. . . . You get enough tickets, and your insurance rate goes up high enough, and you get threatened with losing privileges, something's gonna happen! . . . People *have* been af- fected by housing ordinances. People have found, reluctantly, that they *can* live next door to a Korean, or a Haitian . . . because that's just the way things are. That arena is always to be addressed by the church, and I think that's pretty scriptural . . . recognizing the structural relationships arena.

Though economic factors do not affect them in the same way that they do African Americans, the two rabbis share with the blacks some of the cultural consequences of a long history of violent prejudice and discrimination. Both rabbis serve congregations of mostly well-off business and professional people. Yet strong identification with oppressed Jews of the past and present seems to yield a more macro-structural perspective on moral issues compared to that of other European Americans. Both congregations include recent

Russian political refugees, for example, and Israeli problems are in many ways experienced as their own. Overall, I sense a tendency in both rabbis toward a somewhat higher level of consciousness about moral consequences of social policy than I saw in most other white informants.

When speaking of parish concerns for racial justice, white clergy, as a whole, follow almost the same pattern they show with economic issues: they express concern but describe little active engagement with the issues among their members, as church. A few talk about involvement in con-sciousness-raising agendas. There are also occasional staffing, preaching, and musical exchanges with people of color. Only two congregations have established high visibility in their communities on racial-justice issues, according to their ministers; and these two men talk with great frustration about failures to find dependable ways for fostering both trust-building relationships and cooperation in community projects.

It is clear that the white clergy speak more in terms of understanding, acceptance, and interpersonal comfort with cooperative projects. The black clergy are more focused on changing the life circumstances of black folk, toward more equitable participation in U.S. social options and benefits. Following are some statements from white clergy focused specifically on racial justice.

- Some very personal things: I'm a parent of . . . African American children. We are an interracial family. Living in a multicultural world begins in our house. It begins with how we parent, . . . the experiences my kids have living with two Caucasian parents, . . . where we live, . . . where they go to school. . . . In this congregation . . . racial justice is clearly an agenda, but the flip side is enhancing our life by becoming multicultural, which is a very difficult thing, given our desire also for homogeneity. A Spanish-speaking congregation started in [our area] a year ago, so three of our Spanish-speaking families left to go help that congregation get started. They're extremely energized by having Spanish-lan-guage worship for their kids; we *lost* some of our diversity here. So it's an incredible challenge to find a way for congregations to become more diverse—to see the benefit that comes from being multiracial (we have a Native American pastor here). . . . We do a lot of interprogramming [with churches in other culture frames]. . . . I continue to believe that racism is one of the greatest manifestations of our sinfulness.

- I'm just in the process of reading Studs Terkel's . . . book on race. I'm very aware, as I read that, how much work I still have to do, in terms of my own . . . racism. Now our justice committee is trying to [awaken] some real awareness in the parish in terms of the Native American, . . . so they're gonna do a lot of educational stuff, . . . seminars. . . . That's the focus right now, but we've done stuff on . . . black-white. We have our own warehouse, which is kind of a

bridging ministry that transfers things from the suburbs. . . . It began as somebody dropping a bed off here. . . . What's been nice about that is it's gotten a lot
of people into neighborhoods [where] they never would have gone before . . .
delivering a bed or a dresser. They get to talk with people and find out they aren't
just lazy "no-goods."

 We are basically a white suburb. I'm not sure what would happen if. . . . Well,
we did a thing in liturgy about five years ago. There was a gospel pertaining to
openness to others . . . in fact, I think it was "the good Samaritan" reading. We
hired an actress [black] to play a bag lady. She was out in the parking lot . . .
going through the garbage can and then walked in and sat down in the front row.
People were really angry . . . they thought they were tricked; they felt betrayed
because many of them tried to get her out. . . . I speak a good line. . . . I'm aware
that I have a long way to go with the race stuff.

- [Racial issues] very seldom come up. I think by and large for the majority of this
  congregation it's ignored. When they do come up . . . we seek to deal with them
  in terms of education and understanding and acceptance. [It's an] all-white
  congregation.

- I think the majority of the congregation knows the language [of racial justice]
  but the majority are very, very sheltered [from racial issues] and the majority are
  very racist.

- Several people came to this church in the mid-seventies and late-seventies
  because this church had a commitment to racial justice. People from this church
  marched in Selma, Alabama, including the minister, and there have been serious
  efforts to make [continuing] commitments.

The informant proceeds to describe numerous efforts of his congregation, during recent decades, to cooperate directly in projects with local black
groups. Most ended in confusion, frustration, and discouragement (doubtless on both sides). He thinks there are a number of dynamics working
against comfort and trust building. His church, he says, is unwilling to make
racial justice its full agenda, and so it may be looked at by some in the black
community as less than fully committed. Also his denomination is anti-
evangelical and most African American groups are in a strong evangelical
tradition. He continues,

So I don't feel real comfortable about what we've done. I've had long conversations with several of the active black members. . . . It's a painful issue. There
isn't any question in my mind but what, on the theoretical level, we are very
deeply committed. What would it mean for us to be more than that? That's not
entirely clear. . . . In terms of lesbians, gays, bisexuals, we know what to do;
we've already got fifty, sixty, seventy people in this congregation. What we do
is we affirm them; we welcome them; we make certain that *they* know that

they're part of the congregation. . . . We don't have [that many] African Americans. . . . I think we have people whose good will is unquestionable, but in a practical sense, I don't know what the answer is; I truthfully don't. But we do always recognize Black History Month. We always have Martin Luther King Day celebrations. I think it's a time of great confusion in issues of racial justice.

The "great confusion" the last speaker sees in issues of racial justice is surely not limited to issues of racial justice. The discussion in Chapter 2 alerts us to a major culture-quake, causing upheavals along fault lines in conventionally modern knowledge assumptions. These include confusions about what constitutes trustworthy moral reasoning and what constitutes ultimate truth—the God realm. If the informants themselves are finding solid footing, they still deal with many congregants who are not, and who look to them for sure and simple answers. It is exceptional in this study when a man feels he has concrete sure and simple answers to dispense. Most feel that the best guidance they have to give is as serious co-seekers of truth and goodness. Quite a few report that their members tend to see them as far more liberal than they see themselves. They do not speculate on the basis for this discrepancy. However, it is a common discrepancy wherever one person assumes a set of rules as a base for ethical decisions and another assumes a more social-constructionist stance. To the former, the latter may appear to be departing from responsible moral rigor, rather than being responsibly committed to an alternative genre of moral rigor.

Chapter 6

Administrative Perspectives

Administration is a central concern for all these clergymen. Executive aspects of professional religious leadership often present clergy with unique identity and role strains, in that bureaucratic management techniques (now heavily used in religious organizations) may be seen by both clergy and laity as antithetical to spiritual development dynamics. Administrative duties, preaching, and ceremonial presiding are among the most visible activities of clergy. The men were surely aware of making a vocational choice that included management of organizational structure as part of tending spiritual community. Groups vary as to whether or not clergy are expected to be the executive officers of congregations they serve; but, regardless of polity, few ministers can escape fairly heavy responsibilities for management tasks. Also, the symbolic ritual functions, themselves, become crucial influences in organizational maintenance and tone.

Before, during, and after their clarification of decisions for ministry, many of the informants were steadily accruing leadership experience in academic, industrial, religious, and other enterprises. Yet, in their descriptions of arriving at certainty about goodness of fit between themselves and a clergy calling they do not emphasize, and seldom even mention, attraction to administrative tasks.

ESTABLISHING LEADERSHIP AUTHORITY

It may be helpful here to review some ideas about authority from an earlier publication of mine before looking at what the clergymen say about administration.

At least since Max Weber, social thinkers have distinguished several quite different ways of exerting influence over others in social situations. Raw physical force is one way, and it obviously does not require any social legitimacy or authority to prevail. In general, though, throughout human history social influence has been wielded by those thought by others to have some right to that influence. They are honored, obeyed, and attended because somehow they seem to most others worthy of such regard. The source of their power tends to be traditional types of assignment, rational types of selection, or personal charm.

Certain people arrive at leadership roles because, according to long usage, leadership is expected from the person(s) in the social position they represent (the oldest male, the particular tribe or family, the skill group, etc.) Theirs is *traditional* authority.

Others are identified and selected through rational group processes deemed best for securing suitable persons to wield power in specific ways. This is *legal-rational* or bureaucratic authority—an authority vested in carefully defined abstract roles and, derivatively, in persons officially chosen for their abilities to fill the roles adequately.

But sometimes individuals come into substantial social power merely, or primarily, on the basis of their personal appeal—their charisma, their extraordinary social magnetism.

The first two types may, of course, be held by charming persons; but their essence is in *correctness* of power location (i.e., persons rightfully in the right places have a right and obligation to say what's right and to exert control over others). The third type depends on believability and admirable qualities that are noticed in social exchanges.

[. . .]

It should be obvious that one form of power can be brokered into another and that they often are combined in particular roles or persons. For example, the traditional power of the throne in England is now dependent for maintenance on the legal-rational power of Parliament. A charismatic leader may use power to secure a succession of that power to descendants. Traditional or charismatic authority may be used to construct a democratic bureaucracy. Legal-rational authority may be augmented through charismatic influence. (Ice 1987, 80–81)

Few of the men interviewed discuss their ideas of leadership authority, as such. None uses the standard sociological distinctions to identify types of authority exercised, ideally or operationally. Perceptions on authority are revealed, however, in many places.

When I asked whether they had enough power to do their work as they feel called to do it, only a few hesitated a bit or qualified their yes in some way. Several added that they think congregations are willing to give ministers too much power.

A priest who says he still has far too much power, observes that certain things in the church (like the current priest shortage) may be diffusing the old tendencies to push all power toward the official minister. He muses,

- I sometimes feel I've been born in a graced moment—that I have one foot in the old pre-Vatican Catholic church and was able to draw . . . what was good there, and know that, and be able to see why some of that had to die . . . and then this changing time, which is exciting for me as we're trying new models and methods. I . . . wonder if I'd be as excited if I was a young priest now—only knowing the new and trying to get my bearings for the future. . . . I feel I've *had* all the power . . . and [now I have] the largesse of trying to give it away or hand it off to someone else . . . knowing that by the time we've distributed all the power, I'll be close to being at the end of my ministry. (Laughter) So it's kind of "Are you feeling so good about this because it's the proper thing? Or are you feeling so good about this because you don't have that much to risk? (Laughter) Hopefully it's a little of both.

Other clergymen, who share the belief that they have more than enough power, talk of the temptation to let it accrue.

- I think a good minister is one who is very aware of power and mutuality in this relationship with the congregation. . . . [Clergy] have a great deal of power. . . . People will hand over their power to a minister at every opportunity . . . and [you have] to make sure you're not accepting that but asking people why they don't feel worthy to accept their responsibility or their calling.
- There is power in the office of senior pastor and there is the authority of the office, and because of my persona, I need to watch my seduction into power and accept my exercise of authority.

In making this distinction between power and authority, the speaker had illustrated his point with a story from a man who said his grandfather had power (you simply had to do what he said) and his grandmother had authority (you understood and wanted to accept her direction). That story clarifies the way he is using the words in the interview. Perhaps, more importantly, his allusions to power as rooted in traditional expectations, in role specifications, and in personal qualities (which reflect the classical authority distinctions) show how authority types blend in the same leader. All nineteen narratives show the combined influence of all three types of authority grounding: traditional—rooted in gender, vocation, clergy families, ordination, denomination, institutional religion; legal-rational—

carried in bureaucratic role and job description; and charismatic—intrinsic to interpersonal attractiveness to others. The first two types, especially for male clergy, are pretty much assured by the professional office as it is usually constituted; and these particular informants gain much influence through force of personal presence, which is the third type. Because of the selection criteria used in this survey, this last basis for authority is strong among the men interviewed.

Given leaders may be disposed to innovate and bring about relatively radical change, such as using hierarchical power to give it away and to structure equalitarian exchanges. Of their very nature, however, both traditional and legal-rational authority tend toward hierarchical arrangements and are potent structural forces resisting attempts to bring about sweeping changes.

CLERGY-LAY RELATIONS

Whether a chief executive officer model or a spiritual visionary (or some other) model is informing the style of leadership, hierarchical distancing of the minister from the laity may emerge to interfere with the hopes for equalitarian clergy-lay relations that many informants mention. I'll include a few representative quotations here from responses to a question about appropriate clergy-lay associations. (Much more information about preferred leadership relations will appear in the men's general ideas about administration.)

- I don't see why there should even be the question. . . . It starts to intimate that there's some essence of being a clergyperson that's different, rather than the role of the clergyperson that might be unique. . . . I think [the clergy-lay relationship] should be valued for what it is: an appropriate relationship between human beings. Why would someone ask, "What is an appropriate relationship between a fireperson and someone who is not a fireperson?"

- My responsibility [to laity] I feel is . . . to give good spiritual leadership; that is, to feed the congregation on Sunday morning, to help them in their time of crisis, to make the hospital visits, the counseling, . . . to be approachable. I feel that their responsibility is to the total ministry of the church . . . whatever the church is involved in . . . to wholeheartedly support that; but again that goes back to their time, their talent, and their tithe. I feel like when I'm happy I can make them happy; and when they're happy they can make me happy—kind of a two-way street. . . . We don't always agree . . . but we try to work in the area where we can come together.

- A strong lay team . . . complements as well as corrects and challenges the clergy, the staff. I would want a lay-centered church every time, over a clergy-centered church.

- I believe firmly that we are baptized into ministry; *all* Christians are ministers. I believe there are times when the ordained minister, who is a set-apart minister, needs to take on that role of robe, the robe of office, and be a representative of God. . . . I see a lot of ministers hiding behind a collar, a robe, and I think that's very unfortunate. . . . We put on that robe of office to represent something at a time when people need it—at a time of death. There's something very special and unique about the ordained minister that doesn't seem to come across with another lay person . . . the symbolic function. . . . This is something I had to learn to accept; . . . I was very much opposed to it when I first began. . . . We all are ministers, but there are times when I need to be the *ordained* minister. . . . I do have training in the Bible, . . . theology, . . . church history. I am in a position to be more universal, more of a generalist than many professionals who must concentrate in [say] accounting . . . [or] physical health. Clergy have their fingers in many different areas.

I asked the men what they preferred to be called by members of their congregations. Most prefer the first name, at least with adults. Some say that parents, and also they themselves, like to have the children use "Pastor," "Father," or "Rabbi" before the name or alone. A few talk about the title "Reverend" as off-putting and uncomfortable for them. No one states a preference for being addressed that way (though they say the term remains in common usage).

GENERAL MANAGEMENT

Pastorally, the men reveal quite democratic, equalitarian ideals; the image of co-struggler-helper has strong appeal for them and a great deal of cultural currency in religious institutions. Administratively, many admit to some degree of ambivalence about how to give effective and efficient direction to their congregations without "pulling rank" as the final authority. A few (who, incidentally, differ from one another greatly in personal demeanor, moral perspectives, and theological positions) appear to be remarkably confident and comfortable in the dual role of spiritual leader and organizational coordinator, reporting both a sense of giftedness in this type of integration and reputational feedback that tends to confirm their self-assessment. But most speak of considerable conflict in this area.

A comfortable integrator says,

- I'm seen as, and see myself as, a very good administrator; but . . . I see my role of administrator as giving order to a congregation, . . . not because order is the end, . . . [but because] order creates the climate so that you can do the Gospel, you can gather in worship, you can care for souls, you can empower people to be engaged in acts of compassion and mercy. If a congregation is in disorder, financially or structurally (governance-wise) or its building is falling down, *that* then consumes the energy. A part of the challenge of administration is to not create such a labyrinth of bureaucracy in the congregation that all of the energies of the laypeople go into keeping the bureaucracy growing.

This man describes himself as a fiscal conservative and good fundraiser, who keeps administration lean and avoids costly outside professional help with planning financial or construction projects—all in the interest of what he deems the more crucial functions of religious congregations. He goes on,

> The challenge for me is to empower lay people to lead, rather than to become the dominant leader; and that's a good balance today . . . in an era of the professionalization of ministry. . . . Part of my administrative role . . . is to use the theology of our tradition to create the vision. . . . I see myself as always stretching people beyond what they think is possible, whether that's the impossibility that an urban church can remodel its building on its own resources, which we did; or to build a Habitat House with three synagogues, which we're now doing; or to open our doors to a shelter, which we're now considering.

The next words come from another person at ease with his two roles, but he exhibits a leadership style very different from the preceding one.

- If I think God has given [me] a mandate, I will share that with the congregation and request for them to begin to be prayerful and seek confirmation of what I have said, because God's not gonna tell us two different things.

I asked, "What if they simply would not share that vision? What would that mean to you?" He responds,

> We'd have to wait on the Lord. That's not my battle to win or lose. My job is to set the table. If [the congregation] doesn't eat that's not my fault. All I can do is set it and wait, but ultimately it's God has to do the convincing. So I don't set myself up for victories and losses. That's not my role.

- To me it seems that half my life has been spent tearing *down* institution and the other half is spent building *up* institution that somebody else is going to have to tear down. I'm aware . . . that we can't live in community without some kind of structure, but I'm also aware that structure constantly has to be changed. . . . The whole purpose of the church is to get people into a deeper relationship with God and we keep forgetting that.

This megachurch pastor works in a staff of five full-time religious specialists, though he is the only one ordained. He now thinks several important principles of administration are seeing that (1) decisions are made at the most appropriate level and don't all come to the "top" ("The fewer decisions that have to come to my desk the better leader I am."); (2) decisions are made by consensual, collaborative pooling of wisdom; and (3) there is steady, explicit encouragement for members to be active in community and personal service, rather than primarily in parish concerns. Other clergy are not so wary of top-down models of management.

The following quotation is especially interesting in that the initial language uses the classical metaphor associated with top-down, bureaucratic authority of a legal-rational type. When the man talks about how authority is established, however, he uses the language of the charismatic authority type, emphasizing trust building and leadership by personal credibility.

- I hesitate to say this. . . . If we were drawing a parallel between forms of government, and democracy and dictatorship were the two poles, I see a church as being at neither extreme. It is a democracy in the sense of its own ability to manage things—the checks and balances are laid there; . . . [it is] more dictatorial in that it is run by a strong leader. Some people . . . describe that kind of government as a "benevolent dictatorship." I think that the biblical pattern is for a strong spiritual leader who kind of sets the vision and teaches the vision to the people in that way. . . . I am chairman of. . . . the church board . . . twelve people. . . . The stronger the personalities, the better I like it! . . . Usually at some point they'll say, "Well, what do *you* think?" If I feel very strongly, . . . I'll tell them. But I think their concern in what I feel is based upon relationship built on the number of decisions I have made and the method in which I derive my decisions. I'm not opposed to opposing views, and my being in leadership as pastor of this church is because the church is willing to go in the directions I want to go. If they decided they wanted to go in an entirely different direction, and just asked me to carry it out, I'd go someplace else; and that knowledge gives some weight.

It perhaps needs to be said here that these words come from a man who presents himself quite simply and unaggressively as a sure and steady presence, a person with deeply grounded convictions. He claims never to have taken initiatives in seeking ministerial posts. Groups have sought him out as leader, though he says he has been content to stay where he was already working, and he has been in his present location about twenty years. He comments that ministry has changed quite a bit, compared to his earlier expectations: "Now a pastor almost needs a business degree." But he finds the new demands of his work challenging and enjoyable. Operating with multiple staff and an organization fitting the designation "megachurch," he describes himself as not feeling high stress and "sleeping well." He adds,

> [Trust] gives you a lot of authority. . . . People who . . . pout, or use threats, . . . all those things . . . I abhor as means of governing. We have gone to great extremes to establish checks and balances. I don't plan on usurping authority, but I also don't plan on always being alive or here; . . . and so we have tried to lay protection in all instances. . . . When it comes to financial things, our checks have to have two signatures and none of them can be clergy. Besides the people that actually keep the books . . . we have reports monthly and yearly. . . . We make a lot of emphasis, individually and corporately, on setting a vision of where to go and then working toward that. I believe that everyone must have a purpose that they're aiming at and ways to measure if they're getting there. Far too often if you said to the pastor, "What is your vision for this church?" he wouldn't be able to answer readily . . . [nor would] the lay people. . . . And I think that a business like that would be a failure. I *don't* think that the church is a clergy movement. Developing lay leadership in every area is so important . . . and that's not if the layman can do it *better*. I'd say if the layman can do it 50% as good. . . . [we should] develop that person and give it to them, because we are a layman-centered church.

This last matter is a stickler for many of the informants. They seem torn between perfectionist ideals and strong impulses to delegate responsibility (both as a matter of conviction and because they dislike detail work). Some feel seriously overextended, as well as more strongly called to the aspects of professional ministry they consider spiritual, pastoral, or intellectual. Administrative, and especially clerical, tasks often loom as pestering obstructions to what they envision as authentic ministry. When one man described his reliance on committee structure for administration I asked, "Is that working well for you?" His reply:

- No. No. I've had to be an independent contractor my whole life. *I* have to do *everything*. The biggest burden is the psychological burden of knowing . . . that, when I do something that I don't have full control over, it's going to screw up. It's a waste of my time . . . a waste of my effort . . . and it reconfirms the inappropriate notion that if I don't do it myself it's not going to get done right. . . . It's a very big burden to carry this institution on my shoulders. Huge. I have a president, who is an attorney, who can't write. I have a publicity chairman who can't do a brochure well. . . . Because I don't trust them, they become disabled. Almost nothing would happen unless I made it happen. . . . I need a helper to allow me to be more productive, . . . a messenger, a valet, someone who will do it well and on time, someone who can understand very detailed instructions, . . . and that kind of person is expensive. I would like to spend my time planning . . .

and not also be the person who has to execute. . . . I'll distribute jobs . . . like the guy who sits in the corner office at the law firm.

- My weakness is staff management, I think. I like to give people . . . room to run their own responsibilities. . . . I have more difficulty with delegation for projects than for specialties. . . . Expertise is the critical question for me; if I sense I can do something better than the person doing it, I have a tendency to take over.

- There's a real sense that we're a ministry team here and my task is that I'm the coach. I'm the manager. I'm the person who's going to make us play the game the best we possibly can. . . . I don't enjoy nitty-gritty administration; I want to delegate that off. I want to be in a place where I can work with people to whom I can say, "We need . . ." Well, actually, I want to say, "Please make sure we've *got* enough pencils for the Christian education program." I don't want to have to *do* that. . . .

  This is a very busy, active, professional congregation. People have a lot of need simply for pastoring and caring, which I just cannot do for everybody and don't enjoy doing, except in critical circumstances. I'm really working right now to reorganize that kind of care and support. . . . I should try to empower others to take their responsibility on the team where ultimately I must take responsibility as coach. . . . My role is to help the people do their work in the world. . . . I think I don't assert authority enough. The team approach sounds good, but it's messy and confusing. . . . Sometimes I think I ought to simply say, "I'm in charge and this is what we'll do," if I'm convinced it's best for the group.

A clergyman listing his work frustrations names the following items, among others:

- There's *always* a department or committee that needs nurturing. You nurture that and get it going and another one is going to slacken off. . . . The constant nurturing of the organization of the church . . . the dull and boring meetings . . . people don't think they've accomplished anything. . . . Yet I'm not sure how we have a church without meetings. . . . The desk! . . . is a constant frustration . . . always stuff on the desk. I'm a poor organizer, . . . poor reader of mail. I set it down to get to it when I can . . . and it stacks up. I want to get to it, and but I often don't. . . . I'm fast at the computer . . . I can write a good letter. . . . I'm *not* the best scheduler of my time and priorities.

  A good minister will get as many people involved in programming and ministry as possible. . . . Ideally I'd be better . . . at delegating. A block for me is, "Hey! you're getting paid; why should you ask someone who doesn't get paid, to do something you could do?" Yet people derive real meaning from . . . taking on jobs. . . . Members need to feel ownership in the decision-making process. Sometimes that's a struggle . . . including as many people . . . as possible. "Leading with," rather than "directing" [is my most comfortable style of leadership]. Well . . . in our denomination . . . I don't even have a vote on our church cabinet. . . . Moral persuasion . . . is a lot of power, but it's the only power I have in that cabinet.

The informant says that his mode of influence differs with issues, but he has a tendency to "go first to the pulpit" for trying to create the kind of welcoming community he idealizes. However, he also says he would take matters up with appropriate boards and committees. Like many other men I interviewed, he emphasizes a preference for collegiality, while making references to organizational structure following conventional bureaucratic standards.

Another ambivalent administrator says,

- I'm not real keen on administrative stuff . . . the paper work and some of the committee stuff. Some of the committees are a lot of fun. . . . I'm very tense going into board meetings and I'm very tense coming out. . . . Policy stuff is very draining, . . . heavy duty. . . . My tendency is to look for something humorous and comment on it or to expatiate . . . or tell a joke . . . and you just can't do committees that way. . . . All the paper work I have to fill out! . . . good Lord! it drives me crazy! . . . I came into this work because in ministry people come before paper. . . . I think we should not be bogged down with administrative organizational things. I should be the *spiritual* leader.

This man says he now has a full-time lay administrative assistant, after working many months for such staffing.

In response to my initial question about what makes good administration one minister responded,

- Someone *else* doing it! . . . I think the leader keeps the vision, decides where God calls the congregation to go, checks for concurrence of other staff, and tries to motivate volunteers to develop a lay-caring institution.

- I like to see lay folk shine. . . . that's tremendously rewarding. . . . I don't always have to be the professional caregiver . . . or minister. Now that again is a double-edged sword. They might make decisions I don't like . . . and sometimes you have to live with the consequences of that empowerment. . . . There are times when I would like to be a Henry Ford: . . . "Get out the bulldozer, get out of my way," . . . but I realize . . . you won't be effective very long. You will use up your authority very quickly and you'll find yourself out ahead of the parade all alone.

These last words may be very telling in some ways. Many men use expressions that indicate a view of themselves as leaders "out ahead" of their congregations in vision, knowledge, skills—burdened with convincing the group to come along. The same clergyman adds,

> All kinds of leadership and motivational tactics have to be employed to get things done. You have to be an astute observer of people and know how to motivate people.

- I think I become the motivator . . . and if I'm not a good motivator, . . . if I'm not committed . . . to church, . . . to community, . . . to ministry, . . . it's hard to generate that. If I'm committed to what I teach, . . . what I believe, then it's easy for me to project that . . . to motivate [others].

He feels that his own moral, spiritual, and programmatic commitments set the tone for the congregation. This idea of commitment projection is not only echoed in the words of other ministers, but a number of them have a personal presentation style that embodies infectious, high-energy expressiveness.[1] They may have had this style from childhood and/or developed it according to ideals for ministerial identity. It may have entered into their seeing themselves, or being named by others, as potentially good ministers, according to one common model. At any rate, even in the interviews, a half dozen of the respondents show a steady, fast-paced, expressive output, at such a high level of personal intensity that (whether or not the style is intentionally cultivated) it fits a model of charismatic leadership focused on the motivating force of leader enthusiasms.

In the interviews, however, high enthusiasms and visibly passionate commitments are not the personal styles emphasized as motivational. More has been said, in the chapters on moral and theological leadership, about inspirational influence stemming from steady, credible congruence among a minister's words, acts, and attitudes. Provided the minister's behavior does not contradict the verbal messages, many clergy see preaching as a primary motivational opportunity having strong spiritual and moral influence in a congregation. This is apart from level of expressive intensity, as such.

Several ministers speak about the democratic principles and processes they attempt to foster in their congregations. They are convinced that interpersonal skills, learned in doing church work, can equip members for better community service, in and out of the congregation, as well as for greater confidence and satisfaction in all their personal associations.

They tend to replace terms such as "delegate," "direct," "recruit," and "motivate" with a vocabulary of "mutual empowering," "equipping," and "encouraging."

- I think of the ideal minister as . . . one who knows self, accepts self, and yet doesn't take self too seriously. . . . I think where a lot of ministers fail . . . is in the mutuality; they somehow are more "important," or their ideas or their theology is more "correct" . . . than that of parishioners whom they serve. . . . I really admire ministers who accept the people's traditions and theology. . . . I admire ministers who see their primary identification as that of a servant of the community. I admire and respect ministers who within this sort of role . . . know that things will function fine without them . . . when he or she leaves. . . . They may be missed, . . . but the structure of the church should function. They should be equipping the people and loving the people into believing they are capable to be ministers . . . and are worthy of that calling.

This man claims he resists people's tendency to turn over their power to him and then judge him. His stated ideal for administration is "empowering laypeople" to take their own places in maintaining the church community.

While some clergy admit that they have come to hate the currently overworked word "empower" (which has already appeared several times in their statements), they nonetheless find that it often says what they want to say about administrative goals. It is a word I heard from many of the men.

- Empowering the laity beyond their dependence on the clergy, . . . that's become a real driving force for me . . . to move people into a realm where they're comfortable seeking their own spiritual growth and development . . . as opposed to being dependent on those of us in pulpits . . . or with robes on.

- I think it's . . . empowering . . . for a congregation to have the kind of leadership that returns responsibility to the people in a way that allows them to equip themselves, and to be equipped by the Gospel, . . . to guide the work of the church. . . . It brings out energy in the church. I feel strongly that people have to have ownership of their ministry, . . . their congregation, . . . their witness, . . . their community. . . . A lot of soul-winning comes from claiming our own souls, A lot of our spiritual influence comes from growing in our own spirits. . . . I've learned to value the traditions. . . . Often a congregation does not see their denomination as a resource for living in the today world. I like to try to unlock the tools and gifts of being in a . . . community. . . . Appreciation of being rooted in a tradition gives freedom to enter the public arena with faith in operation. . . . Having a place for people to participate in ministry—that's a real goal for me. That has a lot to do with church growth. If a person comes to your church and there's nothing going on, no clear stated mission, no sense of what we're working for together, . . . you don't have the experiences . . . to make your congregation alive and therefore more appealing. . . . Having a style of ministry that allows people (that positively *demands* that people) carry the load together joyfully, . . . experience their strength, . . . reach out to their neighbors to share in work—I think all of that is the image of the church being equipped.

A man whose commitment to nonhierarchical structure is increasing, talks about the fact that the transition is not easy.

- Hierarchical structure would probably be what I've employed most of my ministry; but I'm at a point now where I am experimenting with different ways of doing things, . . . a flatter, broader, more horizontal structure. We've kind of operated that way this past year . . . with some difficulties. I'm in the process of evaluating what happened. I've not found the mechanism for communicating with the broad structure as effectively as I have with the hierarchical structure. But I think that the benefit of involving more people in dialogue and planning is something I don't want to lose; so I've got to find how to improve upon those skills.

The clergyman who entered professional ministry out of a corporate executive career identifies himself as a person who finds real fulfillment in doing organizational tasks (especially financial coordination) in a business-like, thorough, conscientious way. He says he has a reputation as a very stable, methodical planner who follows through with careful attention to detail.

- I enjoy organizing. I like things in their proper place. There's a running joke with [a colleague] who sometimes moves one of my pens on the desk to see if I notice . . . and I do.

Yet this man, who also feels especially called and gifted for evangelism, names as an administrative ideal "not getting so bogged down by details that we lose vision." He hopes to avoid being tyrannized by procedures, in attending to things that need doing.

A person at the other end of the spread of administrative perspectives is a clergyman who, in ticking off his ordinary tasks, referred to "administrative garbage." I asked whether administrative tasks consume a lot of his time, to which he replied,

- No, not really. I'm not real organized. I don't do it real well. I get enough done to keep [my] head above water. I don't like to obsess on administrative stuff. I like to defer to committees and if it doesn't get done, I let it go, because I don't believe that pastors should be paid to administer churches. That's a waste of gifts. I think a lot of pastors hide behind administration.

"THE VISION THING"

A large number of the clergymen see setting a vision for the congregation as a key aspect of their administrative leadership. This word "vision" enters the narratives frequently, as we have seen in several of the earlier quotations. Mainly, descriptions tend to focus on envisioning concrete programmatic possibilities, though some also deal with creating a spiritual tone for the religious community. The image of minister as special agent-representative-conduit for God's direction is commonly expressed among the nineteen. There are important differences, however, in levels of comfort with this image. Here are some voices that tend to emphasize it:

- I think clergy needs to understand it occupies a position through which God communicates his will and purpose . . . I seek to offer direction as I see the Lord moving this congregation. Sometimes that means that I will suggest that an organization adopt a theme for the year's activities to kind of drive home some point through their work to reach some specific objective that I see the Lord is calling the church to at this time. So through preaching, through the planning process and the church's ministries, a prophetic function of ministry is reflected. It is important to know and agree about what our purpose is. Attainable objectives are . . . the foundation for our organization. Based on that, we're able to establish structure to accomplish our mission. It's important for the pastor to be able to lead in . . . having vision and clarity of purpose . . . and to be able to find willing, dedicated people in the congregation with the skills and the interest to carry out programs.

- The black congregation is a totally unique experience. One has to share, to be involved in it, to really appreciate it, to understand it. . . . It has organization but it has a freedom. . . . it has a looseness, . . . it's not tied to a certain structure. It's never ABC. . . . It has to be that worship, that freedom of expression, allowing God to do whatever He wants to do at that given moment. . . . There is that strong belief among black churches . . . that the pastor is in touch with God, very much in touch with God, and that when he speaks he really speaks as God's representative.

- As a leader, I think I'm a little bit of a visionary; I believe very much in having a vision of where you want to go, . . . planning how you get there, . . . wanting to start new things that were never done before.

- I'm in a very fortunate position, having a group of people around me who complement my skills and give me the freedom to declare the priorities of my position. I can carve out my own job description. I see three primary roles . . . as senior minister: . . . vision . . . and communication . . . and the direction of staff and lay leadership. . . . More and more I feel that my job as leader is . . . to figure out where we're being called to go, to check in with the other staff and lay leadership to see if God is saying the same thing to them, and to motivate our folks.

CAREER ASPIRATIONS

Perhaps this is a good place to tuck in some information about the ministers' aspirations relative to judicatory responsibilities (for example, at regional or national levels of coordination and supervision). Only one man says he would welcome such an administrative assignment. He is a man with low-key presence and sophisticated interpersonal skills developed as a social worker. There are several who allow they'd be willing if called upon. The rest are negative to the possibility in varying degrees. A few, at earlier points in their careers, were assistants to judicatory executives, or were regional administrative specialists, and say they are not at all interested in returning to that kind of work. Some feel strongly called to congregation ministry and see it as a lifelong commitment. Incidentally, one of these, from the age of thirty, has held a tenured contract with his congregation; and another, who led his church through years of explosive growth, envisions spending his career life in the same place. Both of these men are extraordinarily active in community affairs beyond their respective congregations, (though one says he's getting less and less enthusiastic about what can be accomplished in bureaucratically managed organizations.)

A person with previous regional administrative experience observes that there is far too much change in personnel and job descriptions for denominational governance work to be attractive to him. He prefers the greater stability and coherence of parish ministry.

Here are some other voices in response to the query, "Would you welcome judicatory work?"

- I don't have goals like being bishop or anything. I think that would be a curse. . . . I do get a tremendous amount of positive feedback from the people here. . . . The feedback I get from all sides . . . is, "We hope you never have to leave here."
- Supervising work tends to be CEO fire fighting in trouble spots. I wouldn't want that . . . no time to read . . . think . . . grow. As it is, it is confused, difficult work. I wouldn't welcome it; I don't think I could shape it to suit my calling, as I see it.
- Some of those roles I have declined simply because it would take me away from . . . what I want to do as being pastor . . . I wouldn't take [the U.S. President's] job because I'd feel it would be a demotion from what I'm called to do.
- I would probably have to be dragged into office . . . and I doubt that I'd be asked. [In response to my question Why?] A combination of the idea that [judicatory work] tends to be set up for small churches—large churches are looked on not necessarily as successes, but as islands of their own . . . and [I'm] too conservative.
- I feel real comfortable. . . . The calling I'm hearing from people is, "Why don't you go into . . . teaching other people how to pastor as you pastor?" . . . (and

that's been a constant theme among this group of pastors of megachurches, because they're all kind of tending that way . . . to want to supplant seminary). My gut at this point still says that's not my skill; that's not where I'm directed. I personally feel I'm suited best for . . . exactly where I'm at in terms of trying to model a form of parish community where everyone is respected on every level and everyone has a sense of ministry. . . . I . . . think some of the people who are working out their hell now are bishops and denominational heads. No, I would *not* want to [do judiciary work]—at least not under the present structure—and if they chose me to do that they'd have to accept the fact that I wouldn't operate under . . . having to defend everything . . . that comes from [the top] . . . and yet trying to be pastoral and sensitive to where the folks are at.

DEALING WITH CONFLICT

As leaders of religious communities idealizing cooperation and mutual support, the clergymen are called on regularly to resolve conflicts. Conflict between themselves and some other person or persons may be the problem, or they may be expected professionally to mediate tensions between other parties (which may be individuals or sides in some group controversy). I asked all of the informants to describe how they deal with conflict.

In many ways this set of quotations on conflict management would fit well into the chapter on moral perspectives; the attitudes, beliefs, commitments, and operational strategies people bring into relationships (and relationship tensions) are at the heart of moral choices. The same constellation also constitutes a central dynamic in creating and maintaining social structures by way of administrative procedures.

From the statements displayed so far, it is clear that there is a wide range of thinking on administration in general. So it will be no surprise that the subject of managing interpersonal tensions evokes similar variety of response.

Many of the men talk of using fairly conventional conflict-management techniques—bringing to the surface as much information as possible, clarifying issues, facilitating direct conversation involving the parties who have grievances, proposing alternatives, weighing consequences of options. It is evident, however, that few of the men interviewed are themselves entirely unconflicted about engaging in conflict resolution. There is considerable talk about preference for avoidance and reluctance to deal with tensions that arise, though almost all are convinced that's not acceptable, by their own standards. Some have been able to adopt styles of leadership, or specialties in leadership, that pretty much remove them from responsibility for conflict management in their congregations, unless they are party to the dispute.

In virtually all instances of multiple staff, the men interviewed are designated "senior" clergy. So it is telling that many have opted out of explicit counseling and conflict-management assignments where they have had the freedom to do so. Nevertheless, they are in the spotlight position for setting the tone of parish life through inspiring the development of community relationship ideals. Implicit in their sermonizing, officiating, and daily interpersonal relations is their operational orientation toward conflict handling. This comes out in countless ways, whether or not the behavior (or the perception of it) ever occurs at the conscious level. How these men respond to differences of opinion and differences of agenda within their communities is, then, an important piece of information about their administrative views.

In trying to defuse and negotiate conflicts one clergyman mentions use of letters and notes, as well as meetings with involved persons, as techniques he characteristically employs. He says that, whatever the approach, his goal is to build care and respect. He readily confesses that he has a tendency to avoid conflicts. He claims he's trying to do better at getting things out in the open, since he's convinced that it works better in the end. Group-to-group is less anxiety producing for him than person-to-person conflict; his greatest anxiety lies in managing conflict between himself and others.

In the quotations that follow you will see much commonality and much variety. Some clergy want to avoid conflict, and some seem to relish "stirring the pot." Some say they refuse to meet separately with parties to a dispute, and others prefer to work with disputants separately. Some talk almost entirely of conflicts involving themselves; some talk of conflicts among others (where they are in a mediation role). The voices reveal much of the idealism, as well as the anxiety, these men have as they encounter social conflict in their ministerial work.

- My first instinct is always to run and hide and hope it goes away. More and more I'm comfortable in terms of trying to get those in conflict together and set up some kind of structure by which we can deal with it.

This man then proceeded to describe three specific parish cases in which what struck me as very creative plans for resolution were implemented, with mutual satisfaction in two cases, and withdrawal of a party to the dispute, in the other.

- I don't enjoy some of the personnel-management tasks. I'm getting better at that, but . . . it's hard for me to be tough with people I work with. When people get upset with me, I think, "Oh, gee, they're upset. Isn't that terrible! I need to make it well." I'm still learning how to say, "That's not my problem." . . . I have a tendency to avoid conflict, but this doesn't work well. I'm trying to do better to get things out in the open. . . . I think this works better.

- If it's me and another individual, I would go to that individual first. It's hard for me, but I know how important that is. Often that will resolve the issue. They misunderstood something I said and took it a wrong way, or we do not see eye to eye and we accept that. [With] a couple individuals I will try to facilitate their working it out together. I will not be a go-between. I will not say, "So and so said" (It's very dangerous and I then become a party to it because it's not the other person saying it; it's *my* saying it.) but "Can we sit down and talk about this?" [With] groups . . . there's always a gentle hammering away in sermons. . . . I'll bring up conflict over [say] use of . . . a room and how we need to understand that we're about a larger mission here than just where my group is going to meet. Often, though, it's one or two individuals who would be stirring things up, and they're the ones who need to be dealt with. . .

  A year or so ago we had a woman running around like a loose cannon. . . . [She] had severe psychological problems. . . . I was contemplating going to her and saying, "You are welcome in the church but you are not welcome to confront people in hurtful ways like that" . . . and actually inviting her to not be around the church if that was going to continue. I didn't have to. She, . . . in her psychological problem, got into such a depression [that she] never came around again. I'm not real proud of the fact that I haven't really ministered to her.

- Gotta *talk*. Communication. . . . I offer myself as . . . a mediator . . . to kind of referee, and identify the issues involved in the dispute. I found that many times [when] my people understand what the issues really are, . . . the disputes are . . . settled right there with that understanding. From there we're at least able to discuss and negotiate and to come to some agreement based on . . . our common desire to be church, . . . to be like Christ. . . . We can always agree on that, so I like to bring that to the process of resolving conflicts. Sometimes it's difficult to get people to that point because of frustration and anger, but I do think it's important to just pragmatically isolate and identify what these issues are all about.

I asked, "Is your impulse more to enter into situations of conflict or to avoid dealing with them, if possible?"

[My] impulse is to leave it alone. Sometimes I do, but there are situations where I can't, or I shouldn't.

In a different part of the interview the same man comments,

I think of negotiation as pretty formal, structured, hold-onto-my-position . . . watch out! someone's moving in. I don't know if I'm as open as others might be on negotiating. I admire the ability to be willing to put it all out on the table, but it feels a little dangerous.

- I'm not a skilled arbitrator. There are skills for conflict management, . . . and I know some of them and I've used some of them. . . . It's not my job; . . . it's the president's job, and the congregation's, to resolve conflict. My job is behind the scenes, making sure that so-and-so understands the circumstances, and *that* one understands *this* one's circumstances. Happily, we don't have much . . . fighting in our congregation. . . . People have the most problems when they're . . . lacking information. The way I . . . try to resolve potential conflicts . . . is to give people the kind of information which . . . hopefully will have a cathartic effect— that they will see how someone could think *this* way and how someone could think *that* way . . . [that they will have] a willingness to trace the genesis . . . of conflict.

- Well, I do believe that clear stating, and telling if dialogue will help, is important. . . . Some conflicts, in their acute aspect, do pass . . . in time. . . . Sometimes a recognition of the role of time . . . is important to offer. Some things don't have to be settled right away. . . . In a few days you'll see it a little differently. I really don't like to take sides, . . . but I sometimes will determine what's at stake for the church or for the Christian witness and on that basis try to clearly state what I feel is the direction we should be going. . . . You know, mediation is something I can do. It takes a lot of energy. . . . [there are] always big risks with what people bring to the mediation. . . . Usually I'm looking for what are the growth issues present. . . . I really try to get under the conflict they're having. . . . In this church I've had to really model for people clear stating, [of the issues and opinions] . . . getting people's feedback, . . . putting things on the table, . . . going directly to the person.

- I prefer confrontation. I go in, confronting the issues as I understand them, seeking to gain fuller, broader understanding. But my goal in the whole process is reconciliation. So I see myself as offering a peacemaking service. I guess I don't live with a whole lot of baggage if I don't attain that, but I do go for that.

I asked how he might proceed in a situation where parties holding mutually exclusive positions each held those positions as matters of conscience. He replies,

That's kind of a tough one to call. . . . Just off the top of my head . . . and dealing with an issue I don't get my arms around too easily, . . . I guess what I would strive for would be a common understanding of our differences . . . and [I would] seek to live with the tension of that, seeing the work of the church and the work of God's kingdom as still a rallying point, . . . our sense of purpose and mission helping us to rise above the differences that lie underneath. On the other hand, if I saw that that was something that was being divisive in the church and that we could not rise above, . . . then I would encourage the faction that I felt was most out of line (not just with my own personal convictions but with the Word of God and with church polity) to separate and go their own way.

The following words come from a man who finds conflict deeply troubling. He showed a lot of humor and insight during the interview while discussing his struggles to arrive at more confidence in dealing with conflict.

- I have probably not handled criticism effectively. I'm trying to respond to criticism differently. . . . I need to cultivate a better . . . a little more . . . , to handle it more effectively, . . . to not let it get to me.

In order to broaden the focus for discussing conflict I asked, "When conflict emerges among people in the church, what are your ways of dealing with that?"

(Big sigh) Oh my! At times when it surfaces, initially I try to catch my breath and try to step back and look at it objectively. Now I *don't* always succeed. Sometimes I respond emotionally and overreact, say things that are inappropriate, respond in inappropriate ways. . . . There are times when folks, groups, need to be confronted with particular issues. There are times when something will just die down or will change with time. But most of the time it does have to be dealt with. Identifying the issues can be confusing.

This man then recounted several community incidents in which, among other things, jelly doughnuts and the U.S. flag display had figured, although the disputes really were based on entirely different matters.

Today most people in the church are laughing about it. We weathered it, but it could have split the church. When you think of all the things that can split a church! . . . I don't like conflict. I'm uncomfortable with conflict. It's a reality and it's a growing edge for me. . . . I need to not be threatened by it . . . and [to] understand that people are born in all kinds of histories to that conflict.

In the next two quotations an explicitly religious framework is used to speak of dealing with conflict. Both men speak confidently of their approaches, and neither identifies anxiety around the subject. Responding to my question about how he deals with conflict, the first says,

- Well, I think that it's pretty standard. In most cases . . . I try not to operate until I have facts in hand to work with, and once that's the case I prefer to address it head on, not to just dismiss it. I don't enjoy conflict, but I think it's healthy for me and the other people. . . . People can embrace some variations in theological viewpoint and not be out of fellowship, . . . and they may not need to be addressed. . . . However, if it's a conflict over leadership or management, it needs to be addressed. . . . Usually . . . the earlier it's dealt with, the better. If someone is out of line and they're in a position of leadership, they need to be approached . . . by a spiritual pattern. You go to them first. If they refuse to listen to logic and authority, you take one or two persons with you, and if they do not bend, you take it to the church's government . . . that makes a ruling. If they do not [comply], then the whole body has to deal with it; it has to be public.

- I can be tough if I have to be. . . . The toughness is required when the bottom line is it's gonna come on me one way or the other. . . . [Toughness is required in] helping people understand that one of the reasons they had brought me here is to trust me with carrying out what the spiritual mandate may be . . . and that if I'm *not* doing that, it's not really up to them for me to answer to [them], but up to [me to answer to] a higher cause. . . . I think once you make people comfortable with that, they're willing to be more understanding. . . .

  In any family you're going to have differences of opinion, and this is a large family. But that doesn't mean we fall out or we're no longer related; we just work harder at trying to be respectful to each other. I think that's a key word, "respect." Humor is used. . . . Sometimes we try to help people understand that . . . things we're upset about [today] . . . will have nothing at all to do with the sun coming up tomorrow. . . . By my own example I try to demonstrate that a person can admit that they're wrong, say that they're sorry, and it doesn't make them any less of a person. I think another key thing for me here, and for this congregation, is the listening aspect; a lot of people just want to be heard and you have to give them their say-so.

In dramatic contrast with some "risers above the fray" are the next two "plungers into the fray." According to reader preference, quotations may make given informants seem appealing or appalling. It should be remembered, however, that all of the men elicit uncommon levels of respect and approbation in their denominational or regional communities. This does not mean that they have no detractors; it simply means that they embody perspectives that find positive resonance among specific religious populations; and thus they all merit serious scholarly attention.

- I always jump in feet first. Sometimes that's the wrong thing. When there's conflict I go right to the source; I don't dance around the edge; I don't talk to people about other people; I go right to the source and say, "Look this is what I've heard. Let's talk about it." Sometimes it's the wrong way. Sometimes it's the right way. But it's the way I operate. . . . I've learned to pick my battles. Sometimes there's conflicts between groups. I would try to come to an understanding of what's going on and choose whether to make it *my* issue.

When I asked this man if he sometimes just ignores conflict, he told a story (another flag-placement story!) about a man whose wife said her husband wouldn't come to church unless the flag was returned to its former place.

> Here I'm faced with a conflict. I had a decision to make. Do I go to [him] with my explanations, [his] being a World War II vet and what not, and try to duke it out? I chose, in that case, to pick my battles, and *that* wasn't going to be one of them; I put the flag back.

- There's three kinda mutually exclusive images of me in conflict. One image is that I create conflict, I thrive on conflict, I love conflict, I let sermons create conflict, . . . the more conflict, the healthier. That's kinda one image of myself that I have and that others have. A second [image] that some people that know me well [have] is that, yes, I create conflict but I don't want that conflict to be to the detriment of the unity of the congregation, so I seek to manage the conflict . . . and have it be energizing, but not divisive. . . . A third [image] is that . . . I only want conflict around the issues that *I* think are worth having conflict over. . . . I have a hierarchy of what things are worthy of conflict and what aren't, which discounts the values of the community sometimes. . . .

> What I articulate as being important and what I model as being important are mutually exclusive. What I articulate as being important is the *process* . . . for how that conflict is addressed, how people are invited into the conflict, how the conduct of those engaged in the conflict is kinda monitored, how the conflict is resolved, how we know whether the conflict is resolved, what happens to the people if it's a win/lose feeling at the end, what happens to those who lost if it wasn't win/win, when do we seek consensus decision making, and when do we go with the majority rule? . . . I articulate . . . and believe . . . strongly that process is essential. . . . [In contrast,] what I tend to model is that when I'm engaged in conflict and believe strongly in one position . . . I become very articulate, . . . dominating, . . . [and I] tend to, either through verbal aggression or through humor, . . . to want to win. . . . I'm working . . . with that which I value and that which I practice, but they are not yet . . . what? . . . *in sync.*

The final selections for illustrating ideas about conflict management come from a few men who appear to be reasonably comfortable with the prospect of facing conflict situations. They talk about regularly seizing situational opportunities, in day-to-day congregational life, to model and encourage personal respect across differences and to develop democratic discussion. They see the honoring of conflicting opinions, and genuine struggles to understand each other, as key focuses in the healthy dissipation of discord. They aspire to lead communities where plain speaking, critical evaluation, and disagreement are seen as ordinary resources for individual and community growth, rather than adversarial treachery or mere nastiness.

The previous material has provided numerous glimpses of these values; the ministers I am describing now differ from the others in that they report both relatively low ambivalence or anxiety and relatively high confidence about how to proceed. Unfortunately, the quotations available from these men (about conflict management, per se) do not show all the points I make in describing their perspectives. Their thinking is woven throughout their statements, overall, most vividly in their discussion of moral, theological, and social-justice issues. One statement was the last topic addressed in the interview, and my tape ran out. Since I have detailed notes, I include the main points descriptively, but I regret the loss of his exact phrasing.

This informant who, before deciding on a clergy vocation, had preparation and some experience as a human-service professional, stresses the importance of immediately identifying core issues in a dispute. Sometimes he finds it illuminating to talk with mature, long-term members of the congregation, people who may be able to give aid in understanding the history of certain situations. While he mentions the value of venting, listening, and reflecting, as well as trying to lighten up the situation in a number of ways, he also thinks that people need help in seeing that "disagreements need not divide" and "conflicts don't all have to be totally resolved." He emphasizes fostering mutuality as a value that allows all parties to be equally respected, tended, and validated.

Two people contribute the following observations to this cluster of perspectives; though, again, other material on the subject lies in earlier quotations.

- My strategy is to confront [conflict], . . . to get the facts out, . . . to deal with it right then and there. I seek to listen and to understand all aspects of the conflict and to make a decision concerning it and to go on . . . and not be bogged down in the conflict or to be bringing it up. . . . If it's constantly brought up, . . . then it's not dealt with.

- Generally I look for compromise. I like to talk to a lot of people . . . try to get people together to talk to each other, . . . at least get people to understand better what the issues are, what the value identifications are, why I'm taking the position I'm taking. . . . I like to say, "I'm a very good loser." . . . If people vote against me, I'll try to make it work . . . to come together; but I'm still gonna say what I think. . . . If you don't speak out at a particular juncture, . . . people will come along later and say, "Hey! you were there; why didn't you say what you felt?" . . . I've *been* wrong, and some things have worked out very well in spite of the fact that I didn't think they would.

A type of conflict management involving the individual's internal management of conflicting ministerial responsibilities emerged for some of the clergymen as an unanticipated cause of stress. A man talking about some of his surprises in ministry mentioned that the *constant* need to prioritize multiple options *within* his professional life was one of his big shocks. He discovered that the freedom to manage his own schedule is simultaneously the pressure to fill it with the most worthy choices from many conflicting possibilities—often having imponderable consequences and often made under the scrutiny of congregation and community eyes in a small-town setting. He finds this a demanding, consuming responsibility that involves him in never ending micro-management of his ministry. He claims that making these decisions, without losing ministerial perspective, requires a level of spiritual grounding he had not thought of, prior to ordination, as connected with management.

- I didn't realize the way that all the responsibilities pull. . . . It's a very freeing profession, in terms of your time, but I didn't see how the responsibility for that time is so hard. . . . Should I be preparing my sermon as a really quality message, or should I be visiting that shut-in person? Should I be at this denominational meeting, or should I be at home in case there's an emergency? Should I say this word of judgment at this time, or should I be giving a word of love and hope? . . . All of those things . . . constantly pulling. . . . *Constant* need to prioritize. Often there is a drop-in. Someone will stop by, someone [say] on one of the boards, . . . and often that ends up being an hour-long conversation. . . . Initially that felt like a waste of time, but now I know that it's not—that they're stopping by not because they want to check on this, but because they want to check on that *other* thing. There are four women's groups and they all like me to attend their meetings, . . . and at first I thought *what* a waste of time! But most of those ladies are quite elderly and it's a wonderful time for me to be with them.

It is evident that the man lets caring priorities win out over efficiency and order priorities as he manages his own ministry activities, though efficiency and order are not low on his list of important matters.

An informant identified early in the chapter as a "comfortable integrator" of spiritual and administrative leadership talks about how damaging institutional structure seems to be for some folks, yet not for others.

- Some day I think it would be good to do a study of why some of us can make it through systems that are really inhuman . . . and come out pretty well unscathed, and other people go through that and are so angry and twisted and hurt that they never recover. . . . I had this touchstone of this great uncle and a family that took God and religion seriously but not the structure too seriously. . . . They kind of tweaked the system a little bit just to let it know they were still there.

NOTE

1. As a rough, quantitative measure of this difference in the volume of narrative content delivered by different men, I have from eighteen to forty pages of hand-written notes for each speaker, covering interview hours which were the same (four hours) for all of them. Also, while checking notes by reviewing tapes, I needed to interpolate much more missed material from the people with the higher density of output, making the contrast even more dramatic.

Chapter 7

Gender Differences

Given my earlier study of clergywomen, the most common question put to me about my current research is, "Well, what differences are you finding?" Or, "Are you finding any differences?" Characteristically, my response begins with an explanation of why the type of data I gather can't provide scientifically supportable comparisons of clergy populations. My work is focused on the statements of clergy describing their perspectives and experiences in ministry. The statements are presented as intrinsically informative—evocative of insight—whether or not differences are noted. But the interest in gender differences remains, for me and for others.

In this chapter I shall discuss some gender difference issues, display clergy quotations about contrasts in women's and men's approaches to ministry, and describe some of my impressions of differences in the data from my two studies.

DIFFERENCE ISSUES

It does seem to me that the general tone struck in my women's and men's interviews is somewhat different. It is surely true that many quotations could be imagined as coming from either a man or a woman; yet, were a person to read the quotations from each study in their entirety, I suspect gender assignment would be easy, even if all self-references to sex were omitted.

Why does the investigation of gender differences interest us at all, as persons or as scientists? Why the strong emotions around gender studies—over whether they're worthwhile pursuits, whether they're merely political, what certain findings imply, how certain information may be used, what motivation the interests have? Two kinds of response come to mind: (1) Humans are curious; satisfying that curiosity at many levels expands awareness, results in important discoveries, and helps people deal with life more realistically and effectively. (2) Systematic disadvantaging according to social categories, one of which is gender, is reported in history, social science, journalism, and everyday life. In addressing the problematic cultural and structural consequences for personal relationships, we need the best possible scholarly efforts toward clarification of circumstances.

> Failing to recognize distinctions of gender, at a time when gender operates as a set of socially instituted expectations that regulate every aspect of our lives . . . [p]retending that social distinctions and privileges do not exist usually is equivalent to perpetuating them. (Jagger 1990, 2)

> The view that sex is a difference that makes *no* difference given the sexual dimorphism of male and female bodies, given that women and men have different experiences of relationship, and given striking differences in the ways male and female experience and development are interpreted in this culture, is a view that simply does not hold up under close analysis.[1]

Certainly the interest in both professional and nonprofessional opinions about sex and gender differences is unmistakable. Magazines appealing to assorted interested publics regularly run features on the subject. There is much editorializing in newspapers. Book sales for releases such as Deborah Tannen's *You Just Don't Understand* (1990) have been brisk and the books are widely reviewed. Faculty workshops bring in specialists in gendered ways of teaching, knowing, communicating, and relating. Scholarly conferences and associations not only contain multiple references to the significance of gender difference but often have established sessions and sections specializing in gender issues and findings. (One gender difference consistently noted is the different amounts of time and attention men and women devote to reading information and opinions about such differences.)

In a recent "Life" section of our local newspaper an article headlined "Why can't we communicate?"[2] carried a giant color cartoon of a man and woman faced away from each other and a color-boxed heading, "Knowing and allowing for other people's differences can help you be more understanding, allowing you to bridge what can often be a destructive gender gap." More color-boxing at the bottom of the page contained these two small lists of differences, attributed to several sources:

Men	Women
• compartmentalize their lives	• see each aspect of their lives as part of a whole
• let human problems take their natural course	• move toward human problems and attempt to fix them
• express love in actions	• express love in words
• think of their wives as their best friends	• have other women as best friends
• think rationally	• think emotionally
• see relationships as accomplishments	• see relationships as in need of constant discussion and nurturing

The same paper carried a William Safire editorial with an even larger headline, "Father Power Rooted in Ultimate Authority." Safire's editorial included the following sentences,

> Let me tell you what fathers want. We want our intrinsic authority back. This essential prerogative of fatherhood has been stolen from us by children who want us to be their friends and by those children's mothers who insist on shared parentalism. . . . Beyond the pleasures of watching their seed miraculously develop, fathers who make the family effort need recognition as "head" of a household.[3]

There appears to be no lack of interest, or availability of diverse opinion, around the subjects of gender relations and gender differences. Ironically, this interest includes academic and street views that the whole matter of gender differences is poorly substantiated, overblown, and counterproductive as a consideration in social relations.

Human sexual dimorphism is transmitted in gene code differences that are extremely small. Men and women share almost their entire genetic heritage. Yet the biological determination of their sex characteristics has long come to serve as a sorting basis for dramatic differences in socially developed gender experiences.

In recent decades the justice, morality, and developmental health of patriarchal social arrangements have been questioned vigorously by large numbers of men and women seeking equalitarian social justice. It is by no means the first challenge in history, but it has been especially strong and has evoked a steady outpouring of scholarship, political action, and counterforces. There has been much hope and expectation that scholarly studies gradually would stimulate more clarifying exchanges on issues of gender difference as they relate to gender justice. Yet the outcome has been *both* clarification *and* bitter disputes.

Beyond the fact *that* many and complicated gender differences appear to exist, questions of how they come about, how they can be verified, whether they're in any sense necessary, harmful, or desirable, what forms of research are most fruitful in delivering information—these are far less settled and more controversial questions.

Admittedly, people do act with political agendas. Some have a big stake in maintaining the status quo; some are committed advocates of change. If in the academic world we value authentic, honest communication and rigorous critical thinking, we need constantly (as part of scholarly discipline) to examine our social action goals and knowledge criteria.

From a sense of being (in the 1960s and 1970s) on the verge of a structural-cultural shift toward equalitarian openness, many proponents of social justice watched with disbelief, sadness, and disappointment as the accusatory/defensive blaming and anger of the 1980s gathered force and rolled forward into the 1990s. At the same time, official institutional requirements of categorical inclusiveness have been put in place; but, given the cultural climate, they come more and more to be discussed in edgily legalistic terms of "political correctness" rather than "social equity" terms.

Susan Faludi's *Backlash* (1991) carefully documents these late-twentieth-century moves and countermoves around issues of gender justice and gender information. Faludi, Carol Lee Bacchi, and Lehman are among recent voices warning that distortions of information and gender relations may result from focusing narrowly on the *amount* of difference between women and men. The problem they see appears to lie in the largeness-smallness debate, as such, and specifically in how these relativities are misused as political propaganda.

I agree with Lehman and Bacchi (in Lehman 1993: 204) that "We need to move beyond the dichotomous [maximalist/minimalist] debate and focus instead on how society is organized and how we should live, work, and care for our families." I do not agree with them that the sameness/difference framework "derails discussion from a mainline focus on ways to eliminate sex discrimination," *unless* parties to the debate assume that either "maximal" or "minimal" differences, if supportable, would constitute legitimation for traditional domination/subordination gender arrangements.

If the debate is actually about whether lower-power categories need to prove or disprove similarity with higher-power categories in order to "earn" or "deserve" true social justice, then we are caught in moral questions attached to political questions that should be named and addressed explicitly rather than allowed to dominate the conditions of information critiquing without clear identification. This is why postmodern rhetorical and deconstructionist (including feminist) critiques emphasize the importance of including *researcher* background and interests as part of the *research data*.

Lehman's work is a major survey research project measuring and comparing responses from large numbers of Protestant clergy (male and female, four denominations) regarding their approaches to ministry. On multiple measures he finds gender differences that range from small to negligible. He identifies with scholars he refers to as "minimalists." Apart from the findings, as such, I see Lehman's adoption of the maximalist/minimalist interpretive metaphor, and talk of "dichotomous categories," "opposing camps vying for positions," "combatants," "competing assertions," and so on, as setting up an adversarial tone that diverts from his central data and invites the very focus he seeks to avoid.

Lehman explains that (1) "maximalists argue that the sexes are fundamentally different cognitively, emotionally, and behaviorally as a result of the interaction of biological, psychological, and experiential realities that being male or female involves"; (2) "minimalists . . . argue that any perceived sex differences in thought, feeling, or action are basically spurious . . . not endemic to males or females but . . . consequences of the positions men and women occupy in social structure and of the various forms of exclusion from social participation that such locations tend to produce" (1993: 179–180). If this is what the terms mean, how are they "maximalist/minimalist" extremes on a quantitative continuum? And can one not, by abandoning the either/or frame, hold them *both*—these arguments that are said to identify the "opposing camps"? Since social structure and culture form a central epi-genetic dialectic of social experience, they are existentially (though not conceptually) inseparable. Thus, neither scholarly inquiries nor political strategies can afford to focus on indications of cultural *or* structural forces without acknowledging their mutual imbeddedness in all aspects of societal development.

Arguments from both sides of debates pitting culture against structure and "large" differences against "small" differences get used ideologically to support the status quo as well as to call for change. However, attempts to ameliorate situations of social oppression and attempts to gain trustworthy information about their extent, causes, and consequences also participate somehow in the very problems and biases they seek to address. If we are to avoid debilitating discouragement and confusion in both scientific inquiries and social justice pursuits we cannot pretend to be untouched and uninvolved.

Harvard legal scholar Martha Minow in her wonderfully lucid and insightful book *Making All the Difference* (1990) deals with these immensely complex matters in a most helpful way.

Acknowledging and organizing around difference can perpetuate it, but so can assimilation. Separation may permit the assertion of minority group identity as a strength but not change the majority's larger power. Integration, however, offers no solution unless the majority itself changes by sharing power, accepting members of the minority as equal participants and resisting the temptation to attribute as personal inadequacies the legacy of disadvantage experienced by the group. Neither separation nor integration can eradicate the meaning of difference as long as the majority locates the difference in a minority group that does not fit the world designed for the majority. (25)

[. . .]

How can historical discrimination on the basis of race and gender be overcome if the remedies themselves use the forbidden categories of race and gender? Yet without such remedies, how can historical discrimination and its legacies of segregation and exclusion be transcended? Should nonneutral means be risked to achieve the ends of neutrality? A similar conundrum arises over how to acknowledge victimization without repeating the victimization in the process of acknowledging it. (47)

[. . .]

This dilemma of difference burdens people who have been labeled different with the stigma, degradation, or simple sense of not fitting in while leaving the majority free to feel unresponsible for and uninvolved in the problems of difference. Legal responses to the dilemma of difference recreate rather than resolve it. The right to be treated as an individual ignores the burdens of group membership; the right to object to the burdens of group membership reinvokes the trait that carries the negative meanings. (48)

[. . .]

Through deliberate attention to our own partiality, we can begin to acknowledge the dangers of pretended impartiality. By taking difference into account, we can overcome our pretended indifference to difference and our tendency to sort the world into "same" and "different," familiar and unfamiliar, equal and unequal. As we make audible the struggles over which version of reality will secure power, we disrupt the silence of one perspective, imposed as if universal. (389)

INFORMANT VIEWS ON GENDER IN MINISTRY

It may be of special interest now to look at what the informants themselves say about ministerial differences in gender relations and perspectives. What they say constitutes their version of social enactments in and around their lives and enters into their ongoing self-expression in countless ways. As with earlier data displays, accurate documentation of what the men say cannot tell us whether these views are in some objective sense *so* or how frequently such views might be expressed in the whole population of male U.S. ministers. Their words do constitute objective data about their subjective experience, though, and I think you will find their words interesting.

Often, if a minister hadn't already spoken of perceived gender differences, I'd ask a question phrased somewhat as follows: "I know you can't speak for all men or all clergymen, and you haven't known all clergywomen; but as you have come to know clergywomen do you think you see any differences in the ways men and women do ministry; if so, what might they be?"

Mostly the initial response indicates little recognized difference attached to gender, plus a suggestion that any differences are essentially individual variations. Yet after a pause many go on to say more. They are usually careful to note that there are plenty of exceptions to any tendencies they describe. A small number of clergymen launch directly into reports of differences they observe.

One man who says there's "not much difference" mentions that, in his present congregation, when new male clergy arrive they get lots of dinner invitations and volunteered services. Not so with women. He thinks "it's assumed she can take care of herself better—isn't so dependent." He also mentions that many men seem bothered by a certain type of woman who embodies "a kind of free-flowing nurturance combined with true intellectual strength—bright, articulate, high intelligence."

Here are some additional voices.

- I do not recall . . . that the women clergy I have worked with or know do things differently than I do. . . . I really think it's an individual thing, as it is with male ministry. I don't know of any pattern.

- I know women that do ministry in the good ole boy system like some of the good ole boys couldn't even do. I know women who do ministry in a wonderful, relational mode—a very disarming, nonthreatening mode. A good friend of mine . . . has walked into just a hornet's nest that has chewed up and spit out two men since I've been [here]. She's gonna do great there, because her way of doing ministry is so different. But I don't think it has anything to do with her gender; I really don't. I've heard women who are boring speakers; I've heard women who have chips on their shoulders; I've heard women who are fabulous preachers.

- Women in ministry are a new enough phenomenon that they are watched more, . . . given more barriers to overcome, . . . but I'd say . . . women involved in ministry tend to be more focused, more competent, more intuitive of feelings, less comfortable moving in systems even when they recognize the need for systems. The women I've been privileged to work with here have been very effective communicators but, again, have to overcome more barriers to be heard, . . . need to work harder to be prepared. I've had a chance to work with many able people, but the women have been exceptional.

- I have been blessed to have good relationships with women in ministry who I think have been good and outstanding preachers and pastors. I think to a certain extent they've *had* to be better in order to achieve what they have achieved. And that's not fair, but that's real. There is a bias in the church; . . . they've got to be better than their average male counterpart. So it's been my experience that several of them have been good strong preachers and very caring pastors. I think one of the keys is they have not made their femininity an issue; . . . they have remained feminine in their role. They have not tried to become like men or have not gone overboard the other way, but have just tried to stand on their own merit and what they bring to the table. . . . They have probably taken a stronger stand on issues that have directly affected females—the whole issue of rape, incest, abuse—issues that many men may not be comfortable with, certainly in public. . . . They sometimes may share a different working relationship with females; . . . for whatever reasons, they seem to be more comfortable working with a man. . . . I think that's an issue females have to deal with.

- We have what's called a visiting staff position. Somebody who had some money . . . came and said, "I don't want to give it to bricks and mortar; would you have an idea?" I said, "Yeah. Start an endowment that each year we can hire a staff person that we'd never hire full time but [that] might be good for us." So one year it allowed us to hire a [Protestant] pastor who's a woman as our spiritual director for that year. I think [women's] preaching would be more intuitive, more imaginative, more relational; whereas the men's preaching . . . has tended to be more theological, more conceptual. Administratively . . . they [women] might be harsher and tend toward more paper work and more letter-of-the law. I don't think that's inherent; . . . it's that it's just so new. . . . My experience is, at least those who work in the full-time ministry—the nonordained—carry a good dose of anger with them that sometimes can be healthy and sometimes can be very destructive.

- I think that it's individual. I think . . . women are more committed. I don't know why. . . . I have some friends who have women who are assistants, who say they would never have a man again. The loyalty to them, the loyalty to the work, the commitment is unsurpassed. . . . They don't approach things like the men. Women can be more compassionate. They can be more understanding. . . . They tend to be a little more perfectionist, I think, when it comes to organization. . . . If you give a woman an assignment usually every "t" is crossed and every "i" is dotted. . . . They are more ordered, I think, than men. . . . Style [of preaching] is different. Women are not as hell and fire and brimstone as men are, and they tend to see Christ more loving . . . more caring. Men have a tendency to see Christ as the authority; and women see him as authority but also as a mother would love a child with the authority. . . . You find that tenderness in the message—that caring. . . . Women don't tend to be quite as stormy as men; . . . [they are] more quiet, . . . more calming. I have some women in this church who can speak and not raise their voice, but when they speak they're listened to. I have some men who could never get the attention. I have about seven women

[lay] preachers in the church and about seven men . . . getting ready for ordination. . . . I think women are a little more studious . . . they will investigate a little
bit more than men.

The women and men mentioned by this speaker can be ordained at the *local*
level, according to a denominational polity that gives congregations much
autonomy; at the national level, ordination of the women is not approved
in his denomination.

A minister who has had some of his best spiritual experiences with
women clergy mentors says he himself would prefer a woman pastor. He
thinks women's "general concern for quality ministry is higher than that of
male colleagues." They have to prove themselves and he thinks they're
more intentional, more professional, better organized, and clearer about the
definition of personal boundaries in relationships. He is especially struck
by women's greater acceptance of others, approachability, and readiness to
deal with personal relationships. He tacks on the observation, "Men may
not personalize conflict as much." It is unclear to me whether he sees this
as a plus or a minus, or perhaps both.

A minister in a denomination with a long tradition of female ordination
and judicatory leadership says,

- It's very easy to be a great prophet and to ignore your people, . . . to be out leading
  the marches and to pay no attention to the fact that somebody is suffering. . . . I
  think that . . . the male model too often [is] to be preachy; and I think that women
  have brought a more pastoral dimension. I think they've helped to teach all of
  us more of the importance of the pastoral dimension, . . . the community dimension, . . . some call it the spiritual dimension. This has all been very healthy. . . .
  There are some things I'm not as happy with; I think it's put less emphasis on
  preaching and I still think preaching is really important. I think that women tend
  to be more pastoral, less administrative. Women tend to be more open to
  experimentation, to liturgical interests in a service, as opposed to doing preaching.

- I guess I would say, "Yes, I think they do conduct themselves in the ministry
  differently than men, for the most part, because women have got different ways
  of thinking and approaching things." . . . I want to be careful when I say that
  because I don't want to be stereotyping women; but it's just been my own
  experience that if I were to approach it one way, my wife would approach it from
  a different angle—not necessarily wrong, just a different focus. . . . The thing
  that stands out for me is that they're much more relational oriented and
  focused . . . ("they" being the lady pastors). . . . They're not as task oriented;
  they're people oriented, where I think the male clergy tend to be more task
  oriented and find fulfillment in accomplishing the task. Female clergy friends

that I have find much more fulfillment in getting to know people and chatting with them. . . . Unlike some of my male colleagues, I celebrate having my sisters in the Lord in the ministry. I'm like some of my male colleagues [in that] I wonder if *some* of the female colleagues have truly been called to a pastoral ministry. But there are others that are clearly gifted for pastoral ministry and I am excited about that and what it can mean in the life of the church and that's not all platitude to get female clergy to like me. I truly think that they bring gifts and graces to ministry that men don't bring. That's not to say some men don't have those. I see the women struggling to fit that expectation that people put on them and so they seem a bit more unsure of themselves and may be less focused because they're trying to get their arms around something that may be bigger than what I'm trying to do. . . . They're trying to discover their own ministry.

- With our staff, one of the persons is a lady; and we notice that there are often times when she brings more of a lady's perspective than we would have thought. We may be discussing something and she'll say, "Well, the women wouldn't be thinking this way," and we wouldn't have known that because we're used to thinking as men, . . . we wouldn't have known it was a *male* thought. . . . I think there's a difference in a man's and woman's role, somewhat, and they're affected by a couple of factors . . . physical and emotional. . . . A lady is going to be affected by childbearing and there are some things in her care of children in the early stages or in having small children [that may affect her] if they're both working. Society usually gives the preference to the child care person being a lady and so she's going to have to pay more attention to that. . . . It's not a rule but a lady is often going to be a little more sensitive in some areas than a man is and bring some balance in that sensitivity. Plus, there's going to be a particular period of the month where there's going to be some emotional fluctuation more on the female side than on the male.

- It seems that men are more political; and characteristically, from my experiences, they move in that realm more than women, . . . and maybe it's because it's been a male-dominated thing and women don't feel comfortable [there]. . . . Women in this faith seem to be more charismatic in preaching, teaching, prayer. . . . Men preachers tend to follow a more traditional form and method . . . that includes story telling . . . [and] religious clichés. Women seem to be a little more creative in their style.

- She [an associate minister] takes charge of Christian education, youth, . . . membership, and evangelism. She preaches once a month; this is a great load off me. . . . I would specialize in administration; she specializes in care and concern. Overall, I would see males in power roles and females in nurturing roles. Now, I worked with an associate in my former church who was very much into power as opposed to nurturing. Yet I think we had a pretty good partnership in ministry. . . . I do think that . . . there is a good balance, . . . if there can be a good and honest and open relationship, that the male minister and the female minister present a whole ministry, . . . whole leadership to a church. People who are uncomfortable going to her will come to me for counseling, and vice versa. . . . I will point out to her some things that she did not see; she will point out to me some things that I did not see. I think that can be very healthy. . . . If there's good communication, an honest relationship, both of them will expand. I believe that. And I think . . . if they retreat into gender roles they're carrying out all these things that I've said are evil in our society—the adversarialness, power, and violence. That's unfortunate.

- [Interviewer: Do you think there's a difference in the ways men and women do ministry?] Oh, definitely! They [women] don't seem as driven; I find the women I know don't put as much emphasis on "what I do" as "who I am." I find that refreshing and I can learn from that. . . . I know there are women who *are* driven. I think there are those who are *very* task oriented.

- Women are strengthening parish ministry and enriching theology through experience as women and strong interest in feminist theology. These are newly expanded perspectives for the church. Communication of the gospel and of relationships with people comes through these different lenses. Women in public office accent pastoral care—especially woman to woman, though I see men also do this well. I just read *You Just Don't Understand* [Tannen] and found it helpful. I have recommended it to others.

He then goes on to speak of some gender differences he notices among congregants.

Men are harder to interest than women. I take more pains to connect with men. A big challenge in the institutional church is how to connect with men, especially blue-collar men. There are [currently] diminished gender-specific activities. As women have entered formerly male roles, exclusive realms of maleness have been integrated; but men don't enter the formerly female service roles as well. The congregation is working on this. A men's study group and prayer group are active.

This congregant difference is echoed by a few others. Two suggest that certain U.S. ideas of what it means to be a real man conflict with certain conventional ideas of what it means to be a real Christian or a spiritual person, and this conflict may make it harder to interest men.

According to sociologist Bruce Nordstrom, "Men who feel they must be 'self-made,' independent, in control, knowing it all, and rational have a difficult time connecting with spiritual questions and issues (even if, paradoxically, religious institutions are run primarily by men)."[4]

DIFFERENCES IN MEN'S AND WOMEN'S NARRATIVES

The preceding statements together with the quotations on feminist theology in Chapter 4 contain most of what the informants say about gender as such. Now I want to share some impressions I have from comparing the men's interviews, taken as a whole, with the women's (1987), taken as a whole. The women and men have lived and worked in culture contexts that give them many perspectives in common; yet discernible patterns of difference emerge in numerous areas and seem to be more likely attached to gendered life experiences (before and during professional ministry) than to random human variety.

The list of differences I note is not exhaustive; it represents the more obvious items that emerged while I was sifting the material. And such comparisons must be understood as differences in how certain characteristics are distributed across categories, not as distinctions between all people in one category and all people in the other.

Differences are often exceedingly subtle and can "fall through" survey grids that have been constructed without awareness of their nature. Such differences may be minimized or absent in survey findings because of the ways variables are specified. Phenomenological studies and other qualitative research can perform a service in discovering tendencies not yet given much or any scholarly attention. For example, the clergywomen and clergymen I interviewed talk of their "vision for the congregation" and their satisfaction when congregants "catch" that vision. Yet women seem more to be indicating a spiritual orientation—a connectedness with the universe, a vision of hopeful life possibilities and encompassing love; men, more a long-term programmatic direction—a vision of what the congregation might accomplish as a community. A survey item using the broad term "vision" could obscure this distinction, though the divergence in connotation would surely affect relational and expressive dynamics of ministry in important ways. How "the vision thing" is framed may be especially significant at the senior minister level, where Lehman (1993) finds larger differences between women's and men's approaches and where ministers have greater responsibility for setting the tone of community. It should be noted that both Lehman and I find relatively few senior women in multiple-staff parishes. Among my seventeen "successful" women there was only one (compared to nine among my "successful" men). Lehman's split in a much larger group was not that extreme; but he also mentions the striking disparity.

Another factor minimizing or masking gender differences in survey results may be the acknowledged "androgynous" constellation of ideal qualities associated with religious ministry. The androgynous person does not feel narrowly restricted to personal characteristics traditionally considered typical for one sex. While some folk wisdom and some contemporary scholarship regard androgynous humans as especially healthy and mature, androgyny is not a widespread social ideal and often is equated with "sameness" or "gender-neutering." However, the clergy role is a respected example of androgynous expectations for success (as are certain other established roles, such as social worker and health-care specialist).

Thus a "really good minister" is ideally expected to be an excellent preacher, wise and understanding counselor, effective and fiscally responsible administrator, sensitive communicator, articulate teacher, loving care giver; supportive presence, friend, trustworthy moral model, effective liaison with the community and denomination at large, impressive presider at ceremonies, and more. It should not be surprising then if the gender overlap of intentional responses to questions is very substantial for people who enter clergy work, and especially for those considered successful. Yet the narrative "spin" that men and women tend to give their responses often turns out to be quite distinctive and gender related.

While both groups of clergy show personal development well beyond narrowly construed feminine and masculine conventions, the overall tilt of each group of narratives is in traditionally normative directions; that is, men tend more toward rational thought, performance goals, specialized and hierarchical relations, and individualistic ideals of identity and justice. Women tend more toward personal thought, relationship health, integrative and equalitarian relations, and communitarian ideals of identity and social responsibility.

Indications of these tendencies show up in men's talking about youthful searches for a "philosophy of life" and freedom to follow it—principles for deciding, a design for living, contrasted with women's talking more frequently about youthful searches for worthy commitments (developmentally healthy for self and others)—commonly identified in personal, relational terms.

Even in the interview process itself the stronger goal-centeredness of the men's orientation appears. There are numerous comments to the effect, "If I knew how you would be using this material, I could speak more to the point and be more clear." The women seem more comfortable spontaneously choosing their ground for self-revelation around very broad themes.

In my estimation, the most dramatic and far-reaching gender contrast is in primary life orientations. Among the men, fundamental reality assumptions range much more widely across the worldviews used for interpretive reference than they do among the women, whose perspectives cluster more closely around a "new paradigm," *yin* orientation. (Few of the men or women, of course, would identify their positions by using those terms or others I've mentioned from scholarly analyses.) This range of difference is apparent within interviews as well as across the groups and shows in theological, moral, and administrative themes.

The groups of clergy also are quite different in depth of awareness about current worldview issues, as well as about inclusiveness issues (gender, race, sexual orientation, disability, age). For whatever reasons (lesser power status? holistic, integrative perspectives? different seminary interests?), the women's interviews reveal more complex understandings of these discussions—from scholarly writings, journalistic accounts, personal conversations, and experiences. The men's observations range from immensely sophisticated, spontaneous statements to responses consisting of only a few remarks about inclusive language. Variety among the women in this respect is not as extreme, and they are generally more broadly conversant with the pedagogical, developmental, vocational, and relational issues around the topics. There is a clear gender difference, for example, in the salience of gender as a conscious factor in administrative, moral, and theological leadership; it is much higher for the women.

Even in crosscutting categories, such as sexual orientation and race, the "straight" white women talk more extensively, passionately, and knowledgeably about the social justice implications of homosexuality and race than do the heterosexual white men.

(Is the reader holding steady with the consciousness that, for example, a given clergyman might well show vastly *greater* concern for, and awareness of, specific issues of life orientation or multicultural inclusiveness than a given clergywoman?)

Incidentally, a *racial* difference that does not vary appreciably by gender is that black clergy show a higher awareness of racial issues in U.S. society. The black clergy and congregations interact with their surrounding communities at a higher level of intensity than do white clergy and congregations, in order both to service individual human needs and to affect political/economic structures.

As administrators, men appear to develop more formally elaborate and hierarchical structures of congregational management. Admittedly, they are mostly in much larger organizations than the women, but even where the sizes are reversed, the tendencies are discernible. Clergymen seem not to think of administration, per se, in essentially religious or pastoral terms. They are clearly concerned about honesty and accountability, and they want religiously meaningful programs and projects, but administration, theology, and pastoral caring are more explicitly separated for the men than for the women. The more holistic, integrative perspectives of the clergywomen emerge in their greater disposition to talk of merged administrative-pastoral-faith ideals of authentic personal communication in congregation building. This approach is spoken about by some women almost as a type of organizational efficiency. Women often experience formal structure as standing "in the way" of appropriate action, attitudes, and relationships; whereas men more often refer to formal structure as evidence of ministry.

Gender differences appear in the informants' reported and implied modes of interpersonal exchange with congregants. Women's narratives have much more detailed information about members' thinking, feeling responses, interests, and political stances. Clergywomen treat such "pulse-reading" as a virtual requirement for developing effective ministries. Men, as you have seen, frequently report not knowing what congregant positions and responses might be on a number of issues. They seldom indicate dependency on sensing the personal worlds of members for setting direction in ministry.

When male informants talk about feedback they frequently seem to imply unsolicited comments from congregants and colleagues. One says he tends to make very strong statements of his positions and then wait to see whether anyone takes issue with them and gives him feedback. Women's comments about feedback refer to ongoing formal and informal opinion-airing sessions, in which they seek to draw out colleague and congregant views for the intrinsic community-building value of the dialogue and for a sign of serious democratic intentions. This may be connected somehow with the greater number of stated preferences among men for avoiding conflict and greater use among women of expressions such as "everything on the table" and "no game-playing." Women, much more than men, talk of conflict as a natural consequence of human differences and as providing constant opportunities for building trust and strengthening community.

Both women and men value reason and emotion. Among men I find higher trust in the rational. In fact two male informants, who are opposites in many respects, each talk about how important rationality is for them (over emotional considerations) in all aspects of their ministries—theology, moral issues, and administration. The women not only accent emotional elements more strongly than men but tend to integrate them with all aspects of ministry—speaking of rationality and feeling, as well as of faith, caring, and managing *in terms of each other* in deeply integrated ways. Women often hone the rational in order to make passionate and articulate arguments about how love can best be carried out in central societal structures that oppress real persons. Men do this, too, but in my interviews, it appears more strongly among the women.

The women range much further in God language variety. The language they use is more experimental and playful, compared to that of the men—more grounded in personal experiences of the sacred and attempts to catch such moments in creative metaphor. They don't seem to monitor themselves for traditional allowability, so much as for existential authenticity in their lives. All the men and women describe God as loving; but the men's imagery is a more parental type of caring, and the women's reveals a stronger flavor of intimate touching and joining and conversing.

Imagery for ministry is also a bit different—more "doing God's work" for men and more "carrying God's love" for women. With seemingly equal comfort both use the language of "response to God's call." Both men and women like presiding at liturgy. Men's descriptions lean somewhat more toward "enacting and enlivening the beliefs about God's presence," women's more toward personalizing and concretizing God's touch for particular people and situations. Both men and women talk in similar ways about the liturgical sense of connectedness with people of God across time and space. Both men and women say they *love* preaching, but a number of the men agonize over the ever impending hours of preparation. The women talk more about sermon content emerging (fairly naturally and with less apparent pain) out of the dialectic of ordinary life and the texts to be addressed. It is important here to recall that the ministers I interviewed were all recognized as good preachers.

I asked informants to give me brief statements about what certain classical religious terms mean to them. One that evokes different response leanings among men, compared to women, is *prophecy*, which seems to be heard by men more as speaking out against evil, and by women, more as envisioning redemptive possibilities in human relations.

Some men voice fear that God's judgment will be ignored—that religion will be too soft and comfortable. Such a fear is all but absent from the women's narratives but what *is* there is much consciousness about the pain and struggle intrinsic to a life of love lived as a faithful commitment. Struggle is accented by many women as central to community building, trust building, and spiritual development. Both men and women seem to fear religion's becoming too socially conventional.

Many women clergy see pastoral care and counseling in thoroughly mundane nurturance terms. The ordinary daily needs people have for support and encouragement in life seem more expected and tolerable, as well as more fruitful for ministry, among the women. It is more unusual among the men's voices to hear valuing of this level of tending congregants, though you have seen some. More commonly the men describe themselves as gaining satisfaction from pastoral functioning in crisis situations, personal tragedies, extraordinary needs. They more often voice impatience with people's trivial needs for pastoral attention. As I mentioned in connection with Chapter 5 themes, many senior clergymen with multiple associates have opted out of major pastoral-care commitments and specialize in preaching, teaching, and executive functions.

Finally, a few differences emerge from the biological material. In families of origin fewer male clergy informants are oldest or only children of their parents, and even some of these have older stepsiblings. Parental couples are described in more traditional terms among the clergymen—few of the unconventional high-ability-mother-and-warm-responsive-father couples that are more common among the clergywomen descriptions.

"Success" ages in my two studies turn out to be a narrower range for men (a spread of about twenty-five years) than for women (a spread of about forty-five). This may be due to differences in success criteria for women and men or because initially women came into ministry at a wide spread of ages (and some with very high ability came in especially late in their lives).

"Success" locations differ a great deal. Men reputed to be influential are at dramatically more prestigious professional locations than are the women—many more senior ministers, larger congregations, more evident affluence and assistance. The labyrinthian staff arrangements I encountered in setting up some of the men's interviews in very large congregations was a different world from the one I entered to interview the clergywomen.

There are many more single women than single men among the clergy I interviewed. Among those who are married, the median number of children is three for men and two for women. In marital families both clergywomen and clergymen frequently experience conflict between ministerial and family demands. The women tend to use the language of internalized commitments and responsibilities, conflict *within* the call to minister. The men seem more inclined to see family requests, duties, or agreements as competing against the call to minister. One man says,

- Marriage and family has enhanced ministry, but in terms of the traditional idea of giving oneself wholly to God, [it] competes and conflicts, too.

Women seem less concerned about keeping clean lines between friendship and ministry. Women sometimes describe both friendship and professional calling in "mutual ministry" terms. Men more frequently express misgivings about the compatibility of friendship with the pastoral role.

Now back to the matter of how to read these impressions of gender differences: My finding of a great deal more variation in primary worldview orientations among and within men's narratives (compared to women's) overarches evidence that clergymen's perspectives, in fact, tip consciously and heavily toward postmodern, social constructionist, new-paradigm views but not nearly *as* heavily as women's. Likewise, there are men who value the small, ordinary pastoral attentions to congregants' needs, finding them satisfying and spiritually important in ministry; and there are men who work hard at building democratic discourse as the foundation of their administrative approach. Nevertheless, overall, both of these tendencies characterize male informants less strongly and more ambivalently than female informants, judging by their statements.

Men and women unmistakably share biological and social proclivities at a very high level of similarity. All things considered, the clergy interviewed in the two studies are far more alike than different. Though differences, compared with likenesses, may be "small" they color and flavor lives and relationships in experientially important ways. My interest in noting and clarifying such differences arises from no desire either to promote or condemn them. Rather it stems from a hope that we might better understand our human ways and more intentionally attempt a society in which differences are assessed and used cooperatively, in mutual appreciation and respect. My ideal society would provide equal developmental support for male and female persons, and equal access to social participation at all levels of community building.

NOTES

1. Lyn M. Brown, Mark B. Tappan, and Carol Gilligan (in press). "Listening to Different Voices." In W. Kurtines & J. Gewirtz (Eds.) *Moral development: An introduction*, Needham Heights, MA: Allyn & Bacon.

2. Cathy McMullen, "Why Can't We Communicate," *Fargo (N.D.) Forum*, 20 February 1994.

3. William Safire, "Father Power Rooted in Ultimate Authority," *Fargo (N.D.) Forum*, 19 June 1994.

4. Bruce Nordstrom "Love and Power: Sources of Male Resistance to Family Change," (paper presented at the Midwest Sociological Society, April 1987).

Chapter 8

Concluding Thoughts

An editorial in a recent issue of a mainstream church magazine begins, "The time has come to acknowledge that virtually every denominational organization must change. That is not a profound observation, but it has more consequences than we know."[1] Insofar as the editor is right about this (and there appears to be widespread agreement), it obviously implies clergy change as well—affecting and affected by such organizational shift.

Sociologist Max Heirich, talking about social change as construction of alternative perspectives and strategies, notes how changes emerge from redefining issues in different terms, linking people in new ways, or envisioning formerly taken-for-granted truths in fresh metaphors of reality. From inside existing social arrangements, according to Heirich, people work toward reframing issues, which changes much about how social arrangements come to be constructed over time.

Others observe that, for both text and interpreter, language occurs with "horizons"—edges beyond which one does not see—and that truth is formed in the play and interplay of meanings among horizons. The often noted interpretive openness of religious metaphor and symbolism allows a great deal of redefining and reimaging of traditions and faith experiences on a continuing basis.

In the midst of an interview a clergy informant talks about changes he's seen in ideals and structures.

- When I started out, "the times were a-changin' " and the old order was rapidly . . . passing. Everybody was gonna have equal rights and we weren't gonna be so materialistic. . . . The world has changed tremendously and yet the world hasn't changed at all. That idealism . . . became overshadowed with a backlash. We've been through a very materialistic time. . . . Still we *need* that idealism . . . and personally, I must fight cynicism. . . . We haven't conquered racism. . . . When I started out, the culture was fighting communism . . . and I thought communism had some good things to say to us. . . . Ecumenism was very strong when I began. . . . This all has sunken down in a deep morass of institutionalism. . . . When I began ministry the Pentecostal movement was growing by leaps and bounds. . . . [Now] the wave of the future seems to be the megachurch. . . . Younger families are going to them, . . . popular music . . . laid back in terms of demands . . . consumer oriented.

The term *axio-age* (referring to an assumed radical shift in worldview now under way) surfaced at a conference I attended where many people, who were either cited or in attendance, referred to our present era as one of mind-boggling complexification of life possibilities—things to know, things to do, ways to be and relate and say. Individuals and societies appear awash in confusion about whether or how to support and strengthen each other. Many search for simple, clear maps to guide them through complicated times.

Traditionally, clergy have been expected to provide such guidance. Religion has a central social function as the culture form in terms of which ultimate existential questions are asked: What is the meaning of reality? What does it mean to be responsible for our individual and collective freedom? How can we sustain authentic and mutually satisfying relationships?

People making and keeping commitments to God and one another in religious communities want dependable ways they can join together to relive the essential traditions while simultaneously being fully alive to the present moments of their lives. Yet linear continuity of culture forms is hardly a realistic expectation for most of contemporary society in its postmodern ambience (if it ever was).

With new poignancy and urgency ancient religious questions are asked: What is truth? What is goodness? What is ideal community? Denominations struggle with issues of what constitutes core belief and on what authority it is based. Interest in what clergy really think about such matters is heightened. This research is an attempt to deliver such views to the curious reader.

At a recent conference of the Society for the Scientific Study of Religion, sociologist Wade Clark Roof listed some major motifs of postmodern faith narratives. He mentioned these items: Motif 1) discontinuities and continual revisions of culture terms; Motif 2) marginality—the necessary working out of authentic belief positions that take into account one's own minority experience in groups whose dominant shared memories of faith are not one's own; Motif 3) fluidity of membership in groups, causing centrifugal dispersion across groups of both persons and their unique faith stories; Motif 4) mixing and matching multilayered belief systems *within* individuals, in a very serious eclecticism, or what he called *bricolage*.

Roof ended with a plea for taking very seriously the multiple impressions and broken continuities of people's lives and for getting good at story telling. He proposed that as we share our own life-grounded stories and the experienced stories of others, new conceptual integrations and new bases of unity emerge, not just in the realm of religious knowing but also in other realms of knowing.

In a sense, our lives are stories within stories within stories; my "Martha story" is in a family story, in church, school, and community stories, in a nation story, in a world story (and more). Whoever I am, my story matters in the whole, and how I envision the whole of reality matters in how I direct and experience my life.

Theology and social research have seen a renewed interest in the ancient art of story telling. This is not mere invention and fantasy, purely for entertainment, but serious construction of person and event narratives that bring coherence to relationships, intentions, values, and understandings within exceedingly complex circumstances. Roof talked about narrative not just as illustration but as affirmation of webs of significance in life—webs that as multiple levels reveal something of the unities within which people actually conduct their ordinary affairs.

My research is an ongoing attempt to document clergy stories, noting especially the worldview "stories" they draw upon as fundamental truth. I see value in direct exposure to the metaphor ministers use for saying what they think on a spectrum of topics. I also see interpretive value in distinguishing major worldview orientations that lie at the heart of important religious and secular rifts, given that our assumptions about reality transform, to some degree, all knowledge that flows through our discourse.

A steady stream of voices—scholarly, journalistic, political, managerial, pedagogical—have been asserting that the dominant Western World reality paradigm is increasingly counterproductive for supporting healthy human development (individual, relational, or societal). This is a crucial issue for consideration since the Western World's international influence is great, through its economic and political power.

Dominant reality assumptions and values have been identified as strongly hierarchical, authoritarian, empirical, rational, dualistic, individualistic, and competitive. They lean to governance by bureaucratic rule and role entitlements; truth by expert correctness within relatively isolated professional specialties.

Men and women who consciously or unconsciously challenge such a worldview and embrace so-called postmodern alternatives emphasize what they have come to trust as a balancing set of terms for human existence: equalitarian, nonadversarial, partnership arrangements; integrative, holistic thinking; consciousness of the social constructedness of all human systems (including meaning and language).

Thumbnail sketches such as these are distilled abstractions that can clarify important operating premises, but that don't exist so purely in concrete situations and are seldom identified in the numerous arguments they infuse. In real life, worldviews interpenetrate, overlap, and often make masked or unbidden appearances within us and among us. Still they represent interpretive options that prove crucial in structuring objectives and relationships and are thus worth raising for conscious consideration. The split between absolutist ("orthodox-conservative") and relativist ("humanist-liberal") views is said by scholars to be the most intractable current religious cleavage, greater now than denominational divisions.

The continuing species benevolence of any worldview orientation depends on its being held open to correctives from alternatives. Psychologist John Ingram and others describe how, just as modernism was a fruitful corrective to the more romantic and magical thinking of earlier eras, postmodernism is a potential corrective to modernism's excesses of mechanistic, materialistic objectification of life. Yet, just as scientific rational-empirical knowledge could narrow into extreme positivist reductionism, so critical thinking and deconstructionist interpretive techniques could accent uniqueness and difference to the detriment of larger unities, failing to make integrative progress toward a new cultural coherence that acknowledges internal social diversity and uses it for creative synergy.

Ingram says, "It makes a certain ironic sense that the individualism of modernism, as it developed into hyperindividualism, would spawn a segmenting of discourse without the ability to agree on *any* overarching rules. . . . [Postmodernism] cannot comprise a complete model of reality . . . as modernism (which cut off its ideological opponents in a very different fashion) also could not."[2]

Insofar as men and women, for whatever reasons, tend to embody somewhat different orientations to life, a strong case can be made that they also grow and thrive best when fully open to each other's perceived realities and approaches to decision making; that is, when they function comfortably in cooperative interdependence, working together (in the words of Sam Keen 1991) "at the process of becoming conscious and compassionate." My studies convince me that religious communities need the gifts of both clergymen and clergywomen, offered to each other and to congregants through mutually respectful partnerships.

You now have seen a large portion of the data from the clergy interviews. The displays give ample opportunity for sensing the thought and feeling tone of the interview narratives. Readers interested in comparing the men's voices with those of clergywomen may consult my 1987 work. The studies invite the reader to form opinions about the data firsthand. The quotations lie open to further analysis but do not require it for informational value. My central interest, in both projects, has been to discover the fundamental reality perspectives stated and implied through the words of relatively successful clergy who differ greatly in other respects.

In each study, the narrative extracts are set into interpretive frames that help us note certain things about the clergy views. In the clergywomen study, cultural futurist writings are examined; "old-paradigm"/"new-para-digm" life-orientation features are reviewed. Clergywomen's thinking is found to be congruent with emerging-paradigm ideals tilting toward holis-tic, integrative, processual, personal, equalitarian perspectives. In the cler-gymen study the "modern"/"postmodern" version of this worldview distinction is discussed with references to contemporary social and literary criticism focused on language and meaning formation. Quotations from the ministerial men show more mixed perspectives than those of the women. This gender difference appears across theological, moral, and administra-tive leadership statements, but it seems to me most evident in thinking about morality and administration.

Based on the interview content, the men do seem to lean toward what are said to be male-typical perspectives that accent doing, accomplishing, rational knowledge, specializing, fairness, hierarchical relations, and iden-tity through independence; whereas women tip more toward being, relating, personal knowledge, integrating, nurturing, equalitarian relations, and iden-tity through intimate connections. It must be emphasized, however, that both the women and the men, as groups, show fairly "epi-conventional," androgynous personal development; that is, growth beyond narrowly de-fined sex-typical norms.

It is clear that the perspectives of the men range much more widely across the alternative worldviews than do those of the women. In terms of funda-mental orientation to life, there appears to be both greater spread among the men and a lower degree of internal consistency across themes within each man's narrative. That is perhaps to be expected for several reasons.

Though scholarly theology and seminary curricula have been moving steadily toward more dialectical and existential interpretations of texts, traditions, and ministries, conventional male socialization continues to idealize (1) more absolutist foundations for knowledge, (2) manliness and success as achievement of dominance and control, (3) morality by principles of justice, (4) organization of corporate projects by bureaucratic (hierarchical) efficiency.

Also, the public world (contrasted with the domestic and leisure realms) remains more wed to the perspectives and structures of its modern formation; and men have been prepared, traditionally, for competitive success in that public world. The more constructionist, personalized, equalitarian perspectives have, in the past, tended to be associated with friendship, home, family, recreation, therapy, and other private, restorative, or peripheral realms—the world of women, hearth, and "time off."

Sam Keen and other writers about men's lives talk about how hard and painful it is for most men to take seriously their inner, subjective experience and to learn to consult it for doing necessary integrative and relational work. His point is illustrated by the following comments made after I asked a man whether his choice for ministry felt like a good fit. The man initially indicated he had no ambivalence about the choice. Then, after a long hesitation he added,

- I'm like the normal man—the normal, general male that grows up in America. . . . Do they like their job? Do they not like their job? . . . To men that's an irrelevant question; they just *do* their job. . . . They're earning money; they do their job as best they can, and work as hard as they can, and go home. In that sense, I'm not used to being reflective about what I'm doing; I just do it. . . . I'm pretty sure I'd be aware if I *didn't* like it.

It is important to remember, as well, that on the one hand, the yin orientation tendencies, with their integrative holistic impulse, tend to take on aspects of the yang orientation through incorporation, enlargement, and synergy. On the other hand, the yang orientation is disposed more to take on yin aspects as additive specialties, which thus might remain somewhat more conflictual and segmented.

So just from logical implications of conventional male ideals and their association with the dominant Western World reality orientation, we could expect more evident diversity in worldviews among male clergy, working in an institutional setting that officially encourages them to embrace aspects of yin development, which they may nonetheless tend to do according to primary yang perspectives. In moving toward an androgynous development of yang characteristics the women do appear to incorporate them more in terms of fruitful connections with the personalized whole—in yin terms.

Obviously these perspectival, developmental tendencies that show up in society and in the data have potential for adversarial use in the "battle of the sexes": Which is really *superior*? But the differences have the same potential for humane synergy. I clearly reveal my own hopes, beliefs, and commitments when I envision a possible society where men and women in all their individual variety can support each other's authentic forms of passion for truth and goodness, compassion in relationships, and creativity in organizing the tasks of world maintenance. I should like to see the best bio-psycho-sociological (and other) scholarship cooperatively address questions of who we are as men and women, and what we may become— with genuine openness and undefensiveness. I hope for religious communities where people feel free to share their experiences of the sacred, ask their deepest questions, reveal their most troubling fears, make their boldest critiques of social ills. This openness, of course, implies mutual respect and a balance of yin and yang perspectives.

The possibility of a revised cultural unity, stemming not from similarity of life experience but from shared commitment to the values, ideals, and techniques of intentional equalitarian inclusiveness, calls attention to some profound questions at the heart of the implied new intellectual and moral consensus terms:

Can we grow collectively and personally in the requisite respectful attention to each other's concrete particularity—each other's true stories?

Can we embrace human variety as a primary intellectual and moral resource, informing and connecting our fund of beliefs, values, sentiments, and interpersonal skills?

Can we celebrate the richness, and ponder the significance, of our differences while having the disciplined perseverance, courage, and compassion necessary for negotiating the order of our ongoing associations with a certain simplicity of orientation and intention?

Can we develop new spiritual community and mutual personal support with cooperative ideals, equalitarian relationships, and holistic perspectives in life?

Though more and more voices are raised to endorse the paradigm of reality implied in this last question, it is by no means the reigning reality perspective in the U.S. mainstream. It is not at all clear what the dominant social impulses will be, over the years. That is one reason why hearing the views of recognized leaders (like the informants in this research) becomes so important.

The information provided here, regarding clergy perspectives, yields some sense of the range of the men's views. There are, of course, many other statements on these same themes, and other themes are addressed.

Scientifically supportable generalizations and comparisons were not expected and would not be defensible, given the project design. I did not seek support or refutation of specific hypotheses. What *can* be claimed is that a fund of experiential references has been built, relative to clergy perspectives, alerting readers to subtleties of social interaction that ought not be swept into variables that hide their import. I am drawn to the phenomenological approach to research not only because I enjoy doing the interviews—which I do!—but also because I am utterly convinced that sociological inquiry fails to penetrate social reality if it fails to strike a balance between life story reports of intersubjective impressions and rigorously structured statistical comparisons.

The men who contributed their time to the interviews have given us a valuable and memorable gift in sharing their thinking about themselves as professional ministers. I trust that the process has been valuable for them, too. Some indicated that it was.

- I haven't had this kind of chance to talk about myself before.
- Conceptualizing has been a good, helpful experience. It gives needed perspective. I don't take time, otherwise, apart from something like this.
- This is a first for me and it's almost been therapeutic. . . . It's been refreshing to do this.
- I kind of enjoyed it.

NOTES

1. This is from a piece by Edgar R. Trexler in the April 1994 issue of *The Lutheran*.

2. John A. Ingram, "Evangelicals, Postmodernism, and the Future of Modernist Illusions" (paper presented at the Society for the Scientific Study of Religion, 1993).

References

Ammerman, Nancy Tatom, ed. 1993. *Southern baptists observed: Multiple perspectives on a changing denomination.* Knoxville: University of Tennessee Press.

———. 1987. *Bible believers: Fundamentalists in the modern world.* New Brunswick, NJ: Rutgers University Press.

Bakhtin, M. M. 1981. *The dialogic imagination.* Austin: University of Texas Press.

Berger, Peter. 1980. *The heretical imperative.* Garden City, NY: Anchor Books.

———. 1967. *The sacred canopy.* Garden City, NY: Doubleday.

Berger, Peter, Brigitte Berger, and Hansfried Keller. 1973. *The homeless mind.* New York: Random House.

Berger, Peter, and Thomas Luckman. 1966. *The social construction of reality.* Garden City, NY: Doubleday.

Brod, Harry, ed. 1987. *The making of masculinities: The new men's studies.* Boston: Allen and Unwin.

Burke, Kenneth. 1984. *Permanence and change.* 3d ed. Berkeley: University of California Press.

Busse, Richard. 1992. "Human Viability and a World Theology." *Insights: The Magazine of the Chicago Center for Religion and Science*, April, 1, 7.

Capra, Fritjof. 1982. *The turning point.* New York: Simon and Schuster.

Capra, Fritjof, and David Steindl-Rast with Thomas Matus. 1991. *Belonging to the universe: Explorations on the frontiers of science and spirituality.* Harper San Francisco.

Carroll, Jackson, Barbara Hargrove, and Adair Lummis. 1983. *Women of the cloth.* San Francisco: Harper and Row.

Derrida, Jacques. 1976. *Of grammatology.* Baltimore: Johns Hopkins University Press.

Faludi, Susan. 1991. *Backlash*. New York: Crown.

Foucault, Michel. 1972. *The archaeology of knowledge*. New York: Harper Colophon.

Gilligan, Carol. 1982. *In a different voice*. Cambridge, MA: Harvard University Press.

Glaser, Barney, and Anselm Strauss. 1967. *The discovery of grounded theory*. Chicago: Aldine.

Greene, Maxine. 1988. *The dialectic of freedom*. New York: Teachers College Press.

Ice, Martha Long. 1987. *Clergy women and their worldviews: Calling for a new age*. New York: Praeger.

Jaggar, Alison M. 1990. "Feminist Ethics: Some Projects and Problems." *From the Center: A Newsletter*, Fall, 2.

Keen, Sam. 1991. *Fire in the belly*. New York: Bantam.

Kuhn, Thomas. 1962. *The structure of scientific revolutions*. Chicago: University of Chicago Press.

Lehman, Edward, Jr. 1993. *Gender and work*. Albany: State University of New York Press.

_____. 1985. *Women clergy*. New Brunswick, NJ: Transaction Books.

Lofland, John. 1971. *Analyzing social settings*. Belmont, CA: Wadsworth.

McFague, Sallie. 1982. *Metaphorical theology: Models of God in religious language*. Philadelphia: Fortress Press.

Minow, Martha. 1990. *Making all the difference*. Ithaca, NY: Cornell University Press.

Nelson, John S., Allan Megill, and Donald McCloskey, eds. 1987. *The rhetoric of the human sciences*. Madison: University of Wisconsin Press.

Patton, Michael Quinn. 1990. *How to use qualitative methods in evaluation*. Newbury Park, CA: Sage.

Polanyi, Michael. 1958. *Personal knowledge: Toward a post-critical philosophy*. Chicago: University of Chicago Press.

Reinharz, Shulamit. 1979. *On becoming a social scientist*. San Francisco: Jossey-Bass.

Roof, Wade Clark. 1993. *A generation of seekers: The spiritual journeys of the baby boom generation*. Harper San Francisco.

Simons, Herbert W., ed. 1989. *Rhetoric in the human sciences*. London: Sage.

Stanley, Liz, and Sue Wise. 1983. *Breaking out: Feminist consciousness and feminist research*. London: Routledge and Kegan Paul.

Tannen, Deborah. 1990. *You just don't understand: Women and men in conversation*. New York: Ballantine.

Wallace, Ruth A. 1992. *They call her pastor*. Albany: State University of New York Press.

Index

of, 40–47, 186; moral foundations and resources for, 112–17; moral modeling of, 95–104; overview of, 2, 27–30; racial issues and, 129–35, 176; scripture views of, 68–74; sin concept of, 90–93; theological bases of, 62–68; vision setting by, 149–50, 174

Clergywomen: gender differences views of clergymen versus, 173–80; gender relations and perspectives of, 168–73; orientations brought by, 184–85; previous study of, 1–2

Conflict management, 152–60

Congregants: friendships with, 58–59, 179; male versus female, 173; relations between clergywomen and, 177

Critical thinking, 16–17

Csikszentmihalyi, Mihaly, 24

Derrida, Jacques, 18
Devotional practices, 86–90
Dewey, John, 19–20
Dialectical conditions, 16
Diversity, as part of unity, 25

Economic issues, 127–29
Eliade, Mircea, 65
Enlightenment, 19–20
Epitaph fantasies, 111–12
Ethnocentrism, 19

Faludi, Susan, 166
Families of origin: of clergymen, 30–37; of clergywomen, 179
Family life, 47, 50–57
Feminist theology, 67, 81–86
Fletcher, John, 63
Foucault, Michel, 18
Freedom, 16–17
Friendship, with congregants, 58–59, 179

Geertz, Clifford, 21
Gender differences: clergymen versus clergywomen on, 173–80; issues in, 163–68; in ministry, 168–73
Gesch, Lynn, 7
God-imagery: used by clergymen, 75–81; used by clergywomen, 177–178
Goodness, human, 104–7
Greene, Maxine, 16–17

Hargrove, Barbara, 7
Heirich, Max, 181
Homosexuality: clergymen as, 98–99; clergymen's views on, 118–22; social justice implications of, 176
Humor, 65–66

Ingram, John, 25, 184
Islam, 61

Jagger, Alison M., 164
Jewish Reconstructionist Movement, 63
Judaism, 61

Kaplan, Mordecai, 63
Keen, Sam, 186
Knowledge, sociology of, 2
Knowledge paradigms, 11
Kuhn, Thomas, 11

Leadership authority, 137–40
Lehman, Edward, Jr., 7, 166, 167, 174
Leisure activities, 59
Lessing, Doris, 65
Liberation theology, 66–67, 81
Lummis, Adair, 7

McFague, Sallie, 23
Maguire, Daniel, 95
Marital relationships, 46–57
Matus, Thomas, 21, 22
May, Rollo, 65

About the Author

MARTHA LONG ICE is a Sociology Professor Emerita at Concordia College, Moorhead, Minnesota. She specializes in the cultural belief systems of science and religion and is the author of *Clergy Women and Their Worldviews: Calling for a New Age* (Praeger, 1987). She now lives in Spokane, WA.

ISBN 0-275-94968-0

EAN

9 780275 949686

90000>

HARDCOVER BAR CODE